"In *The Space Between*, Eric O. Jacobsen sets himself two goals: to get us to attend to urban space—the space between the buildings in a city or village—and to explain why Christians in particular should care about the quality of urban space. He succeeds admirably on both counts; cities will look different to you once you have read this book. Along the way he also introduces us to some of the most recent writings on urban space, and he offers a compelling explanation of why the urban space of our present-day American cities came to be as it is and why we should be dissatisfied with it. It's a fine contribution to an extremely important topic that has been neglected for too long by too many."

—**Nicholas Wolterstorff**, Noah Porter Professor Emeritus of Philosophical Theology, Yale University; senior fellow, Institute for Advanced Studies in Culture, University of Virginia

"Eric Jacobsen's *The Space Between* is a seasoned Presbyterian pastor's account of the reciprocal relationship between urban form and communal life. As Pope Benedict XVI reminds us, 'Life in society must be considered first and foremost as a spiritual reality.' And Jacobsen, working from a Christ-centered perspective emphasizing both justice and generosity, articulates not only for pastors and laypeople but also for neo-traditional urbanists what religious communities have to gain from traditional towns and neighborhoods, and what they have to give. Highly recommended."

—**Philip Bess**, director of graduate studies, University of Notre Dame School of Architecture; author, *Till We Have Built Jerusalem*

"Jacobsen's book awakens us from our Gnostic slumbers. It reminds us that as embodied beings, we not only move through space but inhabit particular places. And it asks us how we ought to make and dwell in the built environment to the glory of God. *The Space Between* takes us on an eye-opening tour of the places that both shape and reflect us. Readers may never look at their homes, neighborhoods, towns, and churches in the same way again. This is an important first step in reclaiming the *locality* of the local church."

—**Kevin J. Vanhoozer**, research professor of systematic theology, Trinity Evangelical Divinity School

"*The Space Between* presses the argument for the importance of the built environment to the mission of the church, deepening the challenge before us of partnering in the emerging kingdom of God. Jacobsen demonstrates that the church's intellectuals are bringing to bear on the world of ideas the insights of Christian theology and our own intuitive experiences of the places we inhabit. Given the scale of what we have built—from the sprawling exurbs to the troubled cities—there is much to say and do. *The Space Between* opens our imaginations to see that the places we make can and should be sustainable realizations of beauty and places of justice."

—**Christopher C. Miller**, assistant chair for graduate programs, department of architecture, Judson University

"Jesus urges us to love our neighbor, but in many modern cities we have destroyed our neighborhoods, making it much more difficult to know who our neighbors are, let alone love them. In this compelling and beautifully written book Eric Jacobsen tells us how that has happened, why it matters, and what we should be doing about it. This book calls us to think again, and more theological' about the way our built environment shapes our life together. It invites us to consic neighborhoods, we may participate more faithfull

—**Murray Rae**, profes

cultural exegesis

William A. Dyrness
and Robert K. Johnston, series editors

The Cultural Exegesis series is designed to
complement the Engaging Culture series
by providing methodological and foundational studies that address the way to engage culture theologically. Each volume
works within a specific cultural discipline,
illustrating and embodying the theory behind cultural engagement. By providing the
appropriate tools, these books equip the
reader to engage and interpret the surrounding culture responsibly.

The Space Between

A Christian Engagement with the Built Environment

Eric O. Jacobsen

Baker Academic
a division of Baker Publishing Group
Grand Rapids, Michigan

© 2012 by Eric O. Jacobsen

Published by Baker Academic
a division of Baker Publishing Group
P.O. Box 6287, Grand Rapids, MI 49516-6287
www.bakeracademic.com

Printed in the United States of America

Library of Congress Cataloging-in-Publication Data

Jacobsen, Eric O.
   The space between : a Christian engagement with the built environment / Eric O. Jacobsen.
      p.   cm. — (Cultural exegesis)
   Includes bibliographical references and index.
   ISBN 978-0-8010-3908-9 (pbk.)
      1. Christianity and culture. 2. Architecture and religion. 3. Religion and geography. 4. Cities and towns—Religious aspects—Christianity. I. Title.
   BR115.C8J335 2012
   261.5—dc23   2012009190

Unless otherwise indicated, Scripture quotations are from the New Revised Standard Version of the Bible, copyright © 1989, by the Division of Christian Education of the National Council of the Churches of Christ in the United States of America. Used by permission. All rights reserved.

Scripture quotations marked KJV are from the King James Version of the Bible.

The internet addresses, email addresses, and phone numbers in this book are accurate at the time of publication. They are provided as a resource. Baker Publishing Group does not endorse them or vouch for their content or permanence.

12   13   14   15   16   17   18   7   6   5   4   3   2   1

Dedicated to
Conrad W. Jacobsen
1936–2011

Contents

Acknowledgments   9

Introducing the Built Environment   11

Part I: Orientation   29
1. Who Are You?   33
2. Where Are You?   55
3. What Are You?   79
4. When Are You?   103

Part II: Participation   131
5. Family   135
6. Politics   157
7. Church   183

Part III: Engagement   207
8. The Sustainable Environment   213
9. Loving Place   239

Conclusion: A Geography of Rest   271

Notes   279
Index   289

Acknowledgments

When I first began thinking and writing about theology and the built environment more than ten years ago, it felt like I was the only one snooping around in the space between the buildings looking for signs of the kingdom. I have since discovered that I am not alone. In fact there is not room to name all of the kindred spirits I have discovered along the way. There are, however, a number of people who have been especially helpful in shaping and clarifying my thinking in this important area—Howard Ahmanson, Jim Belcher, Phillip Bess, Jonathan and Nate Bradford, Randy Frazee, Griff Gatewood, David Gobel, Tim Gorringe, David Gruesel, Charles Matthews, Ken Meyers, Christopher Miller, Stefanos Polyzoides, Murray Rae, Jill Shook, Clinton Stockwell, Gideon Strauss, Kathryn Streeter, James Van Hemert, Mike Watkins, Summer Wilkes, Cory Wilson, and Nicolas Wolterstorff.

I also want to thank Bill Dyrness and Richard Mouw who helped with the arduous task of backfilling my theological foundation after I had already started building the house. Lee Hardy has been invaluable to this project. He not only provided the illustrations and many photos for this volume, but also has been the intellectual version of the friend you don't have to clean the house for. Lee has seen most of my work long before it was ready for public viewing and has helped put my ideas in their best possible light. And speaking of light, this project would never have seen the light of day without Bob Hosack who suggested it to me over doughnuts at the AAR, Lisa Williams who never fails to astound me with her patient care and attention to detail, and Lance Kagey who helped with the photo editing. And, of course, I want to thank all the folks at Baker Academic who believed that this subject was worth a second book; the First Presbyerian Church of Tacoma for giving me a couple of months to finish the project; and for Liz, Kate, Peter, Emma, and Abraham for allowing me to spend too much time on this project that should have been spent with them.

Introducing the Built Environment

But the LORD God called to the man, and said to him, "Where are you? (Genesis 3:9)

Begin Where You Are

Where are *you*? As you read these words, you are doing so somewhere. This may seem obvious, but bear with me a moment. You may think that the question is hardly worth asking. But since "Where are you?" was the very first recorded question that God asked, let's run with it a bit.

Wherever you happen to be as you read this book, you are most likely in a place that we can call a built environment. So take a second to look around before reading further. Who thought this space through, and what can you discern about their values as you interact with it?

Did they value community very much? How can you tell? Were they thinking of you as a person, as a resource user, or as a consumer?

Think about how you got from the last place you were to where you are now. Was the experience of getting from there to here a meaningful part of your day, or was it a meaningless necessity to get you from point A to point B? Who decided how you would get from that place to this one? Did you have a few realistic options? Or was it feasible to travel only by car?

Questions concerning the physical location and features of the places where you live, work, worship, and play and the way that the various places in your day relate to one another are pretty unusual these days. Many would assert that these are no longer important (or at least not practical) questions. This perspective is rather pervasive both within and outside the community of faith.

Does Geography Matter?

I was reminded of this not too long ago during a discussion about youth ministry. We were talking about the ministry implications of research demonstrating significant benefits to young people who had five nonparental adults involved in their lives. The discussion immediately turned to a question of how we could set up programs at church that would help facilitate relationships between individual youths and five adults at church.

I mentioned that church programs may not be the only way to encourage youth to interact with adults in their lives. It could be accomplished by rethinking the kinds of neighborhoods in which our young people live. Interaction between young people and adults could occur organically if the following conditions were met:

1. Young people lived relatively close to church or in relative proximity to a sufficient number of adult believers.
2. The neighborhood in which the young people lived encouraged social interaction by having good sidewalks, a complex network of streets, and community-enhancing businesses (corner stores, coffee houses, etc.) mixed in with residences.

Although these are precisely the conditions under which young people have been informally mentored by adults for generations, the general response to my idea was that it was hopelessly nostalgic. Not only was my idea well beyond the range of solutions that this group might initiate (with which I agreed) but also there was a strong sense that such a solution was a movement in exactly the wrong direction (with which I disagreed).

We live in a culture that has become convinced that there is no longer any connection between *geography* (where one lives and the distinctive qualities of that place) and our experience of *community*. "Community is about relationships" has become almost a truism in certain circles. Questions of location simply don't matter anymore.

There was some disagreement as to what kind of church programs would best engender meaningful relationships between adults and young people, however. Those who felt that relationships needed to grow more organically, but weren't persuaded by my geographical argument, tended to look to communications technologies to facilitate relationships. Email, social networking websites, and cell phones if used intentionally could allow relationships to be formed irrespective of place.

The perspective articulated in this discussion helps to explain to some extent why it is so hard to get Christians to care about the physical environment that surrounds the places in which they live, work, worship, and play. It explains why we so often make choices regarding where we live without much thought about how far our home is from where we work, worship, and play. And it explains why we build churches surrounded by oceans of parking to which everyone must drive. So long as people can get from place to place in their cars and can stay connected through technology, very few of us care that much about the space between the buildings.

But this is all about to change. Either because gas prices will no longer allow us to drive our cars quite as far as we've been used to or because people will figure out that cyber-community and online social networking friends are no substitute for being in the physical presence of actual friends multiple times per day, questions of geography will become increasingly important over the next decade.

Questions of geography are already important. Every day, questions about geography are being raised in coffee shops, on sidelines, and through letters to the editor within your community. It's just that most of us lack a conceptual framework for putting these questions together. Such a framework is emerging, and it is known by those working on it as the *built environment*. Those who are interested in the built environment often describe themselves as Urbanists.

Although the built environment is becoming an increasingly important subject for discussion, with a few notable exceptions it has not been on the radar for the Christian community.[1] This book is an attempt to remedy the situation by offering a Christian reflection on the built environment.

Via Negativa

The built environment frequently is ignored because the questions considered in this field are very close to (while significantly distinct from) the questions asked in a number of related fields. So the first thing we must do is to clarify what the built environment is *not*.

Not the Natural Environment

One of the easiest ways to begin to get a handle on the built environment is to realize that it can most easily be defined as that which is not part of the natural environment. Things that have come to be without human intervention are part of the natural environment, and things that were created or put into place by humans are part of the built environment. Just about everything that you might see while out on a walk can be put into one of these two categories.

Because the built environment is first understood in opposition to the natural environment, many mainstream environmentalists have tended to ignore it. This is unfortunate, because despite some obvious differences, in many ways the built environment and the natural environment overlap in some rather significant ways.

A section of old-growth forest in the Amazon is part of the natural environment. However, a forest in England is likely to have been planted and designed to look as if it grew naturally. This, technically, makes it part of the built environment. Similarly, the trees planted on a boulevard in a city are part of the built environment. Such observations can make it sometimes difficult to determine which is the built and which is the natural environment.

The difficulty of distinguishing between the built and natural environments may have a good side as well. One danger of maintaining a rigid distinction between built and natural environments is that it tends to obscure the fact that although human beings are distinct from the rest of the created order in many significant ways, we do share some similarities with the other creatures.

The way that humans tend to live on the land can be understood as a kind of habitat that is not unlike the habitats of other creatures. When their habitats are lacking in certain key characteristics, humans tend to languish; and when habitats are in an optimal state, they tend to thrive. One of the benefits of paying attention to the built environment is that it can help us think through settings that support human thriving.

On the other hand, the built and natural environments are connected because it is common for one to become the other. Specifically, all areas that are now part of the built environment were once part of the natural environment. One of the greatest concerns of environmentalists right now is the pace at which the natural environment is being "developed" and transformed into built environment. The rapidity of this pace can be explained to some extent by failures within the built environment. Because we have failed to create environments in which humans can live comfortably in proximity to one another, lots of people are seeking places to live that are far away from other people—aka, the natural environment. This suggests that if we really want to preserve the natural environment, we need to focus some of our attention on the built environment.

Not Architecture

For many people, one of the more surprising discoveries about the built environment as a field of study is that it is not exclusively about architecture. Architecture has to do with the design of buildings and other structures. The field of architecture treats these structures as individual units. People who study architecture employ categories of style (using terms such as Federalist or Georgian) and classify individual buildings and evaluate buildings based on aesthetic and functional criteria. The focus tends to be on the individual architect and the creativity and skill that are made manifest in a particular building. In this sense, we tend to treat architecture as we treat sculptures in a museum. When we say that Los Angeles is becoming an architecturally significant city, what we mean is that Los Angeles contains a growing number of interesting buildings that command our attention.

While buildings built by architects clearly play a significant role in the built environment, much of the conversation about the built environment sets aside considerations about architecture. For one thing, the field of architecture has already received plenty of attention by people who are interested in such things. But the more compelling reason is that a study of the built environment reveals that the spaces between the buildings are equally if not more important than the buildings themselves.

The facade of a particular building is not the only aesthetic contribution that it makes to the built environment. The way that a building sits on its lot and how it shapes the space between itself and the adjacent buildings can be done graciously, or it can be done awkwardly. Architecture is about buildings and their facades, urbanism is about the placement of buildings and how they shape the space around them. Although we occasionally look at the facades of buildings, we live much of our lives in spaces between the buildings.

Architecture buffs can tell you which buildings in a particular city are architecturally significant based on their connection to a well-known architect or by how well they represent a particular movement. But Urbanists do not necessarily recognize distinctions between significant and insignificant buildings. Rather, a distinction is made between things like fabric (or background) buildings and monumental buildings, which both shape the built environment in different ways. Urbanists care about things like corridors and plazas that are shaped by the buildings that line their edges. Those interested in the built environment recognize that a great many of the buildings we encounter on a daily basis have little or no connection to any architect at all.

Not Urban Planning

To describe someone interested in the built environment as an urbanist brings to mind the area of urban planning. But this, too, is off the mark. The field of urban planning emerged in the twentieth century as a way of using rational scientific methods to help solve the problems associated with the modern city. Prior to the development of this particular specialization, cities tended to grow organically around the natural flows of people and goods.

Or, in the case of particularly important cities, public buildings and thoroughfares were laid out with a coherent purpose in mind. Sometimes this purpose involved religious belief—such as the arrangement of pilgrimage sites in Rome. Sometimes the purpose was aesthetic—as with the beaux arts movement in France. And sometimes the purpose had to do with defense. The task of shaping the public spaces of a city around a particular shared value is often referred to as *civic art*. And there are important distinctions to be made between civic art and urban planning.

The purpose of civic art isn't simply to make cities more aesthetically pleasing, but rather to help reinforce and communicate the layers of meaning that have accumulated within a particular city over the years. Civic art supports the monuments (statues, buildings, etc.) that tell the story of a city, as well as the settings (plazas, streets, and squares) that encourage the citizenry to gather and rehearse the story. The field of civic art has a great deal of overlap with the built environment, but civic art is no longer an active discipline.

Like those who practiced civic art in earlier generations, those interested in the built environment are attentive to the stories contained within our cities and towns. They often advocate for the preservation of the important artifacts of the city. Because of an awareness of the story of a city, Urbanists tend also to be concerned that new building projects will be valued not only by the current generation but by future generations as well for making a contribution to the story.

The specialization of urban planning that emerged in the twentieth century marked a distinct break with the tradition of civic art. Whereas civic art often represented an attempt to organize and appropriate the history of a particular place for the present and future residents, urban planning tended to attempt to "solve" the problem of the city, by breaking free from the past using statistics and rational scientific methods to justify initiatives.

Introducing the Built Environment

Urban planning was an attempt to break down the organic movements and flows of the city into abstract categories and to reorganize them in a more efficient manner. As urban planning became normative, those with the power to shape the urban environment typically valued rationality and efficiency above aesthetic considerations or historical continuity. Whereas civic art represented an attempt to enhance the characteristics that made a particular city great, urban planning can be seen as a radical break with a particular city's past.

Those who have an appreciation for the built environment tend to see that the best examples of civic art exist despite the efforts of urban planners in the twentieth century. However, it should also be noted that the field of urban planning has evolved significantly from its beginnings, and many urban planners can now be said to have an appreciation for civic art and the organic ways that cities develop over time. The field of urban planning, although distinct from the built environment, seems to be becoming more sensitive to issues in the built environment.

Enacted Space

Once we locate the built environment conceptually and spatially, there is one more aspect of this realm that we need to have on our radar. That is the aspect of enacted space. Enacted space explains why we cannot always simply go to a particular place and begin to make observations about the built environment. What is most interesting about the built environment is not available for observation at any particular time. We've already noted that the most significant aspect of the built environment is found in the space between the buildings. However, that space becomes interesting only when it is activated by people using it. For this reason, we need to understand the concept of enacted space.

Enacted space refers to the dynamic interaction of people and props in a particular place through time.[2] A baseball field is a *place* designed for a particular purpose. That place is often augmented with *props* such as bases, a pitcher's mound, and equipment. And that space becomes activated when two teams schedule a game and play there at a particular *time*. If we want to understand a baseball field, we should visit it when it is functioning as enacted space. A church is another example of enacted space. A tourist visiting an ancient cathedral when it is empty may not be experiencing the church in its entirety. To really see a church as a place, one must experience it in the context of worship.[3]

Enacted Space

Enacted space is an especially useful concept in its absence. We can look at a municipal map and determine how much public space there is in an area, but it is only on the ground and at particular times that we can see how much truly enacted space there is. It is much easier to build a public place like a park or a plaza than it is to create a successful public space that is regularly enacted. Any number of architects can draw an attractive space; a few can design a place that actually attracts people. We can observe areas where kids endlessly drive around in cars looking for a place to gather, and we can draw the conclusion that we have failed to provide adequate space for them to activate.

Thinking Theologically about the Built Environment

From Garden to City

Sometimes Christians fail to take the built environment seriously because they see the built environment as working against God's purposes. The story of the Bible begins in the natural environment, and everything is "very good." It is only after humanity is punished for its sin and expelled from the garden that the built environment as a project begins in earnest. The sewing together of fig leaves may be seen as a first step in this direction, but the project really gets moving when Cain builds the first city. From this angle, it looks as if the natural environment is a more godly environment and the built environment is stained by sin.

But this quick glance at the story leaves out some crucial details. A closer look shows not only humans but also God at work in adapting the natural environment. Adam and Eve sewed fig leaves together, but it was God who provided them with better clothes. The cities featured in the Bible are not just the ones that Cain built, but also Jerusalem, where God caused his Name to dwell.

But the most important evidence for the importance of the built environment for Christians comes at the end of the story. In John's vision of the coming reign of Christ, he is given an evocative picture of our lives when our relationship with God is fully restored. And that picture is not of a garden or a wilderness, but of a city. The story of the Bible, then, provides an important reminder that whatever we may think of it, the built environment will be an important and inescapable aspect of our future.

It is interesting to contrast these very different settings at the beginning and end of the biblical story. Each pole describes very different conditions, but what makes them similar is the harmony of relationship that obtains between humanity and God, among humans, and between humanity and the rest of creation. In the beginning, there is the nuclear family in a naturalistic setting, taking baby steps toward putting its imprint on that environment by naming animals and collecting food. At the end, there is a human society greater in size and in complexity. And there is evidence of humanity adapting its environment in much more developed ways. We find walls and streets, ships and formal landscaping, and the glory of the nations being brought into the gates.[4]

We can understand the relationship between these contrasting images of harmony among humanity, creation, and God as one of realized potential.[5] The family in the garden is good, but it was never the intent of our Creator for things to stay exactly like this. The city (that includes gardens) provides a clearer picture of what God had in mind for human community and worship when God created us. We can think of this relationship as analogous to the relationship between the acorn and the oak tree. The acorn is wonderful and miraculous in its own way, but we really see the glory of an acorn when it grows into a magnificent oak tree.

We can plot this progression on a timeline. We begin in a garden and end up in a city. In between these two poles we find ourselves somewhere within the flow of human history. The question we first need to answer is, What does faithfulness look like in the space between the garden and the city?

From Garden to City

Creation Mandate

Unlike with the acorn and the oak tree, the kind of progression we observe from the garden and the city includes a good deal of human intervention. God not only created humanity in God's image, he also invited us to participate in the divine plan to redeem all of creation and bring it to fulfillment.

One of the first places we see this invitation expressed is in the first chapter of Genesis, where God gives humanity what is known as the *creation mandate*: "God blessed them, and God said to them, 'Be fruitful and multiply, and fill the earth and subdue it; and have dominion over the fish of the sea and over the birds of the air and over every living thing that moves upon the earth.'"[6] This creation mandate can be broken down further into three submandates.

"Be fruitful and multiply" (or the procreation mandate) has to do with having children and intentionally providing necessary links in the chain of human history. "Subdue the earth" and "have dominion over the animals" (or the stewardship mandate) has to do with enjoying and taking good care of the rest of creation. And last, "fill the earth" (or the cultural mandate) has to do with developing inherent potentials by making something out of creation. When we build a house, paint a picture, arrange a bunch of flowers, or enact a piece of legislation, we are making culture and thus fulfilling our creation mandate.

Part of what it means for us (as image bearers) to worship our Creator is to carry out these three creation mandates. Our participation in the miracle of creation through procreation, our care for the natural world, and our drawing out the God-given potential of the materials of creation can all be done as acts of worship. Each one of these mandates affects our interaction with the built environment.

Serving the Kingdom

Thinking about the creation mandate can be confusing for Christians, because we share this mandate with all of humanity and not just with fellow Christians. How, then, does obedience to the creation mandate count as part of Christian discipleship? This question, and ones like it, emerges out of a particular way of thinking about the kingdom of God.

To fully engage questions of the built environment, Christians must first articulate their understanding of the kingdom of God. There are two fundamentally different ways to approach this issue. The more common way to think about the kingdom of God is called the *two kingdoms approach*. In this way of thinking, there is the kingdom of God and the kingdom of the world. And we can distinguish between what type of work counts for the kingdom

Introducing the Built Environment

of God and what type of work counts for the kingdom of the world (or is worldly) by the type of work that is being done.

According to this way of thinking, worship, Bible study, evangelism, and participating in church programs of various kinds are all considered to be kingdom-of-God work. Working at a bank, fixing pipes, making a movie, and growing crops are considered to be worldly. This way of thinking is called a two kingdoms approach because it makes a very clean distinction between work that is for the kingdom and work that is not. The problem with this approach is that it confuses the institutional church with the kingdom of God and recognizes only church activities as kingdom service.

An alternative to the two kingdoms model can be called the *unified kingdom approach*. This alternative approach recognizes all activities, from worship to plumbing, to be done *coram deo*—or before the face of God. Each one of these activities can be done in a way that is God-honoring or God-dishonoring. If the activity is done in a God-honoring way, it is work for the kingdom of God. If it is done in a God-dishonoring way, it is done for the kingdom of the world (or worldly).

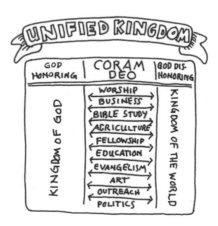

This alternative approach provides a helpful challenge to leaders of Christian organizations. Just because we are doing worship doesn't mean that it is God-honoring worship. To take an extreme example, a church that bars a particular race from worship services is not doing kingdom work in their weekly gathering. However, more important for our purposes is how this alternative way of thinking validates the vocations of countless Christians who are working faithfully in fields that are not formally related to the church. According to this view, there is a distinctively Christian way to approach one's work as a farmer, as a city planner, or in any other profession. Christians who think deeply about and put effort into the built environment may very well be doing important kingdom work.

A Plea for Patience

As you begin to explore the issues raised by a study of the built environment, you will begin to notice that the major impetus in getting this important subject back on our radar has been a renewed critique of America's postwar development pattern known as suburbia. Those of you who have been around a while may already be rolling your eyes. The suburbs have been a popular source of scorn among cultural elites since the 1960s. You might be thinking that despite the mocking the suburbs receive from each generation, they seem to be doing just fine. In fact they continue to be the dominant choice among most Americans when it comes time to purchase a house.

If you think you've seen this critique before and for that reason feel inoculated to the issues about to be discussed, let me ask you not to dismiss this conversation too hastily. Granted, the suburb has been an easy (and perhaps unfair) target for some time now, but in the past decade there have been some interesting developments with regard to who is critiquing the suburbs and why. In the sixties the critique came largely from cultural liberals.

> In the 1950s and 1960s, the ticky-tacky boxes of postwar suburban tract housing were attacked for the conformity and "inauthenticity" of the lives lived therein, with gray-flannelled fathers making their way in the "system" and oppressed mothers "imprisoned" at home with their children. Presumably, authenticity lay in the orgiastic, liberated irresponsibility of urban bohemia.[7]

The suburbs were seen as too conformist and too square for creative and passionate people. But now we are beginning to see some of the most thoughtful and compelling critiques of the suburbs from the cultural right. In commending the work of pioneering Urbanists, Mark Henrie draws connections to classically conservative thought.

> But the critique of the suburbs advanced by such new Urbanists as Andrés Duany, Elizabeth Plater-Zyberk, and James Howard Kunstler is a substantially different phenomenon, and it is not going too far to say that these critics owe something to Burke. Rather than condemning suburbia because it is not bohemia, the new Urbanists criticize suburbia because it is not a *polis*.[8]

To be sure, the bohemian critique of the suburbs is alive and well, but now we are witnessing an entirely new type of critique emerging.

Also, we need to acknowledge that the American suburban experiment is no longer the juggernaut that it once seemed to be. During the recent real estate crisis, houses in postwar suburban subdivisions were hit far harder than the traditional walkable neighborhoods. Additionally, marketing surveys show that more and more Americans prefer living in denser walkable communities than in ones where they are dependent upon their automobiles.

The other potential roadblock to giving this subject a fair hearing is the cultural context in which it has arisen. The current conversation about the built environment did not emerge from the places where new ideas normally gain traction. It did not come from the cultural top, namely, the academy. Nor did it come from the bottom, namely, the voices of an oppressed minority. Rather, it came out of a relatively well-to-do group of practitioners whose primary motive, prior to entering the public spotlight with questions about the built environment, was to make money.

The built environment entered the public consciousness in the late twentieth and early twenty-first centuries through the work of a coalition known as the Congress for the New Urbanism (CNU). New Urbanism rose quickly from an obscure advocacy group to a household name in the span of a few decades. Where the New Urbanist name is recognized, it is often associated with certain projects on which it is perceived to have had a major influence. Notably, these have been Seaside, Florida, which was the set for *The Truman Show*, and Celebration, Florida, which has been the Disney Corporation's attempt at entering the development business. Both of these well-known projects have helped to give New Urbanism a reputation for building nostalgic "pretend" neighborhoods for rich people. Within the academy, the principles extolled by the New Urbanists have been largely accepted by the planning guild, but they claim they thought of the ideas first. The architectural guild has been less kind. Their critique of New Urbanism has been scathing.

This popular and professional critique of New Urbanism has been both misinformed and unfair. Suffice it to say that New Urbanism has had an influence that extends far beyond Seaside and Celebration. There are over six hundred explicitly New Urbanist projects currently in the United States, and many more throughout the rest of the world. Many of these projects are in what would otherwise have been traditional exurban settings, but over half of them are infill projects right in the heart of the city. Many of them are expensive, but there are a great number that are affordable. As Andrés Duany asserts, "New Urbanists wrote HUD's HOPE VI standards and are thereby associated with 110,000 units of affordable housing—virtually the entire supply of the last 15 years, and with a good portion directly designed by CNU members."[9] And New Urbanist principles are influencing much more than the development projects that have been inspired. Practicing New Urbanists have been involved in the plans for reconstructing the Mississippi Gulf Coast as well as Port-au-Prince, Haiti.

The Congress for the New Urbanism is not a lockstep organization. This coalition represents a wide diversity of practitioners and thinkers who come from a variety of backgrounds and disagree on many important issues. I am an enthusiastic supporter of the Congress for the New Urbanism and yet still point out some significant limitations of this movement in chapter 3. In any case, it is my belief that the ideas inspired by the Congress for the New Urbanism are valid regardless of the merits or viability of New Urbanism as a formally organized movement. That is to say, we may not have a Congress for the New Urbanism ten years from now, but ideas that it has put forth and the buildings New Urbanists have built will be with us throughout most of the twenty-first century.

To Change the Way You Look at Everything

In this book we embark on a journey that explores some new developments in both Christian theology and civic discourse that result from a growing awareness of the built environment. I should warn you that this book just might change the way you look at everything. You may have never thought about the built environment in a formal way, but I'll bet that you haven't spent very much time outside of it, either. It's pretty hard to escape. As a dish soap commercial used to claim, "you're soaking in it."

You have most likely lived the majority of your life within this sphere we are calling the built environment. And there is a very good chance that you haven't really looked at it directly. Well, what exactly have you been looking

Introducing the Built Environment

at, then? My guess is that you've been looking at texts (as you're doing now), you've been looking at screens (how many texts have you received as you've been reading this chapter?), you've been looking at signs (telling you at what street you needed to make a turn), and you may even have been looking at some buildings. And a lot of the looking you've been doing has been at speeds of thirty miles per hour or more and from within the bubble of an automobile.

But you probably haven't spent much time looking at the shape of the spaces formed in between the buildings. Those spaces are an integral part of built environment, and that is what I am going to spend the rest of this book encouraging you to look at. Hopefully, in addition to those other things you have been looking at, you've also been looking at people. If there is a legitimate hesitancy about embarking on a study of the built environment, it is that people really are more important than buildings.

As we work through this material and learn to look at the built environment, it is my hope that people become more, not less, important. The built environment is ultimately a setting for people. It is a setting that has the potential to engage you as a whole person, and it is a setting where you can meet and interact meaningfully with other people. Life takes place within the built environment.

Because we live our lives in the built environment, our experience of community is strongly influenced by the shape and quality of that environment. This fact alone should encourage us to be aware of the built environment. However, our attending to the built environment is important for other reasons as well. The living of our lives is not only shaped *by* but also *shapes* the built environment. Where we shop, how we get from point A to point B, where we choose to live—all will ultimately have an impact on what shape our footprint in the built environment will take.

The fact that we are somehow responsible for this built environment is a sobering thought, but it is an empowering one as well. It means that we have the power and the opportunity to influence an important part of culture. As Christians consider the possibility of meaningful engagement with culture, there is often a feeling of discouragement. We can critique movies, music, and literature from a Christian perspective, but only a very small minority of exceptionally talented Christians are ever likely to have much of an impact on these cultural forms. But almost all of us, for better or for worse, have opportunities to engage as well as shape the built environment on a fairly regular basis.

The purpose of this book is to help you look at the built environment specifically in light of your Christian commitment. The built environment is not just a place where our lives are lived, and it is not just a setting that is shaped by the living of our lives; it is also a place where the story of our salvation is played out.

"Where are you?" This question spans the distance between alienation and reconciliation, between turning away and turning toward, between living a reduced life under the shadow of a curse and living a whole life within the freedom of *shalom*. Although the "Where are you?" I addressed to you at the beginning of this chapter was not nearly as profound as that which was spoken by God in Genesis, where you are now does involve many of these same issues.

My goal is simple and straightforward. For those who already see the built environment as an important setting for human thriving and Christian discipleship, I want to provide tools for better understanding and working within the built environment. And for those who are not accustomed to looking at the built environment, I want to challenge the way you have been conditioned to look at everything, so that we can discover new ways that the God who sees everything can change us as well as redeem the world through us.

For Further Reading

Bess, Philip. *Till We Have Built Jerusalem: Architecture, Urbanism, and the Sacred*. Wilmington, DE: ISI Books, 2006.

Crouch, Andy. *Culture Making: Recovering Our Creative Calling*. Downers Grove, IL: IVP Books, 2008.

Duany, Andrés, Elizabeth Plater-Zyberk, and Robert Alminana. *The New Civic Art: Elements of Town Planning*. New York: Rizzoli, 2003.

Gorringe, Timothy. *A Theology of the Built Environment: Justice, Empowerment, Redemption*. Cambridge: Cambridge University Press, 2002.

———. *The Common Good and the Global Emergency: God and the Built Environment*. Cambridge: Cambridge University Press, 2011.

Jacobsen, Eric O. *Sidewalks in the Kingdom: New Urbanism and the Christian Faith*. The Christian Practice of Everyday Life. Grand Rapids: Brazos, 2003.

Kostof, Spiro. *A History of Architecture: Settings and Rituals*. New York: Oxford University Press, 1985.

Mayernik, David. *Timeless Cities: An Architect's Reflections on Renaissance Italy*. Icon ed. Boulder, CO: Westview Press, 2003.

Meinig, Donald W., ed. *The Interpretation of Ordinary Landscapes*. New York: Oxford University Press, 1979.

Myers, Ken. *All God's Children and Blue Suede Shoes: Christians & Popular Culture*. Turning Point Christian Worldview series. Westchester, IL: Crossway Books, 1989.

Wolters, Albert M. *Creation Regained: Biblical Basics for a Reformational Worldview*. 2nd ed. Grand Rapids: Eerdmans, 2005.

Wolterstorff, Nicholas. *Art in Action*. Grand Rapids: Eerdmans, 1980.

Introducing the Built Environment

———. *Until Justice and Peace Embrace: The Kuyper Lectures for 1981 Delivered at the Free University of Amsterdam*. Grand Rapids: Eerdmans, 1983.

Other Resources

Theology and the Spatial Arts Colloquium www.otago.ac.nz/theoart/research/artsbuiltenvironment .html

The Congress of the New Urbanism www.cnu.org

Part I

Orientation

Do you know what this is a picture of?

This is a picture of the most advanced civilization in the world.[1]

Does something about that seem wrong to you? This picture shows a rather unremarkable scene that could be anywhere in North America. You've probably seen places like this countless times and may never have given them a second thought.

More specifically, this is a snapshot of the public realm that most of us have come to expect in our everyday life. In most places throughout history, the public realm was where a country showed the rest of world what it valued and what it was capable of. The public realm is where a citizenry would put its most gracious plazas and its most beautiful buildings.

But the public realm in this country is, with few exceptions, rather unremarkable and even depressing. And this somehow seems wrong to us. Not only does this seem out of order in one of the richest countries in the world, it doesn't seem like a fitting setting for the human species wherever we happen to be. We are, after all, part of God's good creation—the ones made in God's image and the ones called to partner with God in the redemption and fulfillment of creation. It seems like we were made for better than this.

And in fact, we *were* made for better than this. There is a special word for this "something better" condition in which we are supposed to live our lives. That word is *shalom* and it includes our built environment and much more. Shalom can be translated as "peace," but unlike our use of the word *peace,* it means more than just the absence of conflict. Shalom involves restored fellowship with our Creator, human flourishing, justice, and relational wholeness for everyone. And shalom is unmistakably beautiful.

Each one of us carries a longing for shalom deep within. This image of shalom fuels our hope.[2] We respond with a twinge of joy when we see a glimmer of this image in our everyday life. And something just seems wrong when the place that we find ourselves bears not the slightest hint of that blessed condition that is described in the Bible.

In the introduction we looked at a garden and a city as two settings where humanity is shown to be living in harmony with one another, with the rest of creation, and with God. Those settings can be described as being characterized by shalom. But we also noted that we do not currently live in either of those settings. We live somewhere between the garden and the city. The question that we considered then, and will repeat here, is how do we live faithfully between the garden and the city? Or, what should we do in the present time with these longings for shalom?

In the introduction we drew a line between the garden and the city to show how the city can be seen as a realization or flowering of the potential that God intended for the garden. But that line can also be seen as a picture of the possibility for shalom that exists between the garden and the city. When we are obedient to God's command in the context of the communities and places to which we have been called, we often find that we can experience a degree of shalom in the present time. For this reason, this line can be labeled *shalom* or *obedience.*

Of course, "being obedient to God's command" is not always as easy as it sounds. In what ways can we point to the picture shown above in terms of specific acts of disobedience to God's command? And how would a decision

Orientation

to be obedient to God's command translate into specific recommendations for this dismal corner of the public realm?

Between the Garden and the City (II)

The first thing we need is to undergo a kind of orientation. We need to be oriented in such a way that we can begin to see where this shalom line might be located in the context of our places and our communities. And we need to be oriented to see how close or how far our places and communities are from the shalom to which we have been called.

There is nothing unusual about a brief orientation before taking on a new challenge. You may remember participating in orientation before your freshman year of college or getting oriented on the first few days of a mission trip in another country. But it is especially appropriate for us to get oriented before exploring the built environment from a Christian perspective, because the very word *orientation* is steeped in geography and theology.

The word is based on the Latin *oriri*, which means "to rise"—as in where the sun rises. From the West, where this term originates, *oriri* refers to the east. The original context for this word has to do with the *siting* of churches. If you are unfamiliar with this word, siting has to do with how a building is placed on its lot. The altar of a church (in the West) was supposed to be directed to the east, so that worshipers would be facing Jerusalem as they celebrated the Eucharist together. Churches were built with the narthex to the west, and the apse (where the altar was supposed to be) to the east. When the church building had been properly sited in this way, it was said to be oriented correctly.

The orientation that we undergo in this first section has nothing to do with identifying geographical coordinates so that a church can be properly directed toward the east. Rather, we will be identifying a different set of coordinates that will help to determine whether you are properly directed toward shalom. Rather than plotting your coordinates on a directional grid of north, south, east, and west, we will be plotting your coordinates on a grid consisting of four gifts that have been given to each one of us by our Creator to assist in our striving toward shalom.

- The first gift is *embodied existence*. Your body was not a mistake, an oversight, or a barrier to your relationship with God. Rather, your body is part of the "very good" that God declared when he completed the work of creation. You were meant to experience the world through the mediation of your five senses at the speed at which your two legs can carry you. These things don't need to be fixed or overcome in order for you to experience shalom.

- The second gift is a *place in which to thrive*. God not only created humanity good, God also placed us in a good setting. This setting was both sufficient to meet our material needs and a delightful place characterized by beauty and variety. To not be attached to a particular place (or to be displaced) is portrayed in Scripture as a dreadful consequence of sin, and not a marker of freedom. To experience shalom is not to be delivered from place, but to experience sustenance and delight in a particular place as we wait for the good place that is being prepared for us.

- The third gift is the *gift of community*. Community is not a panacea against loneliness, nor is it a strategy for making life more interesting. Community is fundamental to our existence. God reveals the divine self to us as a community of Father, Son, and Holy Spirit. We enter the world as part of a natural community of mother, father, and child. And we are called as disciples of Jesus Christ in the context of the community known as the church. We cannot create community from scratch, nor can we truly leave the communities that shape us. We can encourage healthy community, or we can inhibit it through our actions and decisions. But only God can give us the experience of community that we need.

- The fourth gift is the *gift of time*. When God divided the light from the dark, many believe God created time itself as a fundamental condition of created reality. Time is not therefore a foregone conclusion but is an intentional gift from our Creator. If we miss this basic fact, we are likely to misunderstand time itself and subject ourselves to frustration and disappointment. Some, looking backward, see time as a burden as it accumulates baggage from our history. Others, looking forward, see time as a commodity that can be leveraged as we "create" our own destiny. But as God's people, we can see time as a gift that can be enjoyed as we learn to receive it, attuned to its various rhythms under the careful guidance of the One who gives it.

1

Who Are You?

Human Being or Automobile Operator?

In the movie *Elf,* Will Ferrell plays the part of a human (Buddy) who, due to a Christmas mix-up at an orphanage, is raised by elves at the North Pole. The reality of his situation comes into clear focus when one of the elves lets it slip that Buddy doesn't really fit in because Buddy is a human. As disturbing as this revelation is, it finally makes sense of why he physically doesn't fit in his bed, the shower, or in any of the chairs.

It may very well be the case that many of us need to experience a similar "aha moment" with regard to our built environment. We humans are embodied beings, but for the past half-century many of us have been living in environments designed around the needs of automobiles. Coming to this realization may help explain numerous situations where it felt vaguely as if we just didn't fit in.

Curb Radii

To explore this possibility for yourself, find the closest sidewalk and go to the corner. Look down to where the street turns and note what you see.

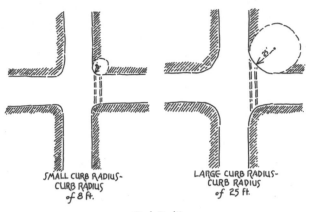

SMALL CURB RADIUS-
CURB RADIUS
of 8 ft.

LARGE CURB RADIUS-
CURB RADIUS
of 25 ft.

Curb Radii

Does the corner look like the diagram on the left or the one on the right? The difference between these two types of turns can be captured by taking a measurement known as curb radius. Curb radius is measured by taking the curve of the sidewalk at the corner as one segment of a circle. If you were to complete the circle and then measure the radius of that circle, you would have the curb radius.

The first drawing above shows a curb radius of eight feet, typical for a traditional pre-WWII neighborhood. The second picture shows a curb radius of twenty-five feet, which is typical for a postwar exurban neighborhood.

The purpose of the larger curb radius is to allow automobiles to travel faster by allowing them to turn the corner without slowing down. Unfortunately, the larger curb radius makes it quite a bit more dangerous for pedestrians.

In addition to the danger of crossing a street that allows fast-moving cars, the larger curb radius increases the distance that pedestrians have to travel to reach the other side of the street. If an eight-foot curb radius creates a forty-two-foot crossing distance, a twenty-five-foot crossing may create a sixty-six-foot crossing distance. The crossing distance is also increased as lanes for traffic are increased; and postwar exurbs also tend to have streets that are four, six, and even eight lanes wide. The larger the crossing distance, the longer the span of time the pedestrian is in danger of being hit by a car.

Pedestrian safety is a significant concern in this country. Every year, roughly four thousand pedestrians are killed, and another fifty-nine thousand are injured.[1] Compare this to residential fires, which in 2009 claimed the lives of twenty-five hundred and injured thirteen thousand.[2]

Concern over residential fire safety has led to numerous requirements for things like smoke alarms and clear access to exits. Why, then, has there not been a comparable set of rules about putting limits on curb radii? Or why do we continue to build streets with multiple lanes for traffic? The most logical explanation is that when we leave our homes, we are expected to be in automobiles. We are not really expected to walk around. That is to say, when it comes to the built environment, humans in their natural state are in a disadvantaged position.

This may help explain why, when we find ourselves trying to navigate the built environment by walking around, we sometimes feel as if we just don't fit in. But we have become so accustomed to "not fitting in" that we hardly notice it any longer and need to do strange things like measure curb radii and count traffic lanes to begin to perceive the reality of our situation.

Pizza and Slice

Another way to help us see the strangeness of our current situation is to use the human experience of certain phenomena as a reality check for our evaluative criteria. This is how we often think about the medical profession. Not all of us know how to do what medical doctors do, because they are trained specialists who work in a complex field. However, as complicated as the medical field is, the product for which that field is responsible (good health) must at some level be perceptible to the nonspecialist. Most people can recognize whether a doctor has done his or her job well, because we have an innate sense of what sickness and wellness look like.

The architect Léon Krier uses the analogy of a pizza to draw out the commonsense aspect of zoning versus traditional neighborhood development.[3] A traditional city, according to Krier, is like a pizza. There are lots of different sizes and types of pizza, and they are generally well regarded. Despite the great variety of pizzas available, there is one rule that governs all pizza. That rule is that one slice of pizza must be representative of the whole. That is to say, whatever kind of pizza you have, each slice will contain most of the ingredients that make it an enjoyable culinary experience. For example, if your friends have ordered a Hawaiian pizza and you receive a slice that doesn't have any Canadian bacon, you are justified in feeling cheated.

Krier claims that cities are like pizzas, and slices of pizza are like neighborhoods. That is to say every neighborhood should contain most of what you love about your city. You should be able to experience and enjoy the city at the level of your neighborhood. This is a rule that in most cases hasn't needed to be enforced. It was a natural consequence of the fact that most people throughout history have experienced the built environment on foot. When a significant number of people in an area don't own cars, the natural consequence is that neighborhoods develop where most needs can be met within a relatively short distance.

As populations expanded beyond distances that one could easily reach on foot, new neighborhoods were formed around the emerging populations on the outskirts. These collections of neighborhoods became towns, and then they became cities. But because people continued to experience them on foot, the basic scale of the neighborhood didn't change much. That is why the traditional neighborhood is considered to be a foundational building block for human community.

However, all of that changed in the second half of the twentieth century in this country. Through a policy tool known as functional zoning, we began to separate the functions of the city into different geographical zones. Hence, the emergence of a residential zone for houses, a retail zone for shopping, an office zone for working, and a recreational zone for playing. This idea may have had some merit, but Léon Krier is not convinced of its wisdom. In his mind, dividing up the city in this way makes about as much sense as dividing up the ingredients of a pizza and serving them separately.

Imagine going to a pizza party and being served a lump of dough, followed by a cup of tomato sauce, then a handful of cheese, and finally a stack of pepperoni slices. This way of "enjoying" pizza may have the same nutritional value as the traditional way, but almost all of the enjoyment of the pizza gets lost in this new approach. In the same way, our "cities" today have many of the same components of their traditional form, but because everything is separated by function, cities today are much less interesting and enjoyable than they were before. What we have now is a rationalized grouping of the functions of the city without a city in the traditional sense of that word.

Embodied Existence

When we stop to think about it, it is very odd that having a body would put us at a disadvantage in navigating our built environment. It is even more odd that we would never stop to ask about the human experience of this ubiquitous automobile-dependent development. From the moment of our creation, God intentionally gave us physical bodies and placed us in an environment that would sustain and even delight the senses with which God had endowed our bodies:

> Then the LORD God formed man from the dust of the ground, and breathed into his nostrils the breath of life; and the man became a living being. And the LORD

God planted a garden in Eden, in the east; and there he put the man whom he had formed. Out of the ground the LORD God made to grow every tree that is pleasant to the sight and good for food, the tree of life also in the midst of the garden, and the tree of the knowledge of good and evil.[4]

Bodily Faithfulness

Throughout Scripture, humans are called to live out their lives and even enjoy their time on earth as embodied creatures. Unlike in many Eastern religions or ancient myths, the body is nowhere in Scripture portrayed as a barrier to faithful living or a liability to our relationship with God. In fact, many of the commands we find in Scripture can be obeyed only by including our minds and bodies in the operation; "you shall love the Lord your God with all your heart, and with all your soul, and with all your might."[5]

When we hear that our bodies are important to human thriving and Christian discipleship, our first impulse is to think of our bodies as a context for applying the truths that we first comprehend through our minds. But this is not the only way to understand this concept. Our bodies can be obedient to God's leading in a more direct way. We can begin to comprehend this clearly in the use of the word *peripateo* in the New Testament. It literally means "to walk," but because it is generally understood as a metaphor about the living of our lives in general, it is usually translated in English as "live." However, because of our tendency to discount the relevance of our bodies to Christian faithfulness, it is a useful exercise to review some of the key verses in which *peripateo* is used, substituting "walk" for "live."

Be careful then how you *walk*, not as unwise people but as wise.[6]

Brothers and sisters, join in imitating me, and observe those who *walk* according to the example you have in us.[7]

As you therefore have received Christ Jesus the Lord, continue to *walk* in him.[8]

Finally, brothers and sisters, we ask and urge you in the Lord Jesus that, as you learned from us how you ought to *walk* and to please God (as, in fact, you are doing), you should do so more and more.[9]

When we think about walking in obedience to God, or like Christ, or in the Spirit, we can begin to see different ways this might happen. Certainly, there are many situations in which our obedience involves applying what we have learned in our minds to a real-life situation in a straightforward way. But there are other situations in which the right thing to do is primarily ascertained through our bodies.

We can push this logic even a bit further. Again, we think of Christian obedience as beginning with abstract truths that we comprehend with our minds and then apply to concrete situations that are mediated by our bodies. But sometimes it is our bodies that initially learn the lesson that our minds then have to grasp. Throughout the Old Testament, God's people were commanded to remember. Some of this remembering involved information that was first received cognitively, such as God's covenant promises or his instructions. However, most of what they had to remember was God's faithful actions toward them that they first comprehended with their bodies:

> Moses said to the people, "Remember this day on which you came out of Egypt, out of the house of slavery, because the LORD brought you out from there by strength of hand; no leavened bread shall be eaten.[10]

> Remember the long way that the LORD your God has led you these forty years in the wilderness, in order to humble you, testing you to know what was in your heart, whether or not you would keep his commandments.[11]

Remembering in this case involves recalling the way their legs ached or their stomachs grumbled as they followed God's leading through the wilderness.

Tacit Knowledge

The kind of information that we can comprehend and know with our bodies is called tacit knowledge. It is a common aspect of everyday life. We cannot claim to know how to play basketball or how to ride a bike from reading books about such things. Rather, to claim that we truly *know* how to play basketball or to ride a bike, we need to have actually done these things with our bodies.

Not only is tacit knowledge a valid form of knowledge, in some cases it can be better or more reliable than knowledge that is primarily cognitive. We can demonstrate this by way of the following scenario. Imagine that you have to get a life-or-death message across a body of water that spans only fifty feet from shore to shore but is too wide to walk around. You need some kind of a conveyer of that message for it to be received successfully. The primary qualification for this role is that the messenger know how to self-propel a human body across a body of water.

One of the candidates for this important role is a fifty-year-old physicist who has the requisite knowledge in the cognitive sense of that word. The physicist can draw you a beautiful chart involving buoyancy and rates of propulsion to explain how a human body moves through water. But the physicist has never actually swum in water. The other candidate is a six-year-old who is just learning to read but who happens to be a very good swimmer. In this case, the six-year-old's knowledge of self-propulsion is not only valid but a more usable form of knowledge. Because of superior knowledge, he would be the better choice for carrying the message.

Once we understand the basic nature of tacit knowledge, we can easily think of a number of situations in which tacit knowledge is to be preferred to cognitive knowledge. Some of the best musical instruments are made by people who rely more on the feel of the materials than on precise measurements. The grading of trees and tobacco is done mainly through tacit knowledge.[12]

Bodily Observations about the Built Environment

As I have demonstrated, our bodies are an indispensable context for Christian obedience. Our bodies may also play a role in understanding certain truths as well as in ascertaining what obedience looks like. These two observations give us permission to "think" about the built environment, not just with our minds, but also with our bodies.

Speed

For thousands of years, the speed at which most people experienced the built environment was fixed by the average person's gait, because the only way for the average person to experience the built environment was on foot. Since the advent of the automobile, all of that has changed. The automobile has not only increased the maximum speed at which we can experience the built environment but has led to the creation of some very distinct settings that are intended to be experienced at differing speeds.

Robert Venturi has suggested that the speed at which we are expected to experience a particular built environment can be understood by paying attention to the way that either signs or our senses are used to communicate pertinent information.[13] On one end of the scale, we have environments designed to be experienced at 65 mph. In these environments, information is communicated to us through iconic shapes and color schemes. At this speed you can see the familiar shape of a big-box store adorned with, say, the trademark Home Depot orange.

This particular landscape changes in scale as we slow down to 35–45 mph on a major arterial road. Here are large lollipop signs letting you know which of the buildings you are passing contain food and where to turn if you want to change your tires.

Driving at 20 mph on a traditional main street, you are still primarily using your eyes, but you are not using them to read signs. From this speed you can see actual merchandise in the plate-glass storefront windows. This environment actually is designed for driving or walking, so you can also experience it walking at 3 mph. As you walk along a typical main street, your eyes can see more detail, and perhaps some of your other senses get involved in communicating to you what is available. You don't need a sign to tell you that you are passing a hardware store or a barber shop; you can read this information more directly by the paraphernalia that you see through the window.

At the far end of the spectrum is the Middle Eastern bazaar or, perhaps, in the United States, a busy neighborhood farmers' market. In this environment, because of the crowds and the sometimes irregular layout of the stalls and the products, you can move only at a very slow pace. Here signs are completely unnecessary because you can see and smell the products that are offered for sale. In this environment touch, taste, and even sound may be used to navigate your options.

One implication of Venturi's observation about the relationship between speed and signs and senses is that the environments through which we travel more slowly engage us more as bodily creatures. The higher the anticipated speed the environment is built for, the fewer of our senses are engaged. At 65 mph only our eyes are engaged, and even then they are not as fully engaged as they could be. Whereas at 1–3 mph our eyes, ears, nose, and even sense of touch can be engaged. Therefore, we can surmise that environments designed for slower navigation may be better suited for the faithful living of an embodied human.

Distance

Not only do humans move on foot at about three miles per hour, but we do so as creatures embodied in a particular way. Our experience of the environment would be very different if we walked on four legs like dogs, or if we could easily transcend the horizontal plane like birds. Jan Gehl claims that our status as "linear, frontal, horizontal mammals" has a great impact on how we experience the built environment.[14]

Because of the way our bodies are shaped, we experience the built environment standing erect and moving forward. We need to think about the built environment in terms of the distance at which we see things right in front of us, in our peripheral field of vision, and above and below us.

The most significant objects that we see directly in front of us are other human beings. Gehl observes how our experience with another person is impacted by the distance at which we see him or her in front of us. He calls this metric the *social field of vision* and notes the difference of experience along certain gradations:

Distance and Intimacy

Sight

- At 330–550 yards we can identify people as humans rather than as animals or bushes.
- At less than 110 yards we can begin to see movement and body language in broad outline.
- From 55 to 75 yards we usually can recognize a person and can note hair color and characteristic body language.
- From 24 to 27 yards, we can read facial expressions and dominant emotions.[15]

Hearing

- At 75–55 yards we can hear shouts for help.
- At 38 yards we can conduct one-way communication using a loud voice.

- At 27–22 yards, short messages can be exchanged.
- At 7.5 yards genuine conversation can take place (as we move closer, the conversation can become more intense).[16]

One of the unintended consequences of the automobile-oriented development that we pursued in the second half of the twentieth century is the way that it has increased the distances at which we encounter one another. It has pushed our homes farther from the places that we work and shop. And because of the large parking lots and wider streets that are needed to accommodate all of those cars even when we are engaged in the same activity in the same place, the distance between us has increased significantly. And where the distance is not terribly great, we are often shielded from one another by the windshields of our automobiles. By increasing the distance between people in the built environment, automobile-oriented development tends to decrease the intimacy that people can have with one another in their environments.

Gehl also believes that our "horizontal sensory apparatus" is key to our experience of the built environment itself:

> Our senses and our locomotor apparatus paint a clear picture of an extremely alert pedestrian who looks ahead and down, but has only a limited field of upward vision. Thus hiding in trees has always been a good idea. Looking down is easy enough, but looking up is another story: we literally have to crane our necks.[17]

This means that skyscrapers and very tall buildings are of very little benefit to the pedestrian on the street. If skyscrapers are designed to be visually interesting, this might be good for postcards but won't typically be enjoyed by pedestrians walking along the streets. Also, this limits the ways that pedestrians can interact with other people who are situated on the higher floors of a building. Gehl claims that above the fifth floor our ability to connect with other people is greatly reduced.

This also suggests that the first floor of buildings is the most important floor for engaging pedestrians. If a building comes right up to the sidewalk and is filled with rich detail and variation, it tends to keep us interested. This kind of visually interesting environment was virtually a foregone conclusion in the traditional downtown or the main street in a small town. But now, one is likely to encounter stacked rows of parked cars or completely blank cement or glass walls when walking in a city or town.

Connectivity

One of the distinct advantages of navigating the built environment on foot rather than in an automobile is that more of your senses are engaged in moving through the environment. As we have noted, the accelerated speeds at which the cars propel our bodies through the environment means that we receive limited sensory input from the landscape outside of our cars. We tend to compensate for this lack of environmental stimulus by supplementing our experience with sophisticated entertainment systems for the interior space of our cars.

As a sensory experience, walking the built environment is fundamentally different. In many cases, one finds oneself enjoying the environment while using one's feet as a method of transportation. While walking to our destination, we may decide to follow a path that takes us by a view we'd like to enjoy or under a tree that is in blossom. One of the joys of navigating the built environment on foot is the ability to choose from among multiple options to get from one place to another.

The exurban environment is not only engineered for the convenience of automobiles but also usually fails to accommodate this kind of sensory exploratory delight that we seek while walking. The cul-de-sac/arterial street layout often dictates just one path to get from point A to point B. Not only is that path often indirect, it does not allow any variation on a whim. The traditional neighborhood grid with small blocks provides a very different experience. In this kind of layout, one can often choose dozens of options for getting from point A to point B. This makes every errand somewhat of an adventure.

The term that is used to measure this different way of laying out streets and sidewalks is *connectivity*. A traditional neighborhood grid has a high degree of connectivity. An exurban subdivision tends to have a low degree of connectivity. Connectivity is measured by the number of intersections per square mile. One hundred fifty connections per square mile is considered to be the minimum for a vibrant community; having twice that is considered even better. The images on the next page show some cities with differing levels of connectivity. They range from a high degree in Portland, Oregon, to a low degree in Forest Hills, Michigan.

Perspective

One of the reasons that the built environment does not always feel very comfortable or enjoyable to experience on foot is that our perspective on foot is

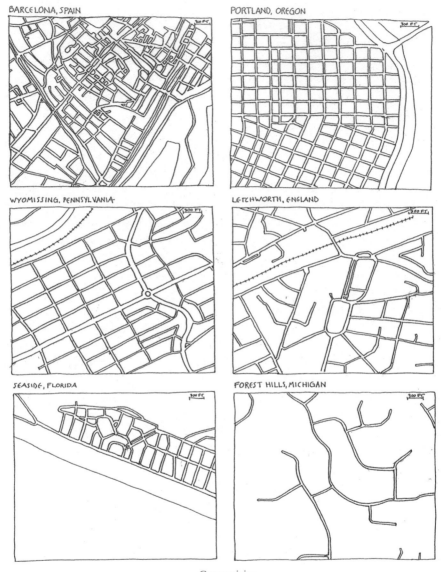

BARCELONA, SPAIN

PORTLAND, OREGON

WYOMISSING, PENNSYLVANIA

LETCHWORTH, ENGLAND

SEASIDE, FLORIDA

FOREST HILLS, MICHIGAN

Connectivity

different from the perspective of those who planned and organized this space. Planners have often formulated their plans first by looking at abstract statistics (traffic projections, census data, growth models) and then drawing out their visions for the built environment on a map that is scaled at something like 6,600 to 1. In some cases, this map is then built into a 3-D model to help communicate the vision to the public.

The perspective of the planning map and scale model is a distinct way of viewing the built environment. It is almost godlike (in perhaps a Greek-god sense) and not like the perspective of the mere mortals who live and move in these spaces. What seems attractive and pleasing at the godlike perspective can be very different from what pleases and attracts us while experiencing the built environment on foot.

For this reason, some of the most insightful commentary on the built environment has come not from planners and other "specialists," but rather from untrained nonspecialists who make their observations about the built environment from the perspective of a human body on the street. One of these commentators is a woman named Jane Jacobs, who has been called one of the most influential voices in city planning of the twentieth century. I return to Jane Jacobs at length later in this book, but I first want to introduce a simple methodology that Jacobs employed throughout her career.

Jacobs practiced what Philip Langdon called "learning through immersion." That is to say, she walked through neighborhoods and observed what worked and what didn't. And she enjoyed riding public transit without a particular destination in mind just to see what she would discover in a city. It is important to learn through immersion when we are first forming impressions about the built environment, and it is perhaps even more important to employ this methodology if our interest in the built environment leads us to accumulate some degree of technical expertise in this area. In many cases, it is easy to convince ourselves of the truth of a particular planning principle even if it really doesn't work from the perspective of the ground.

Inviting People

Jan Gehl asserts the simple observation that people will generally do what they are invited to do in the built environment. Throughout much of the twentieth century, our cities and towns had been inviting people to either drive their cars or stay at home; "interrupted lines of vision, large distances, high speeds, multistory placement and orientation away from people deter people from seeing and hearing others."[18] It may not have been an intended outcome, but the result of this tendency has been to express a rather low opinion of human beings within our public realm.

One task before us, then, is to rethink the public realm of our cities and towns to invite pedestrians to use and enjoy these areas and thus recover some dignity for our species. Again, Gehl has a good read on what a human-inviting environment looks like: "unobstructed views, short distances, low speeds, staying on the same level and orientation toward what is to be experienced."[19]

The Rise of Auto-Oriented Development

It is relatively easy now to raise questions about the wisdom and viability of automobile-oriented development. In retrospect, we can look at the impact that zoning and other policies had on traditional neighborhoods and wonder what in the world we were thinking. Why would we have deliberately destroyed the very things that made city and neighborhood life enjoyable? And why have we developed a built environment in which it is dangerous to navigate as a human being?

I don't think that our intention was to dismantle these things per se. Rather, we failed to consider the impact our decisions would have on these elements, and we were busy pursuing other ends.

Material Factors

There were a few material factors that strongly shaped our thinking in the postwar years. We were flush with wealth, land was plentiful, and oil was cheap. In this context, it made sense to develop a way of life around the assumption of universal automobile use. These particular factors may help to explain why zoning and the decimation of walkable neighborhoods were characteristic of development patterns in the United States and not in other countries during the same time.

There are always new buildings and elements of infrastructure being built, and at the same time, there are lots of old buildings and infrastructure being preserved. The ratio between the former and the latter correlates roughly with the relative wealth available to each generation. In general, a generation with a lot of wealth is going to build more and preserve less. Beginning during the postwar years and extending into most of the latter half of the twentieth century, America was a very wealthy country, and Americans created a lot of new buildings and infrastructure during this time. If it was just a matter of wealth, the aesthetic tastes of postwar Americans would have had a disproportionate influence on the look of the landscape, but when wealth was combined with other key resources, the impact on building practices was unprecedented.

America is unquestionably a spacious country. In many countries it would be unthinkable for an ordinary citizen who wasn't a farmer to have a home on five acres of land. However, in the United States, it is typical to have entire residential areas where it is required that every house sit on five acres of land.

When land is plentiful, there is a premium on being able to develop land quickly and cheaply. The developer who can clear a couple hundred acres and build hundreds of houses at roughly the same time will be able to keep her or his per-house cost well below that of the builder who has to build one house at a time. By the same logic, a company that can get land cheaply on the edge of town and build a fifty-thousand-square-foot megastore will be able to keep prices on its goods significantly lower than its smaller-scale competition. Such economies of scale favored the kind of tract housing and big-box store that blossomed in the latter half of the twentieth century.

An abundance of wealth and land played a significant role in postwar development patterns, but probably the low price of oil had an even greater impact. Because oil was inexpensive, gas was cheap. This made it economically feasible and even reasonable to completely abandon the walkable neighborhood pattern in favor of a form of development that required that every adult drive to fully participate in society. This gave us the boldness to build a transportation infrastructure that focused almost exclusively on privately owned gas-powered vehicles, which gave consumers the confidence to buy a home that was anywhere from fifteen to sixty miles from the place that they worked as well as a car trip away from other necessary amenities for daily living.

Zoning

Zoning in this country technically began in New York City in 1916, but by the end of the Second World War it had become the dominant mode of land-use regulation in just about every city in the United States. A watershed event for functional zoning, however, was a Supreme Court case argued in 1926 that ruled that cities did have rights to restrict land uses according to functional zones.

Prior to this decision, land use was regulated by municipalities, but it was done primarily through nuisance laws. If someone was planning to build something next door to your house that would have been dangerous, noisy, or smelly for your family, the city could have deemed that project incompatible with the residential character of the neighborhood and prohibited it.

The case we examine here came about when the town of Euclid (a suburb of Cleveland) passed a zoning law prohibiting commercial buildings and apartment buildings in a particular residential zone of the town. A local real estate company that owned land in the newly designated residential section had planned to develop that land for commercial purposes and felt that the creation of a residential zone made its land less valuable and therefore constituted an unfair intrusion on its land rights.

Village of Euclid, Ohio, et al. v. Ambler Realty Co. became a landmark case in land-use law. Once it established the precedent that municipalities could restrict private land uses into geographical zones, most cities pushed forward to adopt their own zoning laws.

Euclid v. Ambler cleared the way for a major shift in development patterns and, ultimately, the way most of us live. In addition to this legal precedent, however, there were other institutional factors that helped tip the scales in the direction of an automobile-oriented rather than a person-oriented built environment.

Lending Institutions and Infrastructure Bias

The Federal Housing Administration is a governmental agency created to help Americans own their own homes. This program has been wildly successful in terms of encouraging home ownership; however, during the postwar era, it helped create an institutional culture that had a corrosive effect on the form of the traditional neighborhood. For a home to qualify for an FHA-supported loan, it needed to be new construction. From the perspective of minimizing risk, this was a sensible stipulation. However, the impact that this had on the housing market was that it diverted a huge number of potential homeowners away from older traditional neighborhoods into the outlying suburbs. The FHA has since made adjustments to these kinds of policies, but the impact of such a bias during decades of home building has left an indelible imprint on the landscape.

Another factor was the Federal Highway Act of 1956. This act was initiated by President Eisenhower with the express purpose of creating an interstate highway system that would greatly increase the convenience of traveling long distances via automobile. Such substantial federal investment in road infrastructure established a pattern for development that would persist for the rest of the twentieth century. Throughout most of the century, development decisions were made with the assumption of universal adult automobile ownership. This in turn meant that people could purchase houses farther and farther from their places of work and other destinations to which they required access.

Two Models

From Suburb to Exurb

As these material factors were encouraging more and more automobile use, new development templates emerged that cemented the automobile-oriented lifestyle into our imagination. The first wave of suburban development was the streetcar suburbs popular in the second half of the nineteenth century. Streetcar suburbs were developments located outside of major cities along major streetcar lines. They were geographically proximate to the larger city and were set up so that residents could travel into the city for work and for cultural activities. These early suburbs consisted of relatively compact and walkable neighborhoods. The development was laid out on a grid plan, and the house lots were small.

Over time, this original suburban pattern gave way to what has been called the automobile exurb. What is different about the automobile exurb is that there is no longer a centralized city to which the outlying suburbs must relate. Places for working, places for living, places for shopping, and places for cultural events are all located outside of any city center. And each of these things is strictly separated from the others according to function.

Another difference is that in the traditional suburb, the breadwinner might have to drive or take the train to work, but many of the other tasks of life could be done on foot. In the postwar exurban environment, one must drive everywhere. Besides the single-family house, one of the most characteristic sights in the automobile exurb is the strip mall.

The strip mall provides a clear picture of the lack of connectivity that exists in the exurban environment. In the first place, the strip mall is set back from the street (and perhaps the sidewalk) that constitutes the public realm. The goods and services of the stores in the strip mall are not directly visible to humans on foot but must be announced through the use of bold signs. Strip malls are disconnected not only from the street and sidewalk but typically from neighboring buildings. There is usually a fence or impervious landscaping that prevents movement from a strip mall to a neighboring business. While one might see a whole block of detached single-family homes in a suburb and an exurb, the strip mall is unique to the exurb.

It is important to understand the difference between the suburb and the exurb, because they may help point us to a workable solution for the future. Many people think that being critical of automobile-oriented development means to be opposed to the use of automobiles in contemporary

·THE AUTOMOBILE EXURB·

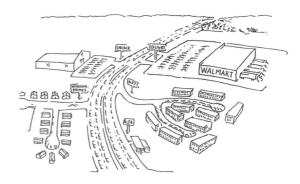

life. But in fact the one doesn't follow from the other. The problem with automobile-oriented development represented by the exurb is that the car becomes the only viable transportation choice for navigating daily life. One needs to get into a car to go to work, church, the store, or a friend's house. The classic suburban environment is different in that those neighborhoods were set up to be navigated by foot, bicycle, public transit, or car. That is to say, people could choose to travel by car if they wanted to get to their destination more quickly or if they had a lot of stuff to transport. But if one didn't want to take a car (or if one didn't own a car), there would still be options for getting from point A to point B.

The important distinction here has to do with the wisdom of constructing our built environment first and foremost at a human scale. One can then make certain adjustments or concessions for automobiles, but not to the point of destroying the human scale. What is most important, then, is to understand how human-scaled neighborhoods work. One can find such neighborhoods in streetcar suburbs, in traditional downtowns, and in small towns. The next section tells the story of how the human-scaled neighborhood has been undergoing a renaissance in the late twentieth and early twenty-first centuries.

The Traditional Neighborhood

Throughout the period of time when the exurban model was being developed, traditional neighborhoods continued to exist and functioned perfectly well in older parts of town. However, because of strict zoning laws, such traditional neighborhoods were no longer being built by developers. Near the end of the twentieth century, people finally began to question the wisdom of the exurban experiment that had dominated most of that century. These critics observed that the quality of life in traditional neighborhoods seemed to remain pretty high, while the exurbs seemed to become less pleasant places in which to live and work as they became more and more crowded and residents began to retreat into the safety of their private homes and yards.

This group of architects, planners, and developers who wanted to offer an alternative to exurban development began collaborating on projects in the 1980s, and in 1993 they formed the Congress of the New Urbanism. They laid out their critique of exurban development and presented a coherent alternative in a Charter of New Urbanism.

> We advocate the restructuring of public policy and development practices to support the following principles: neighborhoods should be diverse in use and population; communities should be designed for the pedestrian and transit as

well as the car; cities and towns should be shaped by physically defined and universally accessible public spaces and community institutions; urban places should be framed by architecture and landscape design that celebrate local history, climate, ecology, and building practice.[20]

Over the past few decades, New Urbanism has become a powerful and well-known reform movement. Although the title for this movement is catchy, it is also a bit misleading, in that what this group is advocating is not exclusively urban and is not very new. New Urbanists advocate community-enhancing development at a variety of scales. By "urbanism" they tend to mean the shape of the public realm that is formed in between buildings. And this group uses a transect model to show what good urbanism looks like along a wide continuum from dense inner city all the way to rural settings.

Many of the ideas advocated by New Urbanists are taken from traditional neighborhood- and town-planning principles that have withstood the test of time. What is "new" about the movement is that building traditional neighborhoods has become a lot more difficult since the onset of postwar exurban development. Whereas things like a coffee shop on a corner of a residential neighborhood, alleys behind houses, and square blocks used to be common features of neighborhood design, all of these things would typically be forbidden by a contemporary zoning code. The newness of New Urbanism is not usually the ideas being proposed, but rather the hurdles one has to overcome to implement them.

One of the more helpful ideas that the New Urbanists have recovered from the dustbin of history has been the elements of a traditional neighborhood. In their book *Suburban Nation*, Duany, Plater-Zyberk, and Speck articulate six features:[21]

1. **The center.** There should be a clear center for activities that residents share in common (shopping, civic, entertainment). The center draws people in and creates connections. The term *sprawl* is an apt moniker for exurban development, because of its spreading, centerless character.
2. **The five-minute walk.** A resident should be able to access most of the needs of daily life within a five-minute walk. This parameter is usually defined as somewhere between one quarter and half a mile and is also called the pedestrian shed. What is so challenging about exurban development is how impossible it is to walk to any meaningful destinations. One can go on a walk for exercise or perhaps walk to a neighbor's house, but walking to the store, hair salon, or coffee shop is not a realistic option.

Pedestrian Shed

3. **The street network.** There is a complex network of streets (usually some kind of a grid) that allows pedestrians and drivers to choose multiple routes to any destination. Exurban style development follows a cul-de-sac-to-arterial pattern, in which most streets terminate in a dead end and direct traffic toward high-volume feeder roads.

4. **Narrow, versatile streets.** Streets in a traditional neighborhood tend to be relatively narrow (one to two lanes of traffic in each direction), and the street includes amenities such as sidewalks, trees, benches, and café tables that support other uses of the street besides driving. Exurban streets tend to be built for the sole purpose of moving automobile traffic as quickly and conveniently as possible.

5. **Mixed use.** Within a five-minute walk in a traditional neighborhood, one is likely to find places for living, shopping, playing, working, worshiping, and enjoying culture. In addition, there are homes for people of a wide variety of socioeconomic status—large single-family homes, small single-family homes, townhouses, condominiums, and apartments. Exurban development is strictly segregated according to house price.

6. **Special sites for special buildings.** Traditional neighborhoods allow structures that are important to the collective identity of the citizenry to have prominent placement. In exurban development, the placement of individual buildings (so long as they meet zoning requirements) is a

function of the market. If you are willing to pay more, you can have a more prominent site.

The Car as Idol

One of the primary barriers to faithfulness in the Bible is not unbelief or even hedonism, but rather idolatry. Idolatry involves placing something in the center of our existence that has no business being there. The path to idolatry is both predictable and surprisingly elusive. It begins with transferring the credit for our well-being from God to something else. When the Israelites had been delivered from slavery in Egypt by the powerful actions of God and were on their way to the promised land, they inexplicably decided to fashion a golden calf from the jewelry that God has procured for them and claimed that object as their savior.

> He took the gold from them, formed it in a mold, and cast an image of a calf; and they said, "These are your gods, O Israel, who brought you up out of the land of Egypt!"[22]

Perhaps part of the dynamic here is that we don't like feeling beholden to a God that we cannot control and would rather give credit to gods of our own making. The gods we make (we convince ourselves) are better, since they exist to serve us. And so we transfer our hope and ultimately our worship from the one true God to various idols.

One problem with idols is first and foremost that they distract us from our worship of the one true God. But the other problem is that rather than idols serving us, we end up serving them, and they continually demand more and more from us.

> Bel bows down, Nebo stoops,
>   their idols are on beasts and cattle;
> these things you carry are loaded
>   as burdens on weary animals.
> They stoop, they bow down together;
>   they cannot save the burden,
>   but themselves go into captivity.[23]

It may be too much to say that the car has been an idol in contemporary American culture. There are some who do worship their cars, but many of us simply see them as a necessary feature of contemporary life.

However, we can see that the automobile has taken on some of the characteristics of an idol for our culture at this point in our history. The car was introduced as a kind of salvation from the burden of embodied existence. Rather than seeing embodied existence as an intentional aspect of the lives God has called us to live, and even as a wonderful gift, we bought into the lie that we needed to be relieved of the burden of our bodies. As the extravagant promises of automobile-oriented development have failed to materialize, rather than rejecting this model, our tendency has been to give over more and more of our resources and efforts to meeting the insatiable needs of our cars. This has led to a built environment that is both ugly to look at and inconvenient to navigate as embodied humans. Perhaps if we could remember that our bodies are good and, in fact, a gift from our Creator, we could begin to build settings that are more useful and enjoyable for embodied creatures.

For Further Reading

Duany, Andrés, Elizabeth Plater-Zyberk, and Jeff Speck. *Suburban Nation: The Rise of Sprawl and the Decline of the American Dream*. New York: North Point Press, 2000.

Gehl, Jan. *Cities for People*. Washington, DC: Island Press, 2010.

———. *Life between Buildings: Using Public Space*. New York: Van Nostrand Reinhold, 1987.

Haar, Charles Monroe, Jerold S. Kayden, and American Planning Association. *Zoning and the American Dream: Promises Still to Keep*. Chicago: Planners Press, American Planning Association in association with the Lincoln Institute of Land Policy, 1989.

Jewett, Paul King, and Marguerite Shuster. *Who We Are: Our Dignity as Human: A Neo-Evangelical Theology*. Grand Rapids: Eerdmans, 1996.

Kay, Jane Holtz. *Asphalt Nation: How the Automobile Took Over America, and How We Can Take It Back*. Berkeley and Los Angeles: University of California Press, 1998.

Levine, Jonathan. *Zoned Out: Regulation, Markets, and Choices in Transportation and Metropolitan Land-Use*. Washington, DC: Resources for the Future, 2005.

Meek, Esther L. *Longing to Know*. Grand Rapids: Brazos, 2003.

Morris, Douglas E. *It's a Sprawl World after All*. Babriola Island, BC: New Society, 2005.

Polanyi, Michel, and Amartya Sen. *The Tacit Dimension*. Chicago: University of Chicago Press, 2009.

Sale, Kirkpatrick. *Human Scale*. 2nd ed. New York: Putnam, 1982.

Other Resources

Walkable and Livable Communities Institute http://www.walkable.org/index.html. This organization encourages communities to support pedestrian-friendly environments.

2

Where Are You?

Place

Take a moment to go back to the question that was asked at the very beginning of this book—"Where are you?" Are you in the same place as you were when you read page 1, or are you somewhere different? Is this a familiar place, or are you somewhere new? Does this place evoke any memories for you? How would you describe this place—is it beautiful, cozy, ugly, or sterile? How many of your senses are engaged with this place—does it smell different from other places? Are there interesting textures to explore with your hands? Have you left a mark on this place—did you decorate the walls or scratch your name on the table? Would this area you are now occupying be better described as a space or a place?

Place and Space[1]

Place, in contrast to space, is a context-specific, meaning-rich concept. Although many use the two words interchangeably, a fairly clean distinction can be made between them. Space is more abstract and undifferentiated than place. Space often is used to express a freedom from or a potential for something—"give me some space" or "we need space for this relationship to develop."

Place, by way of contrast, describes a realm where something significant has happened or is happening; "there's no place like home."

Walter Brueggemann identifies place as storied."[2] One way to easily visualize the relationship between space and place is to think of a college dorm room. Before a student moves in, the dorm room has everything that is needed for college life, but it's generic, undifferentiated space. Typically, there is a desk, a bed, a closet, a mirror, and a light. Within a week or two after the student moves in, this space is transformed into a place. There are pictures on the mirror, a cover on the bed, posters on the walls, and bric-a-brac on the desk. The story of that particular semester of college in that student's life has already begun to be inscribed on the walls.

There is a dynamic relationship between space and place. Place is good, but we sometimes need a break from it. As a person lives life, one's narrative begins to etch meanings on a particular space, causing it to become a place. As the meanings and memories crowd a place, a person may express a desire for more space. This is why we go on vacations to be restored or sometimes long to start over.

Space can be good in and of itself as well. Space is sometimes necessary for personal growth or identity formation within a group. Often we go on retreats not to disengage, but to reconnect with God, with ourselves, or with others. Often, however, new spaces are lonely and disorienting. Strangers finding themselves in this kind of situation long to find a place that they can call home.

The Demise of Place

John Inge discusses how modernity has diminished the importance of place in contemporary life.[3] In ancient and premodern cultures, place was a significant determiner of one's identity. A person typically was born, lived, and died in one particular place and was closely identified with that place (Jesus of Nazareth or Joseph of Arimathea). With the universalizing impulse of modernity typified in the scientific method, the particularities of place began to be perceived as a liability to the modernist project. For an experiment to be valid, it had to be repeatable regardless of the particularities of place. Through this and other developments, space began to be valued more highly than place.

With increasingly faster modes of transportation and communication, place became swallowed up by time. As people could get information and goods from various places and could easily travel, places (and the people associated with them) became less and less important. In the nineteenth century, a person from North America would have to travel on a boat for many weeks to experience the taste of a kiwi or would have to wait months for news from the mission front in interior China. In the twenty-first century, a North American can eat a bowlful of kiwis in the middle of winter while participating in a video conference with missionaries from six continents at once. If you want to make a direct connection with another person today, the most important thing you need to coordinate is the time of your connection. With the cell phone, Skype, and Facebook, your location and theirs are insignificant.

Placelessness

Globalization and the horizontal integration of corporate structures have more recently introduced the notion of placelessness into the modern vocabulary.[4] Big-box chain retail stores and identical, production-built tract houses can be understood as placeless places. These are technically places in that stories are lived in them, but the generic nature and short time span of the buildings make them resistant to holding the stories that are generated there. More and more of the contemporary landscape is being taken over by developments in which it can be very hard to tell where one happens to be located.

Implications

While one would be hard-pressed to try to make a convincing case against the scientific method, improvements in communications technology, or the significant benefits of expanding productivity in industry, it may still be helpful to consider some of the implications of the diminishing importance of place in contemporary life.

As one's connection with a particular place becomes more tenuous, it can be harder to make sense of one's identity. Gaston Bachelard makes the argument in *The Poetics of Space* that our identity is formed by our early interaction with places like the homes of our childhoods. This notion suggests that placelessness might play a contributing role in the current crisis of identity.[5]

The loss of place can have a detrimental effect on our collective and individual memory as well. Places of significance hold memories, and when they are designed with standardized elements or for short-term use, they tend to hold memories less well. To people who have been commanded in the Bible to "remember," this should be particularly concerning. We will explore this theme in more detail later in this chapter.

The boundedness of place has been an important element in relational development. We know one another more deeply when proximity forces us to interact on a regular basis. The contemporary ease by which we can move from one place to another has tended to pull us further apart from one another, rather than bring us closer. Martin Heidegger has observed that in contemporary life "the frantic abolition of all distances brings no nearness."[6] This theme will be taken up in chapter 3.

Ambiguity about Place

Not all of the attributes of place can be considered unequivocally good, however. For some people, place is primarily associated with oppression. A place can signify the stigma of one's identity in a particular context. One woman who encountered Jesus understood only too well that her place carried with it certain restrictions, "for Jews do not associate with Samaritans."[7] A place can evoke painful and destructive memories, and place can provide the pretext for relational disassociation and social stratification—"they ought to know their place."

In many ways, postmodernity has been concerned with navigating the assets and liabilities associated with place. On the one hand, postmodernity has revived an interest in narrative and localism in an attempt to recover some of the richness of place. On the other hand, postmoderns have embraced the fluidity and mobility allowed by modern communication technologies. Modernity brought the radical notion that a son of a blacksmith from Bath could grow up to be a lawyer in London. Postmodernity presents us with the possibility of making up an online identity that needs no correspondence with our actual geographical or demographic particularities. We have yet to discover the implications of this radical dismissal of place.

A Theology of Place

Whatever we may think about place, or whether or not we have given it much thought, place is an extremely important concept in the Bible.[8] From the very beginning of the story to the very end, place plays a key role. In fact, the whole story of the Bible can be quite easily framed around the theme of place.

Creation

The very structure of the account of the creation of the cosmos appears to be geared toward place. We can see this when we arrange the days of creation on a grid—dividing the creation between its first and second halves.

On the right hand side of the chart, we see the creation of objects of various sorts. Corresponding to each of these days of creation on the left-hand side

Orientation

of the chart, we see the creation of the "place" for these objects to exist and move. The stars, sun, and moon are placed within the field of light and dark; the birds and sea animals live in the sky and water; and earth animals and humans live on dry land. The God of creation not only created each creature unique but also seems to have placed each creature in a particular setting that was appropriate to its needs and capabilities.

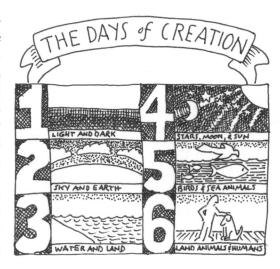

Removal from and Return to Place

When the first humans rebelled against their Creator in sin, the consequence of their rebellion was a removal from Eden—the place that had been created for them. This removal from place signified in a tangible way the fractured relationship with their Creator and their changed relationship with the earth. Their work in the garden had been meaningful and satisfying; outside of the garden, their work becomes toil.

As God begins to reveal his plan for the redemption of humanity, we discover that place plays a prominent role in this as well. God calls Abram to be the object of his covenant love and instructs him to leave his land and "go to the land that I will show you."[9] This command includes a promise to be placed in a good land flowing with milk and honey. A significant part of these early movements in the story of salvation involves arriving at this place, losing this place, and then finding it again.

The identity of the Israelites is wrapped up in their relationship with their God. But even this fundamental relationality is connected to place. It is essential that within the place to which the Israelites have been called, there is also a place for God's name to dwell.[10] Walter Brueggemann suggests envisioning the relationship between God, place, and people as an equilateral triangle, with God at the apex and "the land" and "the people" making up the other two points.[11] Putting too much emphasis on the land or the people leads to distortions, and so a balance must be kept between these two factors.

Redemption and Place

In the New Testament, the coming of Christ affects the role of place once again. On the one hand, the incarnation in a specific locale as well as the journey to Jerusalem can be seen as an affirmation of the significance of place in the plan of salvation. On the other hand, Christ breaks the oppressive power of place by indicating that God can be met in any place: "the hour is coming when you will worship the Father neither on this mountain nor in Jerusalem"[12]; "For where two or three are gathered in my name, I am there among them."[13] This shift can be understood as the specific historical person of Christ taking the place of "the land" in salvation history.

Although one implication of the incarnation is that no one particular place can be exclusively identified with God's presence, through Christ, God continues to meet people in particular places. Although part of Christ's redemptive work in our present age is to redeem us from the oppressive aspects of place, ultimately our redemption will again be rooted in place. Christ promises that he will go and prepare a *place* for us in his Father's home.[14] And one of the markers of Christ's return and the beginning of his reign in glory will be an ingathering of all of God's people. The notion of gathering suggests the specificity of a place.

Town Fabric and Placemaking

The built environment plays an important role in this dynamic process of space becoming place. I've already introduced this topic in our discussion of placelessness. As has been mentioned, certain kinds of environments are conducive to placemaking, and other environments seem to resist this process. If place is to play a role in our redemption, we need to give some thought to the potential for placemaking in the settings we construct as well as the settings we inhabit.

The thing that placeless environments fail to provide—that placemaking quality—can be described as *town fabric*. Daniel Solomon, in his book *Global City Blues*, breaks down town fabric to its three essential functions. According to Solomon, town fabric

1. houses people and provides places for work and their private needs;
2. creates settings for monuments;
3. shapes and defines the outdoor public spaces of a town.[15]

Each of these functions plays a key role in the making of place. We will deal with them in reverse order.

Enclosure—Setting the Stage

Obviously, when we speak about the built environment, we are mostly talking about buildings. And there are a lot of important things that we could say about buildings. However, as we have already noted, the problem is that if we focus too much on buildings, we fail to see the space between the buildings. And it is important that we notice the space between the buildings because it is here where some of the more interesting things in life are likely to happen.

With regard to the space between the buildings, we can identify two fundamentally different ways of assembling buildings.

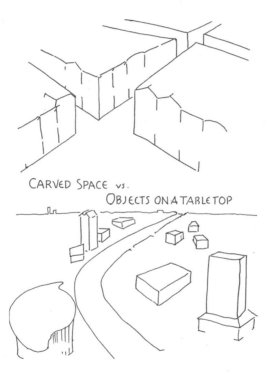

CARVED SPACE vs.
OBJECTS ON A TABLETOP

The traditional way of assembling buildings has been to carve space as is represented in the top half of this image. The way that we've been assembling buildings since about the Second World War has been to arrange them like objects on a tabletop, as is represented in the bottom half of this image.

Because this seems so natural when one is experiencing such a place, it can be easier to see when we adjust the scale and our perspective a bit. This image of Legoland allows us to see carved space in a more recognizable form.

Legoland

The desired outcome that carved space allows the town fabric to achieve is called enclosure. Enclosure provides a sense of protection, and it defines the space in pleasing ways. A sense of enclosure makes us feel more comfortable both when we are moving and when we are stationary.

We can measure enclosure by examining the aspect ratio of a particular place. The aspect ratio is the ratio of the building height to the width between the buildings. An adequate aspect ratio can be anywhere between 1:1 and 1:6.

Aspect Ratio

Buildings that are too low, streets that are too wide, or large parking lots destroy the sense of enclosure. When settings fail to provide an adequate sense of enclosure, we say that they "leak space."

Leaking Space

The majority of buildings constructed in the second half of the twentieth century are guilty of leaking space. There are three primary reasons for this. The first is simply a failure on the part of architects and city planners to understand and appreciate the concept of enclosure. This is in part due to an antiurban bias embedded in our institutions. Most municipal zoning codes require buildings to meet a minimum setback from the street, and they restrict building heights in many cases to a single story. These types of regulations are based on the idea that people would rather be in a rural or small-town setting, where one does not feel crowded by tall buildings.

However, an even more prevalent reason for leaking space has been parking regulations. Most municipalities require a minimum number of on-site parking spaces for each building. This number is usually based on providing one parking space for each user of the building at its busiest time. Because of the minimum setback regulations and because business owners (who also fail to understand enclosure) want their customers to see available parking spaces, the full number of required parking spaces usually ends up right in front of the building. This causes leaking space.

Of course, most of the churches constructed during this period have followed suit and have provided more than enough parking spaces for everyone of legal driving age to have a parking space. It is not enough to simply have ample spaces for a normal Sunday morning; they must provide ample space for parking even on Easter Sunday. This means that for six days of the week, the parking lot is virtually empty, and on Sunday it is only half empty.

A final reason for leaking space has to do with streets that are overly wide. As we noted in the previous chapter, one of the primary goals of city planning during the second half of the twentieth century has not been to create pleasing settings for human interaction, but rather to facilitate the easy movement of automobiles. This goal has often been made manifest in continuing to add as many lanes for traffic as possible. It is not unusual in some cities to see as many as eight lanes of traffic right in the middle of town.

Once we begin to understand the idea of enclosure, we can break this idea further into at least two common spatial tropes. Within a coherent town fabric, we can expect to experience what can be called outdoor hallways and outdoor rooms. In this sense, we can understand a city to be very much like a house with its roof taken off.[16]

The streets of a city with coherent town fabric should feel like hallways. This trope helps us feel more comfortable moving through the city by allowing our eyes to see our destination and by naturally guiding the movement of our bodies.

Outdoor Hallway

The plazas and squares of a city should feel like outdoor rooms. This spatial trope helps us feel more comfortable remaining stationary in the urban environment by providing a sense of shelter.

Outdoor Room

An awareness of the concept of enclosure and of the spatial tropes of outdoor hallways and rooms allows our eyes to see more than just the individual buildings within the built environment. We begin by seeing these distinct forms. But then we begin to see some of the detail within these forms.

One detail we can notice is called *streetwall*. The walls of buildings that form the town fabric work together to form a single streetwall. The buildings don't need to be the same height or of the same period or style, but if their fronts are at the same depth and they are parallel to the street, we have a streetwall. A good streetwall is a pleasing collage of textures, colors, and moods.

Streetwall

Another detail we can notice is known as *streetground*. Streetground has to do with how the ground between the buildings is apportioned. For the streets (or outdoor hallways), streetground can include qualities of the sidewalks, street trees, lampposts, benches, planting strips, parking lanes, driving lanes, and boulevards. The streetground of plazas (or outdoor hallways) can include benches, play structures, trees, fountains, and statues.

Monuments—Sharing Meaning

The second aspect of town fabric, according to Solomon, is to provide settings for monuments. Traditionally, monuments have been physical objects invested with special meaning for the people of a particular area, objects that are somehow elevated above ordinary objects in importance.

Monuments can be works of art—typically, statuary. And monuments can be buildings. Because monuments are most commonly thought of in terms of statuary, we will focus here on the monumental qualities of particular buildings. There are two requisite conditions for the presence of monumental buildings. There needs to be a way to signal that some buildings are more special than others. And these buildings need to be given priority of place so that they are presented to the public.

Traditionally, the buildings that were to be set apart would signal their special status through the use of architectural vocabulary. The height and scale of the building and its prominent features (such as the front door), the use of a more grand style, the quality of materials, and the use of architectural detail would together signal the importance of the building.

Monumental Building

The placement of buildings within the town fabric is the second way that monumental status is established. Monumental buildings can signal their importance by being set back from the right-of-way. Unlike the myriad of buildings that are set back for parking, true monumental buildings are set back for a dramatic effect. Typically, the setback of a monumental building creates a plaza or park for the public to enjoy.

A more elaborate approach to organizing town fabric goes beyond just maintaining an adequate aspect ratio for the sake of enclosure; it also lays out the streets into a coherent pattern. Such a pattern creates axial lines that cut through various sections of the city. These axial lines create focal points on which special monuments (buildings and statuary) can be placed.

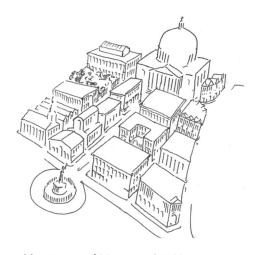

Monuments and Monumental Buildings on Axis

Placing monumental buildings on a formal axis is a characteristic of a very refined phase of civic art associated with the École des Beaux-Arts in Paris. There was a renewed interest in this formal approach in the late nineteenth and early twentieth centuries in the United States. This movement was known as the City Beautiful movement, and it was showcased at the World's Columbian exposition in Chicago in 1893. When one thinks of civic art in this country, one's mind tends to go to the City Beautiful movement.

At this exposition a series of monumental buildings was constructed; formal parks and public statues were organized around axial lines. A plan to extend this model throughout the rest of Chicago was devised by the famous architectural team of Burnham and Root. This led to a number of cities across the United States adopting City Beautiful plans. While these plans led to the construction of some beautiful civic buildings and some gracious public spaces, the momentum for this movement was lost during the Depression and wasn't picked up again.

The use of axial lines brings up another important requirement for monumental coherence. This is the issue of ratio. Solomon described the second function of town fabric as "creating settings for monuments." It is interesting that he doesn't seem to consider the monuments themselves as the most significant part of the town fabric, but the settings. This seems to suggest that it is the other buildings that allow us to see the monuments as special that have a most important role to play.

The nonmonumental buildings to which Solomon refers are known as fabric (or liner) buildings. The fabric buildings can be beautiful or ordinary, but their primary function is to help define the streetwall. If the fabric buildings are playing their role properly, you don't notice them too much, but rather see them as part of the streetwall that helps direct your eye to the monuments. The other important thing to note about fabric buildings has to do with ratio. This means that you need to have a certain ratio of ordinary buildings in order to signal that the monumental buildings are special. I don't think that it is important to identify a precise number that applies in every case, but something like 95 percent of fabric buildings provides a rough approximation.

Fabric Buildings

Orientation

If monumental coherence is a typical aspect of traditional town fabric, the lack of monuments is usually a marker of a placeless place. Placeless places that are underinvested tend to have only generic, featureless buildings as far as the eye can see. However, placelessness is just as much of a problem in wealthier areas. In these kinds of settings, every building wants to be a monument. The only qualifications for achieving monumental status are the cash to pay for it and the hubris of self-importance. Something feels amiss when monumental status is simply granted to the highest bidder.

The fact that placeless places lack monumental coherence may reflect a deeper problem with our public life. It may be an indicator of the increasing privatization of our lives. We no longer care very much about public life or the ways that it is expressed in the built environment. It may also reveal the increasing fragmentation of our lives. For one building to be more important than another, there needs to be some consensus on what kinds of things we find important. Not only is it difficult to establish consensus around religion as being important, it is even doubtful whether one could point to certain virtues such as courage, honesty, and fortitude as being commonly valued.

Philip Bess describes the distinct role that monumental buildings have traditionally played in the city.

> The buildings in traditional cities that shelter the private familial and economic activities—houses and housing; commercial and market activities—are typically backdrops to figural public spaces and to the buildings sheltering those governmental, religious, and educational institutions that exist to promote and sustain precisely those practices and virtues that simultaneously support and constrain the pursuit of private interest. And it is because the goods promoted by such institutions are goods common to the denizens of the city, and necessary for the achievement of its common goals, that such institutions rightly have been regarded as civic. It is therefore neither a surprise nor an accident to find that these "civilizing institutions" have been both prominently sited and architecturally monumentalized in traditional cities and towns. Not merely symbolizing power, architecture in the traditional city aspired to symbolize legitimate authority in general and specific (institutionally promoted) practices and virtues in particular.[17]

Monumental coherence, then, may be the cause of a particular place being placeless, or it may simply be a reflection of a deeper problem. In either case, it is helpful to be attuned to the ways that traditional town fabric employs monuments to reflect and undergird meaning for a particular locale.

Thresholds—Connecting and Enlivening Place

The third aspect of town fabric that we can attend to is that of thresholds. A threshold is a portal or an opening between the inside of a building and the outside of a building. Thresholds allow direct communication between the inside of a building and the outside. The most common types of thresholds that we encounter are windows and doors.

There are other kinds of quasi thresholds to consider as well. A front porch or a patio for a restaurant can be called a *liminal threshold*. This kind of threshold allows easy communication between the realm represented by the inside of the building (even though it is technically outside) and the actual outside of the building. And what's more, these thresholds tend to encourage movement between one realm and the other. Acquaintances are easily invited to come and sit on the front porch or to join the conversation around the coffee table.

Additionally, we can think of visual thresholds as allowing people to see from the inside to the outside of a building and from the outside to the inside of a building. There is some debate as to whether visual thresholds increase connection between the inside and the outside of the building or create more distance by making verbal communication impossible.[18] Another kind of quasi threshold is the virtual threshold represented by the connections that are made between inside and outside buildings made possible by the internet and cellphone technologies. How these technologies really function (or fail to function) as thresholds is yet to be determined. In any case, we can claim that in their current iteration, virtual thresholds tend to decrease the significance of place since they make the location of persons irrelevant.

The important function that physical thresholds play is that they connect the mostly private realm of the inside of buildings to the mostly public realm outside of the buildings. They mitigate our cocooning tendencies by drawing us into the interesting sights, sounds, and smells of the outside world. They also provide opportunities for people on the outside to gain social access to people on the inside. Thresholds help generate the energy of connection that enlivens places and allows stories to be generated.

When we examine a particular stretch of streetwall, we can distinguish between those that are saturated with thresholds and those that exhibit only minimal thresholds. A long stretch of streetwall without any thresholds can deaden the experience of walking in a city and can increase the sense of placelessness. If thresholds are so important to creating and maintaining a sense of place, why have they been so rare in the postwar era?

Orientation

Saturated and Minimal Thresholds

While there may be a number of causes we could point to, the dominant one has been central air-conditioning. With central air, it wasn't economical to have windows open on a hot day, so buildings were constructed with very few windows or windows that didn't open. The primary threshold of any building, no matter how much streetwall it is responsible for, tends to be the front door, and perhaps a garage. While a front door is technically a threshold, it typically encourages communication and passage between inside and outside in only a limited way. One usually has to establish one's right to enter the building (as a customer, a messenger, or a friend) before one can enter the front door. Front doors do not allow or encourage the creation of new connections between people.

Fortunately, we are beginning to realize the limits of air-conditioning in controlling the climates of our buildings. The notion that we could ignore natural heating and cooling elements (sunlight and breezes) because of readily available heating and cooling technologies has turned out to be a wrongheaded and environmentally wasteful assumption. In the past decade we have seen a return to some of the traditional practices for heating and cooling that involve architectural elements such as windows that open and shut. We are also seeing some municipal policies that encourage restaurants to have windows that open onto the sidewalk outside of their building. These changes in direction may provide a way for a return to using thresholds on buildings to enliven public spaces.

Performing the Scriptures in Place

We could say that the three functions of town fabric (shaping public space, settings for monuments, and housing private needs) together increase the liveliness or drama of the public realm. The idea of attending to the dramatic possibilities of the built environment is important because we can think of the built environment as a kind of stage for the performance of a spontaneous civic drama. This may be especially significant to the Christian community, because we are called to participate in public life as witnesses and ambassadors. In fact, we can think of Christian discipleship in general in dramatic terms.

In his book *Theology on the Way to Emmaus*, Nicholas Lash encourages us to think of the range of ways in which we interact with texts. We do different things with different texts. Some texts allow us to interact with them on our own, while others implore us to engage them with others. We carry maps with us as we navigate unfamiliar terrain, we read poems to an audience at a pub, we carefully follow the instructions of an auto repair manual, and we perform musical scores in conjunction with other players. These are just some of the things we do with texts.

What kind of interaction, then, does the text of Scripture require? Is it to be read passively, or is it to be enacted in the lives of believers? Is it to be interpreted alone, or is the Christian community the proper locus of interpretation? To these questions, Lash claims,

> The fundamental form of the Christian interpretation of scripture is the life, activity and organization of the Christian community, construed as performance of the biblical text. Secondly, that Christian practice, as interpretative action, consists in the performance of texts which are construed as "rendering," bearing witness to, one whose words and deeds, discourse and suffering, "rendered" the truth of God in human history.[19]

Lash believes that the Scriptures are meant to be performed in the context of Christian community.

Much of the faithful performance of Scripture takes place in the liturgy of gathered worship, but we can also think of this performance as extending out into the public realm. This is easy to see in the various processionals that Christians have enacted within the public realm throughout the centuries, but this can also be seen in informal ways. Whereas a secular person may use the stage of town fabric to enjoy people-watching or to meet new friends, a Christian may enter that stage to enact compassion or to seek justice. One can even see encouraging or participating in lively street interaction as helping to perform shalom in the public realm. We will explore further ways this concept can be applied in chapter 7.

Memory and Place[20]

A sense of place is important in helping us connect not only with one another in our current time frame, but also temporally with those who have preceded us and those who will succeed us through holding memories. Since churches are often among the oldest structures in a community, they provide a good place for us to begin exploring the role of memory in the built environment.

Walls That Hold History

One of my duties when I was a pastor in Montana was to lead a new members class for those who expressed interest in joining the church. Most of the teaching was done in a room in the Christian Education building, and most of the content was conveyed by way of lecture or discussion. At the conclusion of the class, however, I would walk the class across the churchyard for a quick tour of the sanctuary. As we approached the substantial doors of our 1920s Gothic Revival edifice, I would turn to my group and proclaim with as much authority as I could muster that "this is not the First Presbyterian Church of Missoula." "Right now," I would explain "the first Presbyterian Church is scattered all around this town, probably spending time with friends and family, and come Monday they will scatter farther, to occupy outposts of responsibility for the kingdom in homes, offices, stores, schools, and other important places."

I had grown up with the firm conviction that the church is not the building but rather the people of God. I was simply passing this conviction on to the newest members of our church family. But if our being a church really had nothing to do with this cultural artifact of brick and plaster, why was I so drawn to share with these groups the particularities of our shared life together from within this building?

As I considered what might lie behind this internal tension, I began to realize that there may be a bit more complexity to this issue than I had previously thought. Having been raised and trained in the Reformed tradition, I was somewhat uneasy with the notion of sacred space. Drawing on Jesus's words that "the hour is coming when you will worship the Father neither on this mountain nor in Jerusalem,"[21] and that "For where two or three are gathered in my name, I am there among them."[22] I had a firm conviction that God could be worshiped in any conceivable place. I drew comfort from the fact that there weren't especially sacred places where God would make himself more present than in others. So why did I find worshiping God in cheap, gymnasium-style churches so uninspiring, and why was I so drawn to churches with a bit more substance and durability to them? Why did I value churches that evoked a sense of place?

Memory and Salvation

I found the beginnings to an answer to my question in thinking about the role of memory in salvation history. Repeatedly throughout the Bible we are instructed to remember. "Remember this day on which you came out of Egypt, out of the house of slavery, because the LORD brought you out from there by strength of hand."[23] And God establishes faithfulness by reminding us of God's connection to our history: "I am the God of your father, the God of Abraham, the God of Isaac, and the God of Jacob."[24] What I was coming to realize is that I valued certain kinds of church buildings because they seemed to hold memories better than others.

Sensory, Semiotic, and Patina Memory

As I pushed this idea further, I began to see that buildings hold our memories in three distinctive ways. Visually (or employing other senses), they are the setting for many of our direct memories. We remember the houses in which we grew up through the associative memories that are placed there. I distinctly remember the look of our kitchen from the perspective of the back door, and it will always represent (for me) the notion of home. These kinds of responses represent the direct *sensory* aspect of memory.

Buildings can also hold memories in a *semiotic* way—that is, buildings put us in contact with symbols that can potentially carry meaning for anyone in our culture. These symbols can be intentional, or they can just be typical elements of a place that we interpret in a symbolic (or representative) way. Even if you have never been in a particular hospital before, if it contains elements or symbols that are typical for a hospital, it may evoke memories of your mother's death, the birth of your first child, or other significant life events.

And last, buildings can physically hold memories by recording the collective practices of those who have used the building over time. The worn stairs of an elementary school evoke a memory of students from another era participating in a similar activity. This quality of holding memory in this third way, I am calling *patina*.

Patina is, literally, a quality in silverware where the subtle scratches the piece incurs over time cause the silverware to take on a deeper luster and a distinctive look. Not all flatware can take on this look, however. Patina is a particular attribute of silverware that can hold history. Real silverware exemplifies the idea of patina because it not only endures but becomes more beautiful with use. Plastic flatware does not endure and so never develops patina. Stainless steel endures but often is more beautiful when new (favoring novelty over history), so it represents a borderline case.

The Value of Memory

Memory as Endangered

The problem with many modern buildings is that they are built for a relatively short life span, with cheap materials that break rather than wear, and they often lack the kinds of historical references that we need to generate significant meanings. There are no shopping cart ruts on the floor of Costco reminding me of bygone shoppers of yesteryear, nor will the Walmart where Jimmy got his first swimsuit be around long enough for him to bring Jimmy Jr. to see it. And the county courthouse (circa 1972) that I visited for jury duty does not remind me of anything that I should know about the value of the public realm or our deep commitment to impartial justice, because it looks very much like the office building across the street.

By way of contrast, the church in which I was baptized still stands today as a symbolic witness to God's presence in the neighborhood. The building has aged well and communicates that my baptism was more than a spontaneous accident of history. I can take my daughter there to show her that God continues to be active and faithful in the lives of people today. The act of showing the next generation the places that mark God's faithfulness in our lives is an act of obedient remembering.

I didn't grow up in the First Presbyterian Church of Missoula, but I think that what compelled me to drag my class back outside in subfreezing weather to take a look around the sanctuary is this notion of patina. I wanted them to see how the church being not only larger but more carefully constructed than their private homes showed a deeper investment in our shared life in Christ than we can muster today. I wanted them to experience the centrality of the cross and the prominence of the pulpit as we unpacked some of the bedrock values that connect us to one another and to those who have gone before us. And I guess what I was really interested in was their beginning to see that there is more to God's magnificent plan of salvation history than what is happening in our individual lives at this single point in time.

I wanted them to feel the presence of the saints who preceded them, so that they could resonate viscerally with these words from the book of Hebrews: "Therefore, since we are surrounded by so great a cloud of witnesses, let us also lay aside every weight and the sin that clings so closely, and let us run with perseverance the race that is set before us."[25]

Ambiguity of Memory

Patina is certainly not the only value that we should consider when we think about church buildings, nor is it a value that is always good. The limitation on the value of patina is that memories sometimes can become stifling as well as reassuring. A church that focuses only on its memories and its "important" history can easily become a dead, museum-type church, with no living testimony to God's faithfulness. There are too many beautiful church corpses throughout Europe and North America for us to forget this sobering reality of our heritage.

If I had to choose, I'd pick a spirit-filled congregation in a cheap disposable building over a beautiful empty church any day. However, there are a number of vibrant churches that might gain a new appreciation for their "outdated" facility if they could see their building in terms of patina. And considerations of patina might inspire congregations that are building churches to build them in a way that will hold memories for generations to come.

Place as Gift or Ruse

Patina is a tangible record of the distinct "placiness" of a place. For a well-built building constructed of good-quality materials, patina can make a space more beautiful over time. A good patina can help even a newcomer feel connected to the deep significance of a place.

However, as with almost anything of value, patina too has become commodified and can be bought. Evidence for this somewhat bizarre feature of modern life is easy to find. That coffee shop in the mall looks like it is fifty years old, not because it has faithfully sat at this location for generations, getting gently worn and frayed by regular customers. Rather, everything from the worn wooden floorboards to the clothbound novels on the shelf has been either artificially distressed by a machine or carefully selected at a vintage store to evoke an earlier era.

The word for this kind of "made to look like something it isn't" is *simulacrum*. Simulacra are such a common feature of everyday life that we hardly notice them anymore. The simulacrum, while a convincing and effective part of a marketing strategy, reveals a deeper pathology within the North American landscape. Insofar as the simulacrum serves as a convincing decoy for the way an actual community impacts a particular place, it is also a sobering reminder of the fact that at some level we do believe that even community can be had for a price. The flaw in this kind of thinking is explored in the next chapter.

A sense of place is invaluable in both finding meaning in our everyday life and in human thriving. While simply attending to the built environment does not create a sense of place, often it is in observing the built environment directly that we note the presence or absence of a sense of place. Ultimately, what we will discover is that, just as in the original creation, the best setting for human thriving can be received only as a gift from the Creator.

For Further Reading

Bartholomew, Craig. *Where Mortals Dwell: A Christian View of Place for Today*. Grand Rapids: Baker Academic, 2011.

Brueggemann, Walter. *The Land*. Philadelphia: Fortress Press, 1977.

Casey, Edward S. *The Fate of Place: A Philosophical History*. Berkeley and Los Angeles: University of California Press, 1997.

Duany, Andrés, Jeff Speck, and Mike Lydon. *The Smart Growth Manual*. New York: McGraw-Hill, 2009.

Gallagher, Winifred. *The Power of Place: How Our Surroundings Shape Our Thoughts, Emotions, and Actions*. New York: HarperCollins, 1994.

Gustafson, Per. "Place, Place Attachment, and Mobility: Three Sociological Studies." Doctoral thesis, Dept. of Sociology, Göteborg University, 2002.

Inge, John. *A Christian Theology of Place*. Explorations in Practical, Pastoral, and Empirical Theology. Aldershot, Hampshire, England: Ashgate, 2003.

Jackson, John Brinckerhoff. *A Sense of Place, a Sense of Time*. New Haven: Yale University Press, 1994.

Jacobs, Allan B. *Great Streets*. Cambridge: MIT Press, 1993.

Kostof, Spiro. *The City Assembled: The Elements of Urban Form through History*. Boston: Little, Brown, 1992.

———. *The City Shaped: Urban Patterns and Meanings through History*. Boston: Little, Brown, 1991.

Lash, Nicholas. *Theology on the Way to Emmaus*. London: SCM Press, 1986.

Relph, E. C. *Place and Placelessness*. Research in Planning and Design, no. 1. London: Pion, 1976.

Ritzer, George. *The Globalization of Nothing*. Thousand Oaks, CA: Pine Forge Press, 2004.

Sitte, Camillo. *City Planning According to Artistic Principles*. Columbia University Studies in Art History and Archaeology, no. 2. New York: Random House, 1965.

Solomon, Daniel. *Global City Blues*. Washington, DC: Island Press, 2003.

Unwin, Raymond. *Town Planning in Practice: An Introduction to the Art of Designing Cities and Suburbs*. 2nd ed. New York: B. Blom, 1971.

Other Resources

The Project for Public Spaces http://www.pps.org/

3

What Are You?

Community or Individual?

On the Florida Panhandle, right in the middle of what is sometimes called the Redneck Riviera, sits the little town of Seaside. This charming beachfront town was founded by some of the pioneers of the New Urbanist movement as a way to demonstrate that the principles of New Urbanism could work when applied to an entire community and that such a community could withstand the rigorous pressures of the free market. In founding Seaside, its developers broke with much of the reigning orthodoxy, which held sway among commercial developers and included many elements that would be illegal in most contemporary municipal ordinances. Instead of adding one more ocean resort to this stretch of coast, they decided to attempt to create community out of the elements of traditional neighborhood design.

Seaside aspired to be a setting where placemaking would be possible. The public spaces of Seaside were given the best locations in the community, and they were arranged to take full advantage of the local terrain and to coordinate harmoniously with the street grid. The commercial buildings were concentrated in the center of town, the residential neighborhoods were mixed in use (residential and commercial on the same block), and the housing types were mixed (apartments were allowed to sit above many of the stores and restaurants). The residential lots were small and dense in their apportionment. And the houses sat near the front of their lots, allowing for easy conversation between front porch and street. Each house was individually designed and provided a high degree of visual interest for the pedestrians, who were expected to walk to many of their daily destinations.

According to the standard advice given by "market experts," Seaside should have failed miserably. But surprisingly, just the opposite occurred. All of the lots have been purchased and developed beautifully. Real estate values at Seaside have increased tenfold, while the rest of the region has remained relatively stagnant. The success of Seaside gave some teeth to the New Urbanist movement and caused even unsympathetic developers to take notice. Seaside has shown New Urbanism to be a rare example of an ideological movement that looks as good in practice as it does in theory.

Understandably, I was excited to make my first visit to Seaside. I had learned New Urbanism in the somewhat different setting of Missoula, Montana, but wanted to see the shining apex of the movement on the coast of Florida. Missoula might be better described as a *paleo-urbanist* than a strictly New Urbanist city.[1] It is one of those cities that was developed during an era when we still knew how to design and build habitable human environments, and it was not rich enough or significant enough to be destroyed by the modernist assault in the seventies and eighties. Missoula has gracious public spaces and public buildings, a commercial hub of interesting, individually designed buildings, and charming neighborhoods built at a human scale.

Missoula has its share of disciples of New Urbanism who are aware of the repository of urban charm that it contains. But for the most part, Missoula holds its urbanism unconsciously, and therefore it totters somewhat dangerously close to extinction. At the time I was living there, the municipal code decidedly favored the single-use model for residential and commercial areas, and every few weeks a new box chain retail store opened and a new standardized housing subdivision was being built.

I suppose that in Seaside I expected to see New Urbanism in its pristine form, as its developers, architects, and every one of its residents would have been committed to and personally invested in the tenets of the movement. I expected to see what Missoula could be if it could get its act together and commit to the course of development it had graciously followed before everything was sacrificed around the insatiable needs of the automobile. I wanted Seaside to represent some kind of ideal toward which Missoula could strive. So I was surprised, when I finally got to Seaside, that I was somewhat disappointed with what I saw and experienced there. In visiting Seaside, I found my expectations turned on their heads as I began to perceive Missoula in many ways to be a flawed, but viable urban community, and Seaside to be the "work in progress."

I arrived in Seaside on a chilly night in March. After stowing my bags in one of Seaside's "artist's lofts" (which was costing me $100 per night), I was anxious to walk down to the local pub for a drink and some convivial interaction with the local crowd. I was somewhat surprised, first of all, to find only two places open at 9:30 at night. One was a dance bar with loud music blaring from the door. The other was not so loud and had a charming entrance that made it look a little more hopeful. I went into the second place and was surprised to find it entirely devoid of patrons. Taken aback, I sheepishly made my way to a table that looked as if it should be in the center of the action and resigned myself to a solitary dining experience.

This first impression came as something of a shock, but I wasn't about to let myself be disappointed, not yet. The night was unseasonably cold, and it was a little late for some people to be out. Perhaps I was just a bit off on my timing. I woke up the next morning with a renewed resolve to find the local community at Seaside. I left my apartment at a respectable hour and walked along what looked to be the main thoroughfare to the commercial hub. As I walked, I noted the varied and interesting architecture and the clever way that the sight lines along my walking route invariably terminated with an interesting view. I noticed also that the homes presented an engaging and welcoming face to the passing pedestrian. There were no garages dominating the fronts of the houses, but rather charming front doors and entries. I could see over the picket fences into well-kept yards and could imagine exchanging pleasantries with the residents who might be passing the morning on their front porches.

But there were no residents on the front porches. The only signs of human life that I saw during my walk were the maids and gardeners, who (given the price of my artist's loft) were probably not residing within Seaside. My breakfast was no more encouraging than my dinner had been. I found no informal gathering of locals at the beachside café. The only other people at breakfast with me on this morning were fellow out-of-towners who had come to Seaside for the same conference that had brought me there. And none of the employees who worked at the café were residents of Seaside.

Later that morning I discovered an explanation for my inability to find any people to enjoy the convivial setting of Seaside with me on that day. There are very few permanent residents of this charming beachside community. Of the five hundred or so houses in Seaside, only about twenty are occupied by permanent residents. The rest are occupied only part of the year or on the vacation rental market. As the day went on and the weather improved, Seaside began to come to life, with people filling the restaurants and strolling its pleasant streets. But I now understood that these were not people whose lives were being woven together through these rituals of daily life; these were visitors for the day or for the week, who would never see each other again.

There was very little community being built and experienced at Seaside, but clearly something was attracting people there. I am convinced that the attraction of Seaside may be of a derived nature. As I walked its streets and enjoyed its amenities, I found myself recalling other real communities that took on a shape and feel similar to what I found in Seaside. Seaside was evoking a kind of semiotic memory within me. If I didn't look too closely, I could imagine neighbors having their daily walk to the coffee shop or see the woman who sold me gifts for my family tending her garden later in the day.

Seaside takes the form of real community, but it is really just a vacation resort. There is nothing wrong with a vacation resort, and perhaps Seaside could be included among the more charming of these types of communities. But Seaside seems to aspire to much more. Its developers included a quaint little public school right in the middle of town, as if they did anticipate more of a permanent intergenerational community. But there are no children among the permanent residents of Seaside, and the school has to bus children in to occupy its classrooms. The developers of Seaside recently included a church on the fringe of the community—perhaps again in an attempt to suggest, through a physical structure, a deeper community than actually exists at Seaside.

In chapter 1, I asked, "Who are you?" and we explored the possibility that we are human beings attempting to live our lives in environments that are designed more for automobiles. In chapter 2, I asked, "Where are you?" and we learned that, despite its importance to human thriving, the experience of place is no longer a foregone conclusion and often takes a certain amount of skill and determination to pull off.

The first two chapters, then, are really an exploration of issues having to do with external conditions. In this chapter we turn our focus inward and ask how our own self-understanding impacts our experience of the built environment.

The question posed by this chapter is, "What are you?" and it will be an exploration of how we understand our relationship with others. The question can be clarified by asking, "Are you an individual who desires the experience of community, or are you a particular being who has been created out of community, for community, and who can discover your true identity only in community?" By asking what are you, then, I am asking whether you are fundamentally constituted by your individuality alone or whether your various communities are inevitably part of who you are.

This question's importance has to do with the issue of physical determinism, the conviction that by changing the physical environment in which people live, we can fundamentally change their behavior and attitudes. So far in this discussion, one might get the impression that I believe that by building traditional neighborhoods we can cause people to act more neighborly toward one another or that by paying attention to town fabric, we can cause the kinds of connections and memories that take place in real towns to emerge out of thin air. This is not, in fact, what I believe.

I believe that the experience of community is tragically elusive for us humans. We were created by a God revealed to us as a community of Father, Son, and Holy Spirit. We were created to be in community. As God exclaimed after creating the first human, "It is not good that the man should be alone."[2] And yet, one of the primary ways that sin is made manifest in our lives is by causing divisions in and among us. After yielding to the temptation of sin, the very first thing Adam does is to blame God and blame Eve for his transgression; "The woman you gave to me, she caused me to do this." The second major event in the story is that Cain lashes out against his brother Abel and is cast out from his community. And things continue to disintegrate from there.

If our understanding of the human condition is not rooted in a theology or some other worldview that can account for why we need community and why so many of our individual and collective decisions lead us away from community, it will be doomed to failure. Lacking a strong philosophical foundation, our culture's default conceptualization is to think of humans as rational consumers, individuals who carry around a hierarchy of wants for which they are willing to exchange tokens of value representing their labor or other assets.

Insofar as we act like rational consumers, the market is an appropriate mechanism to adjudicate questions of production and distribution of various goods. But it seems as though the more important something is for our well-being and fulfillment, the less likely we are to act like rational consumers. For these kinds of things we need a more nuanced understanding of how our needs might be met. With regard to community, it may very well be the case that what is needed is the radical intervention of a good God who is powerful enough to break the destructive cycle of sin in our lives and creative enough to weave the disparate strands of our lives into a coherent whole that we call community.

But first we need to return to Seaside to see why this is so. Seaside can be understood as a case study in physical determinism in general, as well as an important laboratory for some of the attempts at recovering a lost sense of community. As we have seen, one of the most compelling of these attempts has been that of New Urbanism.

Perhaps what we see at Seaside is a picture of the prospects for and limits on the New Urbanist movement in its current form. This exploration should in no way be seen as a rejection of the New Urbanism movement. For it is in this movement that I see the emergence of some of the most helpful tools for

---

the recovery of human community. At most, this chapter provides an exploration of how the New Urbanist conversation needs to be extended to include a wider set of voices.

New and Paleo-Urbanism

We will begin with an anatomy of New Urbanism as a movement. The medium of the New Urbanist movement has been rediscovery of a physical form that engenders community and the successful application of that form in a contemporary context. New Urbanists have made a serious attempt at recovering a sense of place. The power of the New Urbanist movement is the market. New Urbanism stands apart from the myriad of failed social experiments in that people actually seem to want to buy what they are selling. Seaside has at least established that point.

People do value charm, they do not mind walking for many of their daily tasks, and they don't need quite as much privacy as the "market experts" tend to think they do. And the wisdom of the New Urbanist movement lies in its willingness to learn the physical form of community from actual human communities, which have emerged and evolved over a long period of time in a particular place.

The pioneers of the New Urbanist movement have been mostly architects and developers who have been able to present some of the traditional concepts of town planning and architecture in fresh and exciting ways. They have challenged the reigning orthodoxies in their respective fields with an admirable degree of success and have begun to turn the tide toward a more satisfying approach to our built environment. Having the market on their side has been essential to the success of New Urbanism in an American context. There are precious few ideas that get very far in this country if they can't turn a profit. Further, maintaining the individual consumer as one's primary constituent is politically safe in an increasingly polarized political environment. It's no wonder, then, that New Urbanism is gaining wide acceptance.

However, these observations also bring to light the weakness inherent in the New Urbanist experiment. True human community does require a coherent physical form, which we have somehow misplaced during the course of the past half-century. The New Urbanists must be applauded for rediscovering this form and for reminding us of this important truth. However, human community also requires a certain critical mass of actual human beings who will inhabit and interact within the physical form over a long period of time. Places like Seaside have developed the physical form of community but have not been able to attract a permanent critical mass of human beings required for true community. The reason for this particular failure at Seaside shows the limitations of depending on the power of the market for its successes.

The market has made Seaside a lucrative and attractive investment for those with enough resources to take advantage of it. But the market has also prohibited the "artist's lofts" from actually being inhabited by artists, and the modest homes from being inhabited by the people who work at Seaside. The market has also restricted the owners of homes at Seaside to the ultra-rich, who have a poor record of maintaining a permanent commitment to any particular community. The market has been Seaside's greatest ally, but it has also been its Achilles' heel. To be remembered as more than a significant "market trend," New Urbanism will at some point have to face some of the other (noneconomic) forces that shape and influence our human existence.

Finally, as New Urbanism has borrowed many of its forms and expressions from actual cities and towns that grew up in history, it will need to grapple with the vision and the values that undergird those places if it hopes to truly appropriate the wisdom to be found there. Most historic American towns (especially in the North and Southeast) were founded on a Christian vision, and the churches in those places have played a central and formative role throughout their development. New Urbanism has been, up to this point, a decidedly secular movement, and perhaps it should remain that way. However, if the New Urbanist movement hopes to have a deep and lasting impact in this country, it will have to figure out a way to bring those distinctively Christian voices back into the conversation that has been initiated. And the New Urbanist vision for new developments (like Seaside) will have to figure out a way to incorporate churches in a more central way than it does now.

As I mentioned above, Missoula is inconsistent in its urban expression and charm. It has some delightful streets, buildings, neighborhoods, and public spaces; but it lacks the consistency and overall coherence of Seaside. However, Missoula has the advantage over Seaside of a permanent community of residents who can use whatever urban amenities are available as a loom upon which they can weave the fabric of the community together. And Missoula has the advantage of having, interspersed throughout the city, a number of significant churches with active congregations who help to anchor and give depth to the urban texture.

Missoula is a typical western city in that the churches were a little late on the scene and have not been afforded a central role in the city, either physically or culturally. Nonetheless, the churches in Missoula are among the city's oldest structures and are decidedly the oldest institutions of continuous use. The churches in Missoula (and the people in their congregations) represent a significant voice in the public square. From the vantage point of a pastor having served in one of these historic churches in the paleo-urbanist city of Missoula, Montana, I want to offer a few observations about faith and urbanism that can inform our understanding about community.

Perichoresis

The God whom we meet in the Bible reveals himself to us not as a perfect unitary being, but rather as a dynamic community of Father, Son, and Holy Spirit. The term coined by the church fathers to describe this dynamic relationship is *perichoresis*.

The literal meaning of *perichoresis* is a "dance around." Colin Gunton clarifies how the fathers understood the implications of this dynamic relationship:

> It would appear to follow that in eternity Father, Son, and Holy Spirit share a dynamic mutual reciprocity, interpenetration, and interanimation.[3]

Although these words are not part of our everyday vocabulary, they are deeply suggestive of a community life that is far more profound than anything we are likely to experience. For our purposes, what is most significant about the perichoretic reality of God is how none of the distinct members of the Trinity is fully who they are without the involvement of the other two. As Gunton explains,

> God is not God apart from the way in which Father, Son, and Spirit in eternity give to and receive from each other what they essentially are.[4]

This is not to deny the distinct particularity of each member of the Trinity. In addition to being part of this dynamic perichoresis, each member of the Trinity is also a particular being. *Hypostases* (or person) is the word the church fathers used to describe the distinct particularity of each member of the Trinity.

Describing the members of the Trinity in terms of hypostases or distinct particulars is different from emphasizing their individuality. Individuality, in the way we are accustomed to using the term, describes that core part of our being that defines us and remains intact regardless of the ebb and flow of things that are external to ourselves, including things like community. The concept of individuality puts us in tension with community, while particularity (or hypostases) can connect us to our communities.

Gunton warns us against moving too quickly or resolutely from how God is in essential being to how we are (or could be) in ours. However, he does think that in some respects, our core identity is at least suggested by who God is in core identity. Gunton does believe that I cannot be who I distinctly am supposed to be completely irrespective of community.

Speaking to the irreconcilable conflict between individualism and collectivism, Gunton states:

> If the notion of perichoresis helps us to rethink the matter, it is by virtue of the fact that, although it envisages close relatedness, it never does so to the detriment of particularity. Rather it teaches that, as made in the image of God, we are closely bound up, for good or ill, with other human beings.[5]

There are two ways that Gunton sees our lives bound up with other people. We are bound up with others whose lives intersect with ours in our present time. And we are bound up with others who have existed and will exist in different times through the passing on (and even rejection of) various traditions and inheritances.

This is a radical thought if we are to take it seriously. Even though most of us experience our lives in the context of some form of community (neighborhood, marriage and family, church), time and time again we demonstrate to others and to ourselves that these communities are really not at the core of our being. When such communities threaten to significantly restrict or impinge upon our individually defined being, we seem to have few qualms about walking away from any one of these communities in hopes of finding a suitable replacement. And it is unclear whether we are less concerned with rejecting traditions that we inherit from the past or with the consequences of our decisions on future generations.

It is the coherence and attractiveness of this possibility combined with our sin nature that so often makes a true experience of community impossible. Fortunately for us, this God who is revealed to us as a being in community also wants us to experience community. God's plan for the redemption of humanity includes redeeming us within the context of community. And, as unsuitable as it so often proves to be, God uses the church as a key instrument for the redemption of human community.

Theology of Sin

In *The Geography of Nowhere*, James Howard Kunstler declares that "community isn't something that you can have like a pizza."[6] He's right, of course, but why? Why can't we buy community as we do other kinds of commodities? Many people claim to want community; and communities, while somewhat rare, do seem to exist in certain parts of this country. What's to stop someone from finding one of these authentic communities, purchase a home in its midst, and secure for himself or herself a communal life? The answer, I believe, has less to do with supply and demand than it does with the sin nature of human beings.

Money represents personal power. The more money that we have at our disposal, the more freedom we have to do whatever we want. This is wonderful if you believe that we will use this freedom in healthy and fulfilling ways. But such unchecked freedom can be perilous, if we consider the potentially destructive power of sin. Sin, according to Luther, is a turning inward—away from God and away from others. We sin when we rebel against our creator and try to make ourselves the supreme being and the lord of our own lives. It is the destructive power of sin, not the design blunders of postwar development patterns, that has ultimately fragmented our communities. And if we hope to redeem and build healthy communities, we must begin with an honest look at our sin nature.

Since the church has retained a vocabulary adequate to handle this particular aspect of our human existence, it has the capability to track more precisely the impact that sin can have on our communities. A popular caricature of the church is that of a community of people who see themselves as righteous while viewing everyone on the outside as sinners. However, a more accurate portrayal of the Christian church is, first of all, a community of sinners. The church is not a hall of fame for the most holy people in our society, nor is it a museum celebrating greatness in our past. The church is a hospital where broken people gather to be healed by grace. People who encounter the church on this basis—as sinners in need of grace—tend to find what they are looking for. People unwilling to acknowledge their own sin invariably miss the very thing that the church has to offer.

In *Life Together,* the German theologian Dietrich Bonhoeffer poignantly describes the process by which people cheat themselves out of a true experience of community through missing the point of church.[7] He uses the term "serious Christian" ironically to describe a person who is more serious than truly Christian, because they come to the church trying to realize some kind of idealized vision of human community rather than trying first to find grace for themselves.

"The serious Christian," Bonhoeffer declares, "set down for the first time in a Christian community is likely to bring with him a very definite idea of what Christian life together should be and to try to realize it."[8] However, in the actual experience of Christian community, that ideal is quickly shattered. The Christian community never lives up to the expectations that people bring to it.

This presents the person seeking Christian community with a crisis. Will she choose to love this actual human community in which she has found herself, or will she choose to love her ideal vision? Is this new community an essential aspect of her perichoretic identity, or is it a commodity with the potential to add a pious element to her individualized identity? The difference depends upon whether she can see in this imperfect community sinners like herself in need of grace. If she does so, she will find first of all the reality of grace as the foundation of this community, and this foundation will hold her up as she encounters her own sinfulness in the particularities of her day-to-day life.

On the other hand, if the Christian decides to love her ideal of Christian community more than the actual Christian community in which he or she has been placed, a predictable cycle of rejection ensues. Bonhoeffer claims that this Christian becomes "the despising accuser of his brethren, then of God and finally of himself."[9] In my experience, this does happen in the lives of many people. Often they will reject not one but a number of Christian communities before they start accusing God, and then self, but in time, the result is the same. In fact, when people join our church because of perceived shortcomings of their former church, I have come to expect that such people will reject us in the near future as well.

As I mentioned above, the Christian church has been especially attuned to this phenomenon because we have retained the language of sin and grace in our lexicon, but some aspect of this basic reality affects every manifestation of human community. A man and a woman who commit to the minuscule community of marriage must choose to love the person that they have married, rather than some ideal partner that they might be tempted to project onto husband or wife. And residents of Missoula or Seaside must come to know and accept their actual neighbors in these communities if it is community that they hope to experience. Of course, not every community is explicitly offering grace to its participants as the church does, but every healthy community will require its members to be more committed to the actual people who make up their community than they are to some abstract ideal that exists nowhere except in their own imaginations.

Askesis

If sin is as universal and pervasive as the church claims it to be, we might expect that no one would be able to truly experience community. It takes a great deal of self-awareness and patience to maintain a commitment to a flawed community. We might also expect every human community to be so flawed by the collective shortcomings of its participants that the very idea of community would cease to be attractive. And yet we do find many ordinary, unremarkable people who do experience community. And we do find in all sorts of human communities surprising examples of beauty, eloquence, and wisdom that seem to be beyond the scope of that particular collection of people en masse.

How is it, then, that individuals who are not particularly self-aware or patient do discover and enjoy some form of community? And how is it that such commendable achievements arise out of gathered groups of flawed people? One possible explanation for this phenomenon has to do with what is known in the church as *askesis*.

Askesis evokes a long-standing practice within the church, but it is reintroduced in a more general way by Eugene Peterson in *Under the Unpredictable Plant*.[10] According to Peterson, askesis has to do with limitations or a beneficial confinement. The word *ascetic* is derived from this same root, but askesis is not limited to the ascetic practices. Askesis, according to Peterson, "is a calculated and deliberate interference with this god-lust, this god-presumption," that besets us as fallen humans.[11] Askesis can be involuntary, like a medical crisis or imprisonment. And askesis can be voluntary, like joining a monastery. But askesis doesn't need to be as dramatic and explicit as taking monastic vows. Often, askesis can be discovered by simply taking account of the particular conditions of one's local context.

Now think of askesis as descriptive of the kinds of good limits that contribute to a lively built environment. A city in Montana is a good place to talk about askesis, because it has one of the lowest per capita income earnings of any state in the nation. Many people experience community in Missoula for the simple reason that they cannot afford not to. They cannot afford to take long vacations at exotic destinations, and so for a significant portion of the year they are forced to make do with the amenities of the local setting in the company of their ordinary neighbors and fellow Missoulians. But this limit, often quite unconsciously, builds intimacy with the city, the land, and their neighbors. And this limit ultimately builds community.

An important point for the New Urbanists to keep in mind is that historically one of the foundational reasons for the lively urban environment has been people's lack of resources. The lords and country squires could afford to place some distance between themselves and the commoners, but everyone else used (and ultimately enlivened) the urban settings because they had some need that they couldn't afford to meet in any other way.

In Missoula, I lived in a neighborhood that met many of the conditions of the traditional neighborhood extolled by the New Urbanists. The buildings are laid out at a relatively high density, there is a good network of sidewalks,

Orientation

and there are some lovely public spaces and charming coffee shops within easy walking distance from my front door. I used to love to walk to the park and the coffee shops and would go there when I had time or money to spare. But when I really would take advantage of the good sidewalks and the proximity of our houses is when I would pop over to a neighbor's to borrow a tool or an ingredient or to ask for help with picking up and moving some furniture. As much as I enjoyed these little exchanges with my neighbors, if I'd had more disposable income, I would probably have kept a better stock of food on hand, purchased all the tools that I needed, and not have worried about the $25 delivery fee for furniture. I came to realize that one of the things that makes Missoula a hospitable urban environment is that it is made up of people who have to get along because they need one another.

Another place where Missoula has benefited from the askesis of her poverty has been in the preservation and development of the downtown. Missoula has a charming and vibrant downtown. There are interesting local stores that inhabit beautifully restored buildings representing a variety of architectural styles and periods. The downtown is a popular destination for visitors as well as locals and makes a significant contribution to the local economy.

However, the charm of downtown Missoula is the result, in part, of a period of economic distress. Missoula has never had a strong economy, but in the 1980s, it was in a serious recession. Whereas other, more economically viable, cities were modernizing their downtowns, it was just barely surviving. Cities that could afford to were tearing down the "outdated" buildings of their downtown areas and replacing them with modernist buildings replete with mirrored glass, featureless design, and oppressive scale. In Missoula we had to keep our outmoded buildings because we couldn't afford to tear them down. These old buildings had the advantage of relatively cheap rents for tenants, and so during the eighties they began to be occupied by an eclectic mix of local businesses.

If nothing else, these local businesses were able to maintain these downtown buildings and keep them clean. But as they began to turn a profit, they were able to make minor repairs and upgrade their buildings for commercial use. By the time the modernizing trend of the eighties had run its course and people were once again interested in historic architecture, Missoula found itself with a goldmine of historic buildings, as well as a strong core of businesses to use them. Over the next decade, these local businesses began to undertake serious reconstruction of many of the downtown buildings. Other cities, which had poured money into their downtowns in the eighties, found themselves with business cores made up of unattractive high-rent buildings. Even if they wanted to return to historic architectural styles, they could not afford to. In the meantime Missoula enjoyed the bones of a vibrant and interesting downtown.

Besides being an interesting example of a fortunate accident of history, this account makes an important point about how community is built. A rich and varied built environment must be built over generations, because any one generation can make only a limited contribution to the environment. Each generation will also have blind spots (stemming from limited understanding and imagination as well as from the sin nature of the residents) and therefore, any one generation should not be allowed to have too much influence on the built environment. Money, as we have seen, empowers the individual to pursue interests and passions but also can exacerbate the consequences of sin. On a communal scale, money allows a particular generation to express its insight and even wisdom, but it can also glaringly show its blind spots. Community that is built slowly over the generations provides a kind of check and balance between the generations, and the limit of time seems to soften the destructive impact of collective sin. This particular insight has now been incorporated into the planning community under the name of *piecemeal urbanism*.

Money is a mixed blessing when it comes to the built environment. Certainly, it takes a good deal of money to build and sustain many amenities. One visit to a bankrupt lumber town is sufficient to demonstrate that point. But money can also act as a kind of prophylactic against the very amenities available in the built environment. The urban life provides a kind of askesis for those who live in the city. Limitations on space force people in the city to live near one another and to share public space throughout the year and thus build intimacy. Limitations on time mean that the people of one generation can exert only so much influence on their physical environment—they have to learn to accept and even value what has preceded them through the built legacy of previous generations.

But those individuals and communities with too much money can obliterate the healthy limits of space and time. They can spend money to put distance between themselves and their neighbors, and they can change the face of their built environments too quickly. As John Updike puts it, the rich often "like to demonstrate they can afford to be elsewhere."[12]

The members of the Christian community are by no means exemplary in respecting the limits of money or time. We are just as likely as any other collection of people to have the absentee superrich in our ranks. However, the church can have a kind of anchoring influence on its community through its sanctifying of time in a particular place. In a culture where everything from worldwide financial markets to grocery stores is open twenty-four hours a day, seven days a week, throughout the year, time becomes irrelevant. The church, by setting one day a week apart as sacred time, and by marking the year with its church calendar, can be one of the only places in a neighborhood where time and season have any meaning. The church also, in the midst of a fluid culture, represents a living tradition that goes back much further than just one generation. Even a new church in a new residential area can tie the neighborhood into a tradition that is thousands of years old and can bring much-needed depth and perspective into a community.

A local congregation can also provide a witness of permanence and connection among the disparate individuals within a community. The church not only provides a place for the community to gather week by week and deepen the bonds of their relationships but continues to gather even as members of the community come and go. The church gathers on my behalf, as it were, when I cannot be present in my local community. And I can achieve some degree of connection with my local congregation by gathering with the local church in whatever town I happen to find myself on a particular Sunday. The church can pray for members when they are out of town, and the church often will visit its shut-in members on a regular basis. The church ties major life events (birth, death, marriage) to the ordinary, Sunday-by-Sunday, in-season-and-out life of a local congregation. I will not marry a couple in my church if they are not members of the church, not because they're not "in the club," but rather because we want a wedding ceremony to be an affirmation (or a beginning) of a long-term relationship with a community that will support the marriage.[13]

The Idolatry of Community

As part of my job, I counsel couples as they prepare to get married. In this process, I routinely ask each person why they want to get married. I've heard all kinds of answers to this question over the years, and I must admit that I have been encouraged by most of the responses. But when I discern that one or both partners want to get married because they want to have a "happy marriage," then I get concerned. It has been my observation that anyone who strives for a happy marriage not only will fail to achieve this goal for themselves but will deprive their spouse of one as well. An indispensable ingredient for a happy marriage is love. Love, by definition, puts the needs and wants of the other above one's own needs and wants. Anyone who hopes to get a "happy marriage" for themselves by some kind of a contractual agreement with another person has not even begun to understand the concept of love.

Truly happy marriages tend to come about when both partners put aside their own needs and purposes and concentrate their efforts on serving their spouse and meeting his or her needs. While it is true that in most cases this approach to marriage does lead to a happy and stable marriage, these ends can never be the goal. This is in fact one of the main reasons that I am a strong advocate for abstinence before marriage and against cohabitation before marriage. Both living together and having sex before marriage suggest to me the notion of a "try-out" before the commitment of marriage. Both actions seem to imply a cost-benefit approach to the sacred covenant of marriage. The message of both premarital sex and cohabitation is, "I will marry you only if I can be convinced that you will bring me maximum pleasure and minimum inconvenience." I greatly prefer maintaining an element of risk and trust in the marriage covenant. It seems to me that couples who are willing to make a commitment to each other without knowing all of the pertinent details concerning pleasure and inconvenience are more likely to stay together when those particular details change over the course of a normal human life. The question that I want to hear a young person ask is, "Is this a person whom I can fruitfully celebrate and serve?" rather than, "Is this a person who will allow me to get what I want?"

Now, as a Christian, I believe that one must be willing to go even further than this to discover the full potential of the sacred covenant of marriage. I tell Christian couples that they cannot make even the happiness of their spouse or family their highest goal but must make their relationship with God a still higher goal. As Christians we are commanded to have no other gods before the God that we meet in the Bible. Idolatry is the condition in which we put something (or someone) in a higher place than God. In the previous chapter we considered the possibility of the automobile as a societal idol. The more recognizable forms of idolatry in our culture involve money, sex, and power. But we are just as susceptible to making more benign objects (family, church, nation) into idols. We are just as guilty when we put our love of money over our love of God as when we put our love of our family over our love of God.

This prohibition against idolatry protects the integrity of our worship of God. But it also protects us as well as the object that we may be tempted to worship. Money can be very freeing and bring us many comforts when it is kept in its proper place. But money destroys us when we worship it by making it our highest aspiration and the object to which everything else is sacrificed. A happy marriage and a healthy family can be some of life's greatest joys. However, our families and our spouses will get suffocated by overattention or crushed by pressure if we try to make them our gods and place all of our hopes and expectations upon them.

These final points, I believe, provide the most plausible explanation for why we "can't have community like we have a pizza." Perhaps the notion of *community* is one of those elusive ends that cannot be pursued directly. Those who plunk down a couple million for a home at Seaside may be trying to secure for themselves community, but they will never find it until they are willing to make a commitment to one place and to be good neighbors.

And perhaps even a dedicated New Urbanist practitioner cannot create community, no matter how hard she or he tries, because even good urbanism cannot withstand the pressure of being the highest aspiration in an individual's life. And when our community becomes an idol, it too can become toxic. Our communities, as well as the individuals within them, need protection against idolatry.

Church at the Center

Seaside in economic terms is a shining success. Seaside as a practical example of many of the truths behind the New Urbanist theory is an invaluable asset. But Seaside does not provide the kind of real community that is experienced in many "inferior" paleo-urbanist settings like Missoula. In this sense Seaside shows some of the possibilities as well as some of the limitations of the New Urbanist movement in its current state. Insofar as the New Urbanism is about getting the physical components of community life right so that people will want to seek out this life in their consumer choices, New Urbanism can be declared a success and can expect many years of enjoying the fruit of that success. However, insofar as true community (or lack thereof) is dependent on nonmarket forces such as redemption, interdependence, and selfless service, the New Urbanist movement lacks the insight as well as the experience necessary to deal with such realities.

To understand these inhibitors to and incubators for human community, the New Urbanist movement will have to look beyond its vanguard of architects, builders, and government workers. New Urbanism will have to begin to listen to the voices of teachers, psychologists, and, yes, even pastors if it ever hopes to become more than a market correction and instead be the long-term cultural project to which it aspires. While it is true that over the past half-century we have hamstrung most of our efforts at community through poor physical design, we cannot fix the problem by focusing our efforts only at the physical level. A community is a living organism of human relationships and must be built and maintained through human interaction.

More important, New Urbanism is going to have to figure out a meaningful way to include the church and the Christian community in its vision for a restored urban life. The inclusion of a church in Seaside represents a significant step in that direction. But the church in Seaside also represents some of the potential missteps that can be made when the proper role between church and community isn't rightly understood.

The church in Seaside is beautifully designed, carefully crafted, and in many ways an impressive building. It is the tallest building in Seaside and terminates the view from a major boulevard by taking advantage of axial lines. The church is set back on a generous lot to distinguish it from the private buildings in the vicinity. It is significant that the developers of Seaside devoted so much attention and so many resources to create a space for the religious needs of the community.

But the particular form that this church in Seaside has taken also demonstrates some of the shortcomings that the New Urbanist practitioners have had in understanding the Christian church and in incorporating the church in meaningful ways into the community. I see at least three areas of concern. The church in Seaside is naked—it is designed in a town-hall style and doesn't contain any explicit religious symbolism. The church is anonymous—it isn't connected to any particular denomination. And the church in Seaside is marginal. It has not been afforded a spot in the center of town but is relegated to the fringes. We'll examine each of these shortcomings in some detail.

There are a number of Christian churches that have consciously avoided religious symbolism in their buildings, to avoid any temptation toward idolatry. However, I suspect that the church in Seaside has not left the cross out of the church for such theological reasons. Insofar as the church represents a human attempt to encourage people to be good and to celebrate beauty and ritual, it can be easily accepted by the secular culture. But the cross is not so easy to swallow. The cross disturbs us because it reminds us that all is not well in the world. And the cross reminds us that we are sinners in need of salvation. Perhaps the designers of the church in Seaside left out the cross because they wanted to highlight the human-aspiration theme of the religious impulse while playing down the sin-and-salvation theme of the church.

However, a naked church—without a cross—is going to have a hard time communicating the reality of sin and the stronger reality of grace to a community that needs constant reminders of these vital themes. A church that tries to "clean up" the symbolism of its faith in this way would be subject to H. Richard Niebuhr's stinging critique of liberal Christianity: "A God without wrath brought men without sin into a kingdom without judgment through the ministrations of a Christ without a cross."[14]

But what places like Seaside need, as we have seen, are clear reminders of sin and grace, so that the limits on and prospects for genuine human community can be more clearly understood. A naked church can too easily be seen as representing no more than human aspiration and potential in some kind of vague spiritual realm.

Orientation

The fact that the church in Seaside is not associated with any specific denomination is also problematic. This is not to say that I would want to put forward my Presbyterian denomination as the ideal church for Seaside. I'll be the first to admit that the very idea of denominations is counterproductive for the unity of the church. However, given the fact that the church currently finds its expression in a multitude of specific denominations and has not yet figured out how to reunite under one major umbrella, simply not affiliating with a specific denomination is not a viable solution.

A church not tied to a particular denomination is not rooted in history. At first this seems like a cleaner place to start, but, as the failed experiment with modernist architecture has taught us, to reject history is to reject the ordinary human beings who inhabit history. Modernist architects failed to make a connection with the people who were to use and enjoy their creations, because they ignored thousands of years of collected wisdom in favor of their own original ideas. In the same way, a church that tries to transcend the contingencies (and, yes, even irrelevancies) of a specific denominational affiliation will find that it will fail to gather a viable human community.

I have found that I can worship and be nurtured in my faith in almost any denominational setting where the basic tenets of the Christian faith are upheld. I have had meaningful worship experiences in Roman Catholic, Greek Orthodox, Episcopalian, Lutheran, Methodist, Calvary Chapel, and Baptist churches. Ironically, there are a number of "nondenominational" churches that have taken on most of the characteristics of historic denominations except explicit identification. I find the denominational character of these nondenominational churches a positive development. Where I have the hardest time making a connection is in the anonymous chapels that are found sometimes in hospitals and on hotel grounds, where I am "free" to tailor some kind of worship experience that suits my particular needs. In these settings, freedom seems to mean isolation from any wider community that might sustain me from the richness of their traditions. These places embody individualistic "freedom," not perichoretic participation.

When it comes to the issue of a church in a neighborhood, its association with a particular denomination can be seen as a kind of positive askesis. The denominational affiliation represents a limit with respect to inflexible traditions, theological boundaries, and the eclectic personalities that have gathered around the particular church. But it is precisely through these kinds of limits that we can ever have a true, flesh-and-blood experience of community. Every attempt to clean up the messiness of a particular denominational tradition is a move toward abstraction and away from real human community.

The final problem with the church in Seaside has to do with its location. The church is the tallest building in Seaside, it is set apart from the other buildings in its immediate area, and a view of the church terminates a major commercial boulevard. However, the church is not anywhere near the center of town, as it might have been in a traditional American town, but is at the very edge of Seaside. This issue represents perhaps the thorniest issue with regard to the role of a church in a neighborhood. On the one hand, separation of church and state requires that a particular church not be given preferential treatment in the public realm. On the other hand, true freedom of religion must allow for the fact that for some people, their religion is more than just a fringe activity; it plays a central role in all of life.

The issue of church-and-state relations is complex; unfortunately, there is no "objective" and "value-neutral" way to address this problem. Any approach to the placement of the church implies a set of theological assumptions—spoken or unspoken. One area where differing theological assumptions can lead to radically different understandings has to do with the meaning of the word *spiritual*. A common understanding of this term involves the assumption that human life can be divided between the physical and the spiritual. The physical realm of life has to do with those things that can be seen or touched—our bodies, the work of our hands, and our sexual relationships. The spiritual realm has to do with those areas that cannot be directly touched—our abstract thoughts, our emotions, and the nonsexual aspects of our relationships.

In this bifurcated understanding of human existence, God is relevant only to the "spiritual side" of our humanity. This is the secular corollary to the "two kingdoms" view of the kingdom of God that we encountered in the introduction. As you may recall, this view makes a sharp distinction between the things that God cares about (worship, Bible study, evangelism) and the things with which God is less concerned (agriculture, business, art, politics). We can look to God to help with the "spiritual" things. But with regard to the physical aspects of our humanity, we are left to our own devices. According to this approach to spirituality, God comforts our minds and our emotions in church on Sunday but has nothing to do with our daily work or our sex life.

A more elaborate version of this same basic idea is implied in the popular notion of the "well-balanced" human being that we see routinely displayed on the walls of student health centers and other offices of the helping professions. This concept is usually illustrated with a picture of a human being in the center of a circle divided into four parts. The parts of the circle are labeled physical, emotional, intellectual, and spiritual. According to this scheme, the "well-balanced" human being is one who has cultivated health in each of these four areas.

These kinds of approaches to human spirituality find their origin in ancient Greek understandings of the human personality and their corresponding dualistic religious systems. However, the Christian affirmation that God took on human flesh and was born in human history cannot be reconciled with either of those two approaches to spirituality. The Gospel of John tells us that the Word (Jesus) became flesh and dwelt among us. If physical human flesh can contain God, and if God can live an ordinary human life and work as a carpenter, no longer can we easily divide human existence between the physical and the spiritual.

Christian spirituality therefore must oppose both of these popular understandings of spirituality. According to Christian theology, there are no particular "spiritual" areas of life. *Spiritual* means simply all areas of life that we have yielded to God's care and direction. Singing hymns in church is spiritual, but so can be working in our gardens or having sex with our spouses if we have invited God into those areas of our lives. Similarly, for the Christian, the problem with the "balanced human" concept is that it puts the human being in the center of the diagram. This is precisely how orthodox Christian theology portrays sin—me and my needs in the center of my existence, with everything else (including God) relegated to the fringes. Christian conversion can be understood as allowing Jesus Christ to resume his rightful place in the center of our lives and allowing the other aspects of our human personality to be shaped and directed around his will.

We can see how for someone who thinks of spirituality as a contrasting notion to physicality, or for someone who takes a "balanced human" approach to spirituality, a church set apart, on the fringe of a community, makes perfect sense. It's there for those who are "into that sort of thing" as the need arises for a "spiritual" experience. But for the Christian with a more incarnational understanding of spirituality, it makes more sense for the church to be right in the center of the activity where people live and work. Or, if that is not possible, the church should be an integrated part of the neighborhood in which it is located. For the Christian who is concerned not to let money, entertainment, family, or even community become idols, the church must remain a visible counterpoint to these seductive counterfeit gods. We need to be reminded that God alone is worthy of our worship and that all other aspects of human existence will be enhanced if we get this one basic relationship right.

Community as Gift

I have come to the conclusion that community is a very elusive concept. The way that we even use this word in our contemporary culture is confusing. At one time, community meant the people that you lived near. Currently, community seems to mean people with whom we share an interest or an advocacy with no expectation that we live near or even have met anyone in our "community." We mostly hear the word *community* with various qualifiers, such as gay community, bicycling community, or even Christian community. To talk about community as a physical place or a setting for real human relationships, as the New Urbanists have taught us to do, is revolutionary.

But even with this restored understanding of the physical aspect of community, we find it elusive. I think that Kunstler is right in his notion that we cannot buy community. But I would even take his idea one step further in saying that we cannot even build community. True community requires wisdom, grace, and time. We can acquire wisdom simply by paying attention to the collective experience of humankind as it has tried to hammer out strategies and settings for living harmonious lives in proximity to one another. This collective repository of human wisdom took a major blow in the past century because of the influence of the modernist movement, which tried to ignore history. New Urbanism has been one of the positive forces that have helped us move beyond this dark period of the twentieth century. But still we see many mistakes being made all across the country as we continue to build inhospitable human environments based on modernist errors.

But community also requires grace. We humans are too self-referential and too impatient to willingly put aside our personal desires and agendas for the sake of the greater good. We need the limits that financial and geographical restraints put upon us in order to discover the joys of community life. Sadly, those who can transcend those limits because of an excess of financial resources can miss out on many blessings of community. We also need forgiveness from our neighbors, whom we will invariably offend in the course of living in close proximity to one another. And as it is nearly impossible to offer grace until we have experienced grace, the theological promise that God provides grace freely is foundational to many communities.

Last, community requires time. The shortcomings of Seaside are not surprising or even deplorable. One would be hard-pressed to find any examples of a thriving human community that was "developed" in the span of two decades. Most utopian experiments in creating ideal human communities in a short period of time have been abject failures. I think that Seaside actually has good possibilities of becoming a viable human community, but it will take time. True human community takes generations to form, to draw out the wisdom from each generation and to illuminate some of the blind spots.

It is for these reasons that I have become convinced that we (meaning any collection of living human beings) cannot build community. I believe that

Orientation

community must be received as a gracious gift. All community must be received as a gift from our Creator and Redeemer, from those that have preceded us, and to some extent from the neighbors who live near us. Building community means first of all to recognize it where it exists and to cultivate a sense of gratitude for it. Out of this gratitude we can begin to encourage what is good in our communities and to oppose that which is destructive. What we cannot do is reject our communities to pursue some kind of abstract and idealized community that is devoid of human messiness.

This chapter began with the question of what we are. Are we individuals or are we particular beings who come from and are called to be in community? And the answer to our question, if we are looking through the lens of Scripture, is clearly the latter. Wherever there are people, there is community. We must start there. Our particular community may need a major overhaul of its zoning codes, or it may need some more visiting among neighbors. If it is a place in the United States, it probably needs both. In either case, the church and the Christians in that community have a distinct and vital role to play. I know from experience that this is true in Missoula, and I suspect it's true in Seaside as well.

For Further Reading

Bellah, Robert Neelly. *Habits of the Heart: Individualism and Commitment in American Life*. New York: Harper & Row, 1986.

Bonhoeffer, Dietrich. *Life Together*. Translated by John W. Doberstein. New York: Harper & Row, 1954.

Goizueta, Robert. *Caminemos con Jesus*. Maryknoll, NY: Orbis Books, 2003.

Gunton, Colin E. *The One, the Three, and the Many: God, Creation and the Culture of Modernity*. Cambridge: Cambridge University Press, 1993.

Schwartz, Barry. *The Paradox of Choice: Why More Is Less*. New York: Ecco, 2004.

4

When Are You?

Storied or Static?

As part of our new members class at my church, we always have a session on basic Christianity. I used to begin that session with a brief quiz covering the essentials of what it means to be a Christian. The form of this quiz was a half sheet of paper filled with check boxes of various actions and attributes, with instructions to check all boxes that are essential to being a Christian. The check boxes include a range of things from "having a daily quiet time" to "going to church" to "being baptized."

After giving ample time for them to take the test, I would announce that there are really only two things required for being a Christian. The first is to repent of our sins and the second is to believe the good news. I then would take them through various Scriptures showing Jesus and the apostles proclaiming this basic message.

I continue to hold such minimalist convictions about what it means to be a Christian, and I think that it is important to ground our faith in this simple starting place. However, I also recognize that limiting our faith to *only* repenting and believing may prevent us from experiencing the fullness of faith that God intends for us and can limit our ability to engage in the world.

Clearly, the center and beating heart of the gospel message is to be found in repenting and believing that "God proves his love for us in that while we still were sinners Christ died for us."[1] Having said this, we need to also recognize that there is a bit more to the story of God's interaction with his creation that we need to attend to. Some have framed this fuller account of the story of the Bible as a *four-chapter gospel*. Chapter one is creation, chapter two is the fall, chapter three is redemption, and chapter four is the eschaton (or second coming of Christ).

The problem of overfocusing on the middle two chapters of fall and redemption isn't that they are in some way flawed or insufficient for salvation, but rather that the other two chapters help to bring richness and color to the hope that is promised in the middle two chapters.

We explore here how a more nuanced understanding of creation and redemption impacts how we understand and engage the built environment. To correct this general oversight, we pay attention to the impact of time on our faithful experience of the built environment. We begin by looking at the large span of time covered by the broad story of redemption, which takes us from the creation to the end of time. Then we narrow our focus a bit and look at the various ways we experience time in the moments of our everyday life.

"When are you?" sounds like an odd question, because we always experience our lives in the present. So the answer to the question, "When are you?" can always simply be, "I'm right now, thank you very much." However, in light of our discussion of the four-chapter gospel, we may want to rethink how we answer this question.

The question of when are you can also be thought of as a question that draws out our historical awareness. That is to say, we can say where we are with respect to our location along the story line of our lives and the larger story that transcends our own. If we were a story's characters who had an unusual amount of self-awareness, we might be able to reply to that question by saying that we were right in the opening scene, or at the climax, or just before the resolution.

And, in fact, we may be more like characters in a story than we may have previously thought. Alasdair MacIntyre sees story as foundational to human life. He claims that our behaviors cannot make sense outside of the intentions that guide them and the settings in which they take place. "We cannot, that is to say, characterize behavior independently of intentions, and we cannot characterize intentions independently of the settings which make those intentions intelligible both to agents themselves and to others."[2]

When Cinderella finally meets the prince, and the two of them become lost in a reverie of mutual delight, she suddenly leaves him for no apparent reason. It is the context and setting for her decision to leave that make her actions intelligible.

Now, unlike Cinderella's, our stories are rooted not in an imaginative narrative sequence, but in actual history.

> A setting has a history, a history within which the histories of individual agents not only are, but have to be, situated, just because without the setting and its changes through time the history of the individual agent and his changes through time will be unintelligible.[3]

These histories are presented in the genre of narrative, and so MacIntyre categorizes all human actions as "enacted narratives."

Keeping in mind the grand narrative of salvation history as a four-chapter gospel, we might say that we look backward to creation and forward to the eschaton. And in the meantime, we are witnessing the realization of the power of sin being overcome by redemption.

Wisdom

One of the benefits of expanding our understanding of the story backward to creation is the truths that we can learn from what has preceded us. These kinds of truths can be accounted for under the heading of wisdom. In this section, we look at wisdom as an important strand in the Bible.

Wisdom and Creation

What difference does it make that our story doesn't begin with sin and redemption but is preceded by God's act of creation? First, this sequence reminds us that the original creation was good. It is easy to overlook this fact when we begin our narrative of salvation with the crisis of our sin.

Second, it causes us to wrestle with a fundamental question: Did sin do irreparable damage to creation? Or does creation continue to bear evidence of its goodness? It is my belief that the goodness of creation was not completely destroyed by sin and that we can see evidence of a good creation all around us. Rather than destroy creation, sin has distorted creation. And, more important, every aspect of creation can be redeemed.

One of the implications of the enduring goodness of creation is that we can learn truth from observing the world. Traditionally, theologians have spoken of God's truth being expressed in two books. There is the book of creation and the book of Scripture. Both speak God's truth, but they do so differently. Scripture is a more reliable form of truth and speaks more clearly to the meaning and ultimate goal of the things we observe in the world. Scripture, then, must always help correct and clarify what we observe in the world.

The two books of God's truth are not in opposition to each other. Scripture itself bears testimony to the fact that truth can be discovered through our interactions with the world. The strand of the Bible that most clearly asserts this reality is known as the wisdom tradition.

Because the wisdom tradition draws on God's role in creation and providence, it invites us to learn truth experientially, through interactions with the natural world. To support such a claim, Albert Wolters directs us to a Wisdom section in the primarily prophetic book of Isaiah.

> Listen, and hear my voice;
> Pay attention, and hear my speech.
> Do those who plow for sowing plow continually?
> Do they continually open and harrow their ground?
> When they have leveled its surface,
> do they not scatter dill, sow cummin,
> and plant wheat in rows
> and barley in its proper place,
> and spelt as the border?
> For they are well instructed;
> their God teaches them.
>
> Dill is not threshed with a threshing sledge,
> nor is a cart wheel rolled over cummin;
> but dill is beaten out with a stick,
> and cummin with a rod.
> Grain is crushed for bread,

but one does not thresh it forever;
one drives the cart wheel and horses over it,
but does not pulverize it.
This also comes from the LORD of hosts;
he is wonderful in counsel,
and excellent in wisdom.[4]

The wise farmer knows the fine distinctions between how to plant and tend to dill, cumin, barley, and spelt. He knows this not from reading Scripture, but from his interactions with the natural world. And yet Isaiah declares that "their God teaches them."

The farmer has gained experience planting and tending these crops year after year, but we can assume that he also has inherited wisdom from his forefathers based on their experience with these crops. The name for this accumulation and passing on of wisdom is traditioning. Much of the wisdom from which we derive both private and public benefit comes from traditions of various kinds. Such traditions can take the form of collected knowledge, and they can take the form of communal practices as well.

It is important to note that not all traditions represent embedded wisdom, and not all traditions contribute to human thriving. Traditions can embed sinful notions and practices such as racism and the oppression of vulnerable members of society. Traditions, therefore, are not irrefutable, but they usually warrant our careful consideration. When Jesus came to declare the good news of freedom from sin and the promise of new life, some of the strongest resistance to his message came from those who wanted to uphold tradition. Nevertheless, we must acknowledge that God can and does speak truth through tradition.

Wisdom and Human Culture

Wisdom is typically associated with knowledge that is gained through interaction with the world—especially the natural world. But, as we consider implications of this reality for the built environment, we also need to acknowledge that wisdom can be found in the cultural and political worlds. We can begin by asking the question of whether wisdom can be found more generally in culture. As we move further away from the natural world, can we envision wisdom being somehow embedded in the spaces and institutions of the city?

The eighth chapter of Proverbs seems to suggest as much.

Does not wisdom call,
and does not understanding raise her voice?

On the heights, beside the way,
    at the crossroads she takes her stand;
beside the gates in front of the town,
    at the entrance of the portals she cries out:
"To you, O people, I call,
    and my cry is to all that live.
O simple ones, learn prudence;
    acquire intelligence, you who lack it.
Hear, for I will speak noble things,
    and from my lips will come what is right;
for my mouth will utter truth;
    wickedness is an abomination to my lips.
All the words of my mouth are righteous;
    there is nothing twisted or crooked in them.
They are all straight to one who understands
    and right to those who find knowledge.
Take my instruction instead of silver,
    and knowledge rather than choice gold;
for wisdom is better than jewels,
    and all that you may desire cannot compare with her.[5]

This passage suggests three places within the public realm where we might find wisdom.

Wisdom can be found *where the paths meet*. This is where the word *trivia* comes from. *Tri-via* means, literally, three paths. Where three paths connect is where people from differing towns interact. They are not friends, family, or even neighbors, so they must speak about things that are of common concern.

Where the paths meet is where we talk about trivial things. When I was growing up, my mother was an inveterate grocery-store-line talker. She could get into a conversation with anyone at any time when she was in the grocery store line. Much of the time, what my mother was doing was bragging about her children, but this is also where she might find important information about the best teachers at school or where to find a mechanic who could be trusted. While at one level such conversations might seem trivial, we must be open to the idea that some of what is being passed back and forth between people in the grocery store line is wisdom.

Wisdom is also to be found in high places. Before the onset of modern communication technologies, the higher you went, the broader your audience could be. A king giving a speech from a balcony could be heard by everyone assembled in the plaza below. We might think of such "high places" today as the discourse of public intellectuals. Venues for this kind of speech are newspaper editorials, press conferences, important speeches, and books that gain a wide reading. While not everything we read and hear from public intellectuals is true or even consistent, we can acknowledge that there may be distinct truths to be found from such sources.

Wisdom also speaks at the city gates. In a traditional city, this is where the elders would sit for political decisions. We find wisdom embedded (hopefully) in the statutes and policies crafted by our public officials. The city gates traditionally also housed the market. So we can think of city gates today more generally as the marketplace. We can analyze the market to learn about the desires, hopes, and fears of the general public. And here, too, we should expect to find some wisdom. As we observed in the previous chapter, the wisdom of the New Urbanist movement may be affirmed by its market successes.

The Common Blessing of Wisdom

The wisdom tradition not only asserts a wide variety of settings from which we might discover wisdom but also suggests a broad range of people who can appropriate as well as pass on wisdom. Wisdom is not the exclusive domain of Christians. Since all people interact with the world, all people have access to sources of wisdom. Such public wisdom cannot tell us ultimate truths of God's character or even lead to salvation, but we must acknowledge that for many practical matters, non-Christians can be repositories of wisdom. We will explore this concept more fully under the heading Common Grace in chapter 6.

Proverbs 8 tells us that wisdom calls out in a loud voice to all humankind. This is not an appeal to wisdom for the benefit of an insular group of believers. From this we can surmise that God cares about public life. God wants public life to be infused with wisdom. God wants wisdom to inform our interpersonal interaction in the public realm (citizenship), to direct our business practices, and to shape our leaders and the policies they enact.

Wisdom for public life is one of the ways that God blesses humanity. Just as God provides air to breathe, water to drink, and food to fill our stomachs, God also provides wisdom to govern our public life. And when public life is informed by wisdom, we truly experience blessings.

Traditional Architecture

Not all wisdom is gathered in books and in the practices of the community. Wisdom is also embedded in the very walls of a community. The built environment, therefore, is a distinctive kind of repository for the wisdom of tradition. This has to do with its durability. A context-appropriate and well-constructed building can be instructional to the next generation that wants to learn how to construct a good building, but such a building can also provide direct benefit, such as shelter and beauty, to the next generation, regardless of whether particular skills in construction are passed on. The kinds of buildings that are good candidates for being repositories of wisdom tend to fall under the heading of traditional architecture. There are two ways of understanding traditional architecture.

Vernacular

Because different parts of the world encounter different patterns of weather and different expressions of cultural patterns, different patterns of buildings tend to emerge in different locales. Alexander, Ishikawa, and Silverstein speak of such particularities in the built environment as a kind of pattern language.[6] Such patterns reflect different uses, tastes, and local conditions. Traditional building based on these kinds of organic patterns is known as *vernacular*.

A barn in a particular town in Switzerland looks similar to other barns in town, but different from the blacksmith's shop. However, the barn in Switzerland looks different from a barn that serves a similar purpose across the world in Japan. And in many respects the barn in Switzerland looks more like the blacksmith's in Switzerland than the barn in Japan.

That particular kinds of buildings in particular locations take on a distinctive look has to do in part with utilitarian concerns. A barn needs to be spacious, with large doors, relatively dry, and easy to clean. And a barn in Switzerland needs to be well suited to withstand a mountainous climate.

In this respect the barn is acting as a durable repository of the wisdom of tradition that works in a particular location. Usually, this kind of wisdom is passed on directly from one craftsperson to the next. A builder who has all of the skills and knowledge of how to build the kinds of buildings in his or her community will pass on that wisdom to a child or an apprentice working alongside the builder.

But there are other reasons for the distinct look of buildings having to do with taste. Often, the collective tastes of people in a particular area become inscribed in the buildings as well. This can be an almost imperceptible process and doesn't spread so directly from one builder to the next.

This "traditioning of taste" tends to follow a sequence of steps:

1. A builder takes a traditional style and adapts one aspect of it.
2. If no one else likes it, it becomes a quirk on the landscape and is soon forgotten.

Orientation

3. If someone else likes it, he or she copies it in his or her own building.
4. If a number of people copy it, it becomes a style.
5. If the style becomes beloved, over time it becomes a tradition.

The informal influence of such utilitarian and aesthetic considerations on the building practices in a particular place is what drives vernacular architecture. Traditions of vernacular architecture account for why barns in Switzerland look the way they do. There are vernacular traditions that account for individual buildings as well as vernacular traditions accounting for the way the buildings are laid out in a place.

High Style

Because of the informal way that these traditions are passed on, vernacular architecture is sometimes called a low or folk tradition. When traditions become supported by institutions and certain people begin to be trained as professionals who are experts in the tradition, we enter the realm of *high style*. Much of what we think of when we think of architectural history is a study of the high style of design and building practices. High-style architectural traditions include Georgian, Federalist, Gothic, Romanesque, Baroque, Victorian, Arts and Crafts, and a whole host of others.

High-style traditioning is passed on not so much from builder to apprentice, but from trained architects in formal training programs as well as professional organizations. High-style architecture can also include practical wisdom, as this form of traditioning can also incorporate "best practices" from a wide swath of building projects. Many of the distinct features that define a particular style also serve a practical function.

Valuing the Past

One of the interesting aspects of the traditioning process is the way that traditions can be improved as each generation takes a fresh look at old problems and proposes new solutions. Traditions can also respond to changing conditions over a period of time. However, even in such cases, the basic assumption is that much that is good and wise is embedded in the traditions and that traditions should be taken seriously.

This assumption began to be widely challenged by an intellectual elite around the beginning of the twentieth century. Partially in response to the great strides that were taking place in science and industry and partially in response to the ways tradition was perceived to have contributed to various iterations of tyranny, tradition began to be viewed with suspicion.

Whereas past generations understood themselves to be making their contribution to the repository of tradition, this new generation understood itself to be sweeping away the past and starting over again on a new and more rational foundation. Within the field of architecture and urban planning, Daniel Solomon has described this impulse as the *architecture of erasure*; "what the architecture of erasure erased was, in fact, the history of American urbanism, the record of the way American cities were built from their first settlement until World War II."[7]

CIAM

The intellectual foundation for this architecture of erasure was developed through a series of meetings that took place between 1927 and 1933, which led to a movement known as the *Congrès International d'Architecture Moderne* (*CIAM*). This movement has had a major impact on the way cities have developed to the present day.

The conclusions from the *CIAM* were expressed in a document known as the Athens Charter; in it we see three elements that would become hallmarks of modern city planning.

Expert Culture

The first of these elements can be described as *expert culture*, the conviction that for every conceivable problem, there is an expert who is best suited to solve the problem, regardless of any consideration of practical skill or knowledge of local conditions. In its explanatory notes for paragraph 74, the Athens Charter states, "The principles of modern town planning have been developed by the work of countless technicians: technicians in the art of building, technicians of health, technicians of social organization."[8]

Expert culture explains to some extent why so many questionable, untested ideas continue to shape the way cities and towns have been constructed during the second half of the twentieth century. The public and public officials have been unwilling to question the sage advice of the "experts" who are backed by professional qualifications.

Function

The second legacy of *CIAM* is an attempt to rationalize the city into four basic *functions*—housing, work, leisure, and transportation:

Town planning has four principal functions, namely: first, to provide the inhabitants with salubrious housing, that is to say, places in which space, fresh air, and sunshine are plentifully guaranteed; second, to organize work-places so that instead of being a painful thraldom, work will regain its character as a natural human activity; third, to set up the installations necessary for the good use of leisure, rendering it beneficial and productive; fourth, to establish links between these various organizations by means of a traffic network that facilitates movement from place to place while respecting the rights of all. These four functions, which are the four keys of town planning, cover an immense field, since town planning is the outcome of a way of thinking applied to public life by means of a technique of action.[9]

The kind of zoning that led to the *Euclid v. Ambler* case involved the fairly simple separation of buildings designed for residential use from those designed for commercial uses. The influence of *CIAM* led to the complete fragmentation of the American city into even more precisely defined functions.

Technology

A third legacy from the *CIAM* is the belief that *technology* holds the key to finding the solution to the most pressing problems that we face. The most important of these technologies has been the automobile, but this device is by no means the only technology upon which our hopes have been pinned: "Mechanical vehicles ought to be agents of liberation and through their speed, to bring about a valuable gaining of time."[10] Although the vast stretches of land that make up our country and our love for freedom of the individualized variety partially explain our unwavering devotion to the automobile, such pronouncements of the *CIAM* helped to cement our commitment to building cities and neighborhoods around the requirements of the automobile.

This commitment to the viability of technological solutions also explains why it was so easy for a whole generation of architects to scrap millennia of the accumulated wisdom of vernacular and high-style building practices. It was assumed that modern heating and air-conditioning systems could solve any problems created by non-context-specific building practices.

Modernism and Folly

While in chapter 1 we saw some of the practical and historical reasons for the development of the automobile exurb in the American context, here we see how the *CIAM* provided much of the intellectual foundation for the various choices that have been made. When thinking about the built environment, it is important for us to be aware of these particular legacies as they relate to things like wisdom and tradition. Even as we see some of the specific solutions of modern rational planning come into question (such as the automobile exurb), we can note how these more general tendencies continue to be embedded in our culture.

Take the issue of parking regulations, for instance. If a developer wants to obtain a permit to construct a supermarket, she will most likely need to provide a certain number of parking spaces on her lot based on the square footage of the store. If she were to ask the person responsible for enforcing that regulation where that number comes from, she would most likely be directed to the municipal building code. If somehow she were able to gain an audience with the author of that building code and ask where that number comes from, the author would most likely make reference to a book of architectural standards that he learned to use in his planning program. And there is some speculation among professional planners whether the person who truly knows where the numbers come from is the one who wrote the architectural standards or the professor of planning who teaches how to use such tools.

The Bible extols the value of learning wisdom from the natural world and from human culture. The Bible also contrasts the merits of such knowledge with the fate of those who ignore wisdom. Those who ignore wisdom are referred to as fools, and the convictions that they cling to are known as folly.

> The mind of one who has understanding seeks knowledge,
>   but the mouths of fools feed on folly.[11]

Unlike the informal traditioning practices that were passed directly from builder to builder, expert culture defers to the specialization of "experts," whose "expertise" becomes calcified into municipal codes that are enforced regardless of whether or not they make any sense. As we have noted, in many cases these influential people gain their authority from a proficiency with abstract knowledge and often lack practical skills or knowledge of local conditions. So, whereas one might be tempted to think of an "architectural standards" reference book as a repository of wisdom, there may be much within the pages that is better characterized as folly.

Embedded Wisdom

The modern movement of architecture has left us a legacy of buildings that very few people like and public spaces that are devoid of life. However, in some ways the more worrisome legacy of the modern movement has been a kind of knee-jerk impulse to dismiss the wisdom of the past and look for the next futuristic/technological solution to current problems. Some of the more interesting and helpful contributions have come from individuals and communities that understand how to value the wisdom of the past. There are two general ways this wisdom can be brought to the table.

Appreciative Inquiry

In light of the overreliance on so-called experts in shaping the built environment, a crucial task that lies before us is a rediscovery of learning wisdom that grows from the bottom up. As was mentioned in chapter 1, this is the kind of thing Jane Jacobs was doing, by learning through immersion. We need to recover the ability as a culture of demanding to know whether something really works or makes sense instead of relying solely on the opinions of irrefutable experts.

One technique that represents a positive step in this direction is known as *appreciative inquiry*. Appreciative inquiry has emerged out of the field of organizational behavior, but it can be usefully applied to the built environment as well. It provides an alternative to the "problem solving" approach to engendering positive change.

Problem solving, as the name suggests, focuses on problems or what is not working. Once the problem is identified, then a variety of solutions are proposed. These solutions are then evaluated in terms of some rational criteria such as cost versus benefit. The problem-solving approach is usually done from the top down. Often it is the experts who get to define even the problem, and in all cases, the rational criteria determine which solution will be attempted. Many of the failed initiatives in urban planning over the past few generations can be attributed to this problem-solving approach.

Appreciative inquiry, by way of contrast, begins with what is working. The first step for appreciative inquiry is to ask the population who will be most impacted by the potential change what they think. With regard to the built environment, appreciative inquiry asks local residents what is working, what has worked, what they are proud of, and where they see potential. Often appreciative inquiry doesn't lead to radical change, but rather identifies obstacles that prevent the local population from solving their own problems or recommends resources to encourage those who are doing good things. Appreciative inquiry lends a kind of organizational legitimacy to what would otherwise probably be referred to as simple common sense.

One of the more successful ways that appreciative inquiry can be quickly harnessed for a particular location is through a community brainstorming session known as a *charette*. Whereas many public meetings are little more than formalities to give the sense that the public is being listened to, a charette is a carefully designed forum that circumvents many of the reasons people become frustrated with public meetings. At a charette the stakeholders and the experts are brought into the same room so that technical questions don't hold up the process. And at a charette ordinary citizens can see how their ideas contribute to the draft proposal that is hammered out before their eyes. The charette has transformed how many people understand the public process, and charettes have been the driving force behind countless successful public projects in the past two decades.

Preservation and Pragmatism

Another place where we are beginning to see a return to learning wisdom from the bottom up has been in the historic preservation movement. The contemporary historic preservation movement began as a reaction against the excess of the "architecture of erasure" legacy of the modernist movement. The architecture of erasure encouraged the wanton destruction of old, "outdated" buildings in favor of modern buildings that were more rational and up-to-date. It wasn't long before some people began to notice that these rational and up-to-date buildings were uglier than the old buildings and in many cases didn't function nearly as well.

Such impulses led to the historic preservation movement. This movement begins with the assumption that if a building has survived for a great number of years, there must be some reason for its durability. Either it is particularly loved by its community, it is extremely well constructed, or it serves an indispensable purpose. In any case, the historic preservation movement shifts the burden of proof from those who want to save a building to those who advocate its destruction.

We can see the positive contribution of the historic preservation movement in the saving of places like Old Town Pasadena. Despite having a gorgeous stock of residential and commercial buildings, Old Town was looking shabby in the 1970s. The first attempt to remedy the situation involved a typical "urban renewal" strategy out of the modernist playbook.[12] Four blocks of residential neighborhood were razed, and in their place was built a huge, monolithic building, surrounded by an ocean of parking.

Soon after, a developer purchased a commercial building in Old Town with plans to destroy it and build something more current. Because of what residents had witnessed with the previous urban renewal project, this time they were ready to put up a fight. A group called Historic Pasadena was formed, and it lobbied to block the developer from destroying the commercial building. Instead, the developer would be allowed to alter the interior of the building to make it usable for his business, but he would be required to keep the exterior intact.

From this point on, preserving historic buildings in Pasadena became a priority, and most of the remaining stock of buildings were kept intact. Just protecting the buildings from destruction, however, would not be enough to ensure their viability. They also needed to be attractive to potential investors.

One issue was parking. We learned in chapter 2 that too much parking can destroy town fabric. Because Old Town was initially developed before the onslaught of automobile culture, parking was not adequate for potential customers. The fact that the buildings came right up to the sidewalk was good for the urban form but also meant that the only parking available was the few street spots in front of each building. And those spots were barely enough for the employees.

In other cities, the municipal code would require new investors to put a parking lot in front of each of the buildings, but this would destroy the historic character of the area. So the city of Pasadena came up with a novel parking strategy called "Park Once." Instead of assuming that people would need a place to park in order to access each store in the Old Town independently, the assumption was that people could park once and access multiple stores. The city amended the parking code to meet the parking needs of the district, rather than of each building.

Instead of requiring developers to build a parking lot for their building, each would have to contribute to a parking fund that would be put toward building parking garages behind the buildings. The second step of the strategy was to free up the spots in front of the stores for customers to use. This involved putting parking meters on the street and charging for parking.

Many business owners resisted this idea, because they felt that it would cause their customers to gravitate toward the mall, where there was free parking. The city officials struck an ingenious deal with the business owners. They would allow the building owners on each block to determine whether they wanted meters installed. If they agreed to the meters, all of the revenues would be used to maintain and make improvements on the block. The revenue that came in for the blocks that adopted meters was used for regular street cleaning, historic lampposts, charming street furniture, and cobblestone pathways. Initially, a few blocks voted for meters, but in time all of the blocks got on board.

Preserving the historic buildings and solving the parking issue turned out to be a winning combination for Old Town Pasadena. Not only did it encourage new investment and recover a charming shopping district for the residents of

Pasadena, over time it has become a regional destination for all of Southern California. The story of Old Town Pasadena provides a good example of employing wisdom in the built environment.

What is especially interesting about this case is how a compromise was reached between the historical heritage of the area and current needs. As historic preservation has become a more powerful force in our culture, the danger is in a tendency to preserve the past and ignore current needs. It is easy for historic preservation to adopt a curatorial (or museum) approach to the past. Preservation is not about treating the built environment as a kind of museum for how we used to live. Historic preservation is about honoring that which we have inherited from the past in order to provide settings for human thriving in the present and in the future.

This provides a good jumping-off point for us to move our focus from creation as the first chapter of the story to the eschaton, which is the fourth chapter of the story.

Restoring Shalom

As important as it is to seek wisdom by thinking back to creation, that is only one part of the story. At the other pole, we see the shalom setting of the coming eschaton. When Christ comes to reign in glory, we will all experience shalom in our everyday life. In the orientation to part 1, we explored the relationship between the garden of Eden and the city of the New Jerusalem. We considered the idea that the human society in the city represented the realized potential of the family in the garden. Between the garden and the city, we depicted a trajectory, which was a direct path from one harmonious state to another. That line represents the biblical concept of shalom, and it represents the development of human community and culture in perfect obedience to God's will.

It's important to note that this future state that is promised in Scripture may very well be an earthly place. In fact, it may take place on this earth on which we now live our lives. Many Christians are becoming more comfortable with the idea that followers of Jesus are not going to spend eternity floating around in some kind of ethereal remote location, but rather are going to experience redeemed existence in the very physical setting of a new heaven and a new earth.[13] This is different from how evangelical Christians had thought about the promise of eternal existence for generations.

A key to this significant paradigm shift has been a reconsideration of the provocative text in the second half of 2 Peter 3:10. As the King James version

(KJV) has it, "the earth also and the works that are therein shall be burned up." One common way to understand this text is that the earth and sky (heaven) are completely annihilated and then later replaced with a brand new heaven and earth.

However, another possibility, and the one that some of the more contemporary translations have, is that the earth and everything on it will be "disclosed" or "laid bare." That is to say the fire will not annihilate the entire earth, but will refine it by burning away everything that is unworthy.[14] This newer translation seems to fit the context better as the author had just made a parallel reference to the destruction of the flood, which wreaked havoc on creation, but didn't annihilate everything.

This eschatological paradigm shift helps to combat some of the Gnostic tendencies inherent in evangelical theology. Evangelicals have sometimes been tempted by the notion that what it means to be spiritual is to deny or ignore those aspects of our lives that have to do with our physical existence. However, when we think of eternity in the context of a real physical place, we tend to take the physicality of our lives more seriously in the here and now.

Another bit of good news implied in this trajectory is that human history is not just a random sequence of events but has a purpose and directionality. We understand that God is working out God's purposes in human history and that the end of the story is one of goodness and delight. The question for us is, What do we do with the knowledge that God has a direction and a purpose for human history? Do we simply wait quietly for God to carry out the plan, or are we somehow supposed to be involved in this activity?

The creation mandates suggest that humans are somehow supposed to be involved in carrying out God's plan for all of creation. We are called to participate with God in the redemption of creation. We do this by being obedient to God's revealed will in Scripture and by faithfully seeking out our particular vocation in fulfilling the creation mandate. We cannot cause God's kingdom to come by our actions, but we can experience some of the goodness that God desires for us as we remain faithful to his will for our lives.

The Crisis of Sin

Of course, the ideal of humanity maintaining perfect obedience to God's will is just that—an ideal. The reality of our situation is one of greater and lesser degrees of sin against the will of God, with obedience being more the exception than the rule. The salient question for those of us living between the garden and the city, then, becomes how we respond to sin.

We can see various ways of responding to that question illustrated in the image below. Sin is represented by the vector from the shalom line to the right. It is not hard to bring to mind examples of the consequences of sin in our everyday life. We see children being exploited, the environment being ravaged, and evil people being rewarded for destructive behavior all around us.

Garden to City (Part III)

Nostalgia

One of the most natural responses to the discouraging and fearful consequences of sin is *nostalgia*. Nostalgia is represented by the curved line that doubles back to the garden. When we feel disgusted at some attribute of contemporary life, we often think longingly of an earlier time before such terrible things existed. This might be based on a memory from our childhood or on stories our grandparents told us. But really, the logical extension of such thinking takes us all the way back to the garden. If humanity is getting worse and worse, it must be a good thing to get back to the time before all of these things started changing.

Nostalgia may be behind some of the overzealous efforts at historic preservation, but within the Christian community, nostalgia often comes in the form of a longing for a romanticized rural life. We can see nostalgia coming out in paintings that depict idealized pastoral scenes and in home decor that evokes the kitchen of a farmhouse. As we discover in the next chapter, this impulse may also be behind some of the exurban housing types that project a kind of rural setting for people who are not farmers.

The problem with nostalgia, for biblical Christians, is that it ignores the urban images of shalom we find in the Bible. It denies the fact that creation was not meant to be only preserved, but also to be cultivated and developed in good and wholesome ways.

Orientation

Revolution

Another way to deal with the squalor and messiness that sin brings to our lives is the route of *revolution*. The revolutionary instinct is to clear everything and rebuild from scratch according to more rational criteria. This response is pictured as the vector arrow that does not originate in the garden. The revolutionary instinct can involve literally clearing away the past—such as by bulldozing old buildings or whole neighborhoods. It can also be expressed in clearing away practices or traditional ways of thinking about things.

The problem with the revolutionary approach is that it tends to ignore the repository of wisdom that is embedded in both the old buildings and the old traditions. Revolution is an attractive option, because it seems so definitive, and it is relatively easy for one agent to bring a significant amount of change in a short period of time. However, the lack of wisdom in much revolutionary change soon becomes evident, and such endeavors tend to look dated and dilapidated very early in the process.

Redemption

A third option for responding to the reality of sin in our midst is the way of *redemption*. Redemption is represented by the short arrow pointing back to the line of shalom. A balanced understanding of redemption recognizes the naïveté of nostalgia as well as the hubris of revolution. It strives for obedience to God by seeking shalom, but not by putting that in tension with the good development of human community and culture.

Albert Wolters uses the example of a baby's development to illustrate this concept.

> Earthly creation preceding the events recorded in Genesis 3 is like a healthy newborn child. In every respect it can be pronounced "very good," but this does not mean that change is not required. There is something seriously wrong if the baby remains in its infancy: it is meant to grow, develop, mature into adulthood. Suppose now that while the child is still an infant it contracts a serious chronic disease for which there is no known cure, and that it grows up an invalid, the disease wasting its body away. It is clear that there are two clearly distinguishable processes going on in its body as it approaches adolescence: one is the process of maturation and growth, which continues in spite of the sickness and which is natural, normal, and good; the other is the progress of the disease, which distorts and impairs the healthy functioning of the body. Now suppose further that the child has reached adolescence when a cure is found for the sickness, and it slowly begins to recover its health. As the child approaches adulthood there is

now a third process at work in its body: the process of healing, which counteracts and nullifies the action of the disease and which has no other purpose than to bring the youth to healthy adulthood, in which only the normal processes of a sound body will take place. The child will then be said to be restored to health after these many years.[15]

In the same way, redemption doesn't want to return humanity to the garden, but rather to bring it to the appropriate place of development that humanity might be if sin hadn't intervened. Redemption takes seriously the goodness of creation and the hope of the eschaton. Understanding this basic trajectory of our task will help to guide our thinking as we contemplate what faithfulness looks like within the built environment.

Already and Not Yet

As we think about participating with God in the redemption of creation, we must strike a balance between taking responsibility for our role in faithful obedience to the creation mandates and trusting the sovereignty of God, who has promised to bring the divine will to completion. The eschaton is not some kind of an abstract future that looms far beyond the distant horizon but is rather a dynamic state that exists beyond our linear time. Rather than us simply traveling toward it, the eschaton is also breaking into our world in various signs of the coming kingdom.

We saw the beginning of this in-breaking when Jesus came in the flesh, and it became firmly established when he gave his life on the cross. It will be fully realized when Jesus comes to assume his rightful role as king. We see evidence of the coming reign of Christ throughout our everyday life. Part of what Christian faithfulness involves is being attuned to evidence of this in-breaking as it occurs.

Eugene Peterson has likened this activity to bird-watching in an otherwise ugly place. Most people see only the ugliness, but the learned bird-watcher has trained his or her eyes to see the rare specimens of birds that are in evidence all around.[16] Biblical Christians need to attune their eyes to evidence of God's kingdom breaking in where others see only chaos and tragedy. And biblical Christians need to calibrate their lives and their work in response to the truth of God's unstoppable kingdom rather than the falsehood of common perceptions.

Theologians describe this in-between time of our existence as the "already and not yet." We live in that nebulous space between Christ's first coming in

Orientation

the incarnation and his second coming to usher in his kingdom in power and glory. Christ's victory over sin, death, and the devil is already accomplished. However, as we wait for its full realization, our lives continue to be marked by heartbreak and pain.

Rhythm—Living Faithfully in the Present

This leads to a third aspect of the "when are you" question. We understand faithfulness to involve looking backward with gratitude to a good creation and looking forward hopefully to a coming eschaton, but how are we to think about faithfulness in time as we experience it in the present? We know that we are to work toward the redemption of creation, and we may have some ideas as to what the goal of such redemption looks like, but how do we set about this task within the framework of each particular day of our lives? To answer this question we need to think a bit further about the concept of time itself.

One of the great ironies of contemporary life is that it is the technologically advanced countries with time-saving devices and organizational efficiencies that tend to have the most harried and exhausted populations. In the less "developed" countries we find people relaxing and enjoying the passage of time. What is the reason for this strange state of affairs?

Colin Gunton thinks that part of the problem is that in the developed countries, we tend to think about time as a commodity that we can control.[17] Our metaphors for time betray this perspective. We purchase "time-saving" devices and we seek efficiency in our use of time in the same way that we talk about fuel efficiency in our cars. Such language betrays the fact that we think of time as a tangible and malleable substance that we can "save" and "spend" at will.

But Gunton argues that time is not like a material commodity that we can gather, save up, and then use at will. Time, rather, is part of God's good creation, and it is given to us in a particular form. Time is given to us in rhythmic flows. Cultures and communities that are less enmeshed in technology tend to adjust their individual and communal practices around some of these flows, whereas more "developed" countries think that they can leverage technology to ignore the constraints imposed by the flow of time. The former are practiced in receiving time as a gift, and the latter seize time as a reward for their cleverness.

At the beginning of this chapter we addressed the question "When are you?" by thinking about our temporal location within the large span of time between creation and eschaton. Now we can address that same question from a more focused perspective. We can think about the when of our lives in terms of our location within the various rhythms of the day, the week, the year, and even the life span.

In the introduction, we were introduced to the concept of enacted space as a dynamic interaction of people and props through time in a particular place. James Rojas divides the time element of enacted space into natural time that tracks the movements of nature (daylight and seasons) and abstract time that is governed by human decision (normally, clock time).[18] Here, we catalog some concrete examples using Rojas's two categories and then we will expand his conceptualization to include some rhythms that are keyed to God's interaction with creation through salvation history.

Abstract Rhythms

One of the most common, and even inescapable, rhythms that we face is the rhythm of the market. If I want to drive up to Seattle to visit my parents, my first consideration is planning my journey to start after about 9:30 in the morning so that I can avoid getting stuck in traffic. I have to wait until that time because a great many people have jobs in Seattle that start between eight and nine in the morning.

The rhythms of the market explain why there is heavy traffic on the roads between 7:00 and 9:30 in the morning and between 4:30 and 6:00 in the afternoon. This rhythm is not precisely a daily rhythm, because it tends to occur only from Monday through Friday. There are some seasonal variations of this rhythm, especially during Christmas, when shoppers turn out in huge numbers to grab the best deals on the day after Thanksgiving.

Another set of rhythms (that are tied to the economic rhythms of the community) are the rhythms of entertainment. There are the rhythms of the various sports seasons that can build up slowly before the events themselves (spring training, draft picks), and they can rush toward a dramatic conclusion (March Madness, the World Cup). We experience rhythms of the big screen (summer blockbusters, Christmas movies) and rhythms of the small screen (*American Idol* finals, the network "sweeps").

For students, there is the rhythm of the academic year. The "year" begins in the fall, and the pace of the fifteen-week semester or ten-week quarter shapes one's life more than do the months or seasons of the year. For some of the population, one's day is governed by the rhythms of public transportation. The scheduled arrival of a popular bus, train, or light rail route causes a kind of frantic gathering as people from all directions converge on the station. Similarly, when a train stops at a major station, the waiting area swells up like a wave over a tide pool and then empties out just as quickly. In this form

Orientation

of transportation, as with the automobile, sometimes knowing the schedule will get you to your destination more quickly.

Natural Rhythms

As Rojas suggests, the above abstract rhythms don't capture all of the things that govern our days and seasons. The other kinds of rhythms that he mentions are the rhythms of nature. These, of course, aren't completely disconnected to the above rhythms. The traditional working day is from nine to five because that is when there is the most daylight. The weather is the reason that baseball is a summer sport and basketball is a winter sport.

The most obvious natural rhythm that impacts our lives is the daily rhythm of the sun coming up and going down. We've already mentioned the connection between this rhythm and the rhythm of the working day, but the presence or absence of natural light affects more than just our patterns of work. Public places like parks can be delightful on a sunny day and menacing in the dark of night. Beaches can be teeming with energy in the middle of summer and quite desolate on a cold winter's day.

One of the legacies of *CIAM* is the dream that through technology we could overcome the contingencies of these natural rhythms. And to some extent the rhythms of nature have become less determinative of our activity. With artificial light we can play baseball or work in our office until late into the night if we choose to. However, try as we might, it doesn't seem likely that we will ever come close to eradicating the influence of natural rhythms on our lives. Ocean cities will need a lot more lifeguards in July than they do in November regardless of technological developments.

The span of human life generates a kind of demographic rhythm as various groupings of people make their way through various life stages. From a societal perspective each life stage caries with it a potential cost or benefit to society. We have felt the effects of this kind of rhythm as the baby boomer generation has ballooned its way through various stages of life. A need for more schools was followed by a glut of productive labor, which is being overtaken by concern for Social Security and health care. Some of the mistakes that we have made in investment decisions and resource allocation have come from thinking primarily of humans as fixed in the prime of their working years.

Sacred Rhythms

The kind of time that is not mentioned by Rojas is that which is governed neither by "nature" nor by human decision. From the perspective of the biblical narrative, the events that we experience in our lives are not the result of chaotic forces of nature or reflective of the inevitable march of human progress, but rather are an unfolding of God's plan for the redemption of all of creation. This plan is centered on the ministry of Jesus Christ, who put on human flesh and came to earth to bring this plan to fruition. John makes it clear that the salvation effected through Christ is of neither natural nor human origin: "But to all who received him, who believed in his name, he gave power to become children of God, who were born, not of blood or of the will of the flesh or of the will of man, but of God."[19]

As we explored earlier in this chapter, we believe that creation is being guided toward a final goal by a loving God. That is to say, the various strands of natural history, political history, and our history will reach their fulfillment and will be harmoniously resolved in the eschaton. That notion has an effect on how we "hear" the various rhythms we've been describing. Rhythms that are more complex can be easy to misunderstand, but the rewards of training our ears to hear them can be significant. The busy signal on a phone has a simple kind of rhythm. But it is different from the rhythm we hear in a symphony. As we learn to recognize the way a symphony works, we come to expect that even seemingly incongruous strands will be resolved by the end.

Sacred time can be hard to distinguish from natural time and abstract time because so often these terms encompass the same events. What makes sacred time unique is that it involves an assumption of coherence and directionality in various events. And it posits a God who interacts with the world in very intentional ways.

We have already noted that the natural rhythm of daylight causes a concentration of productive human activity during the day. From this perspective, the day begins with the sun coming up, because that is when we can start accomplishing our work. The day is the unit of time that is significant. Night is just an interruption, a non-day. Night becomes significant only insofar as it can be manipulated to behave like day (via electric lights, etc.).

But this is an overly anthropocentric way of looking at reality. We see a helpful contrast to this perspective in the account of creation given in Genesis. In what seems to be a quirky poetic device, each day of creation concludes with this kind of summary statement, "and there was evening and morning, the first day." Our first impulse is to see this as a kind of minor error. We want it to say, "there was morning and evening, the first day."

But according to Eugene Peterson, this is no mistake, nor is it a quirky poetic device. There is important theology embedded in this repeated phrase. According to Peterson, the Jews saw the day as beginning in the evening as a way of asserting God's sovereignty.[20] Humans, as we have seen, are unique among God's creatures in that we have special work to do. We are to participate in God's creation of and sustaining of the universe by fulfilling the cultural mandate.

However, despite this honor, we are, like the rest of creation, finite creatures. We have important work to do, but we cannot work continually. Every day we must rest if we are to continue working. Every day we need a minimum amount of sleep. This is one way that we are different from God. God doesn't need to rest as we do.

> He will not let your foot be moved;
>   he who keeps you will not slumber.
> He who keeps Israel
>   will neither slumber nor sleep.[21]

This difference between who God is and who we are should have a significant impact on how we see each day.

When we see the day beginning in the evening, the first thing that humans do is rest. That means when we awake with the sun and begin our work, we acknowledge that God has already been at work through the night. Our work is not an independent force but rather is joined to the work of the One who initiated our work with a command.

Rest, then, is not an interruption of that which defines us and gives us meaning. In some ways our daily rest does a better job of anchoring our true identity. Our identity begins with an acknowledgment of our dependence upon God, and only then can we participate in God's work with our effort. We take up the issue of rest in more detail in chapter 9.

Tied to the rhythm of each day beginning with rest and then moving into work is the weekly rhythm that also begins with rest and the acknowledgment of God's sovereignty. This cadence is marked by the practice of gathered worship on Sunday—the first day of the week. The practice of gathering regularly for the purpose of worshiping God has deep foundations in the Bible and Christian history: "And let us consider how to provoke one another to love and good deeds, not neglecting to meet together, as is the habit of some, but encouraging one another, and all the more as you see the Day approaching."[22]

The expectation that God's people gather regularly for worship is linked to a more explicitly communal practice. That is to say, one can remember the Sabbath alone, but to gather for worship, one must coordinate with other worshipers.

Although the gathering for worship is so ordinary as to be hardly noticed, Nicholas Wolterstorff encourages us to think more deeply about what is going on in this particular practice:

Every Sunday for almost two millennia Christians have left their homes, their places of work and recreation, and assembled to perform the liturgy. When the liturgy is finished they return to their homes, their places of work and recreation. Seven days later they repeat this pattern of assembling and dispersing. The temporal dimension of this familiar yet curious systolic-diastolic pattern invites reflection. What is the significance of inserting this one-plus-six rhythm into the flow of time?[23]

Wolterstorff already hints at his take on this question in his choice of adjectives. "Systolic-diastolic" likens the pattern of worship to a circulatory system. The heart is both central and essential to life, but it in no way encompasses all that is involved in human life. Humans eat and sing, they write novels and they fix cars, they make love and they ride bikes. The heart isn't directly involved in any of this, but without the heart none of it could happen.

We can think of worship as playing a similar role. As we gather for worship we are cleaned up (forgiven) and revived by finding our place once again in the grand story of salvation history. And we are sent out again after gathered worship to continue our worship individually or in smaller groupings by faithfully doing our work in the world. Unlike the heart analogy, there are a number of things that happen in worship that have intrinsic value for human life. Worship must never be only instrumental. The act of ascribing glory and honor to God our creator and sustainer is a fundamental human practice and does not derive value from its effectiveness in sustaining other practices. The regular celebration of the Lord's Supper (or Eucharist) is also an indispensable aspect of what happens when God's people gather. We explore Christian worship in more detail in the next chapter.

The traditional church calendar presents a yearly rhythm of celebrations and seasons. The essential elements of salvation history are reiterated each year as churches follow the calendar through Advent, Christmas, Epiphany, Lent, Easter, Ascension, and Trinity. The specifics of these special days and seasons notwithstanding, this practice helps communities that are attuned to such things to distinguish between ordinary time (feral) and celebratory time (festal).

Within the realm of sacred time there is a corollary to the stages of life mentioned above. However, when it comes to marking key moments in our life journey within the community of faith, we do not focus on relative cost and benefit. Rather, the community of faith marks key moments as celebrations of covenant faithfulness. Baptism (or dedication) represents God claiming the helpless child with (undeserved) covenant love. Confirmation (or believer baptism) represents a child moving into adulthood by claiming the covenant promises for himself or herself. Christian marriage is a celebration of two individuals asking God to bless the covenant promises that they make to each other. And the funeral is releasing one's earthly body to the earth while confirming that one's life is secure in the hands of a faithful and everlasting God.

Hearing the Music of Life

Knowing how to experience time as a gift is one of the primary challenges of modern life. We are tempted to forget our history and the inheritance that we have received from those who have preceded us. We project our anxieties and our dreams into a future that doesn't exist yet. And we constantly seek new ways to reshuffle the events and encounters of our day in order to cram more stuff into our waking hours. But these strategies, as we have seen, often cause us to make decisions that are foolish, and they cause our lives to feel harried.

One helpful way to counteract this tendency is to take cues from our experience of music. Music is one area of modern life where we have been able to retain much of the experience of time as a gift. We can think of a song as a collection of pleasing sounds, harmonies, and word pictures. Each of these elements contributes to our enjoyment of the song. However, what really makes the song work is how these things are presented to us in time. The melody consists not only of the various notes in the song but also in their sequence and in their timing. The song has a dramatic shape involving tension and resolution.

In our music, unlike much of the rest of our lives, we are not tempted to gain efficiency by rationalizing these flows. We would not take kindly to a suggestion that we should group all of the like notes together in the song. If we have a favorite part of the song, we wouldn't want to listen just to that moment in the song without the parts of the song that lead up to it as well as follow it. We would not appreciate the offer to gain time by doubling or tripling the speed of the song. The way a song presents itself to us in time is an inescapable aspect of our enjoyment of that song.

In a similar fashion, we would do well to think about our creaturely existence as being lived in the context of a beautiful song. Reducing salvation to an abstract moment where the problem of sin is fixed by the application of redemption misses the fullness, beauty, and drama of God's plan to redeem all of God's good creation. To reject our placement within the flow of salvation history by nostalgically longing for an earlier time or trying to erase that past increases our sense of control or reduces our anxiety in exchange for a replacement song marked by banality and ugliness. To try to "fix" the problem of time by pursuing efficiency and time-saving strategies is to risk missing the glorious melody of each day as a gift. A key aspect of understanding the built environment is to be able to hear the music of everyday life.

For Further Reading

Alexander, Christopher. *The Timeless Way of Building*. Center for Environmental Structure. New York: Oxford University Press, 1979.

Blake, Peter. *Form Follows Fiasco: Why Modern Architecture Hasn't Worked*. Boston: Little, Brown, 1974.

Brand, Stewart. *How Buildings Learn: What Happens after They're Built*. New York: Viking, 1994.

Lane, Belden. *Landscapes of the Sacred: Geography and Narrative in American Spirituality*. Baltimore: Johns Hopkins University Press, 2002.

Lynch, Kevin. *What Time Is This Place?* Cambridge: MIT Press, 1972.

MacIntyre, Alasdair C. *After Virtue: A Study in Moral Theory*. 2nd ed. Notre Dame, IN: University of Notre Dame Press, 1984.

Peterson, Eugene H. *Working the Angles: The Shape of Pastoral Integrity*. Grand Rapids: Eerdmans, 1987.

Scully, Vincent Jr. *American Architecture and Urbanism*. Rev. ed. New York: Henry Holt, 1988.

Vanhoozer, Kevin J. *The Drama of Doctrine: A Canonical Linguistic Approach to Christian Theology*. Louisville: Westminster John Knox, 2005.

Wolfe, Tom. *From Bauhaus to Our House*. New York: Farrar, Straus & Giroux, 1981.

Wolters, Albert M. *Creation Regained: Biblical Basics for a Reformational Worldview*. 2nd ed. Grand Rapids: Eerdmans, 2005.

Part II

Participation

In many respects, we can see the twenty-first century as a rediscovery of the built environment. After pursuing a radical experiment with automobile-oriented development during the second half of the twentieth century, by the end of that century a concerted effort was made to recover some of the practices of building neighborhoods that had been forgotten during that period.

These neotraditional (or New Urbanist) projects began to spring up throughout North America. The characteristics of a traditional neighborhood have already been listed, but in many respects the more interesting question is what happens next. The automobile-oriented subdivision, so the argument goes, can inhibit the formation of deep and multinodal connections among neighbors, because life is divided between activities that take one far away from one's neighborhood and time inside one's home that turns its back on the neighborhood. Although there are numerous exceptions to the rule, in general it has been observed that subdivisions don't encourage neighborly behavior.

We addressed in chapter 3 an important question: If we begin building neighborhoods again with stores mixed in with residences, a walkable scale, a clear center and edge, etc., will people who come from two generations of the more privatized subdivision all of a sudden begin acting more neighborly? The assumption that we can cause certain behavioral changes through changing the built environment we called physical (or material) determinism, and the evidence from the first couple of decades of a return to neotraditional neighborhood building demonstrates that it is not such a simple thing to change human behavior patterns.

We can think of the requisite components of community, therefore, in terms of hardware and software. *Hardware* refers to the buildings and other physical aspects of a particular place. *Software* refers to the people who enact the communal activities and practices in that place. Another term for the software component is *agent*. The question of who causes (or prevents) community from forming is a question of agency.

In part 1, we discovered that God always acts as the primary agent. In many respects, the first thing that we must not fail to do when considering the built environment is to begin with gratitude. We must see our embodied selves, our placement in a particular environment, our community, and even time as gifts that we receive from our creator. Once we are rooted in gratitude and grace, we can begin to think about ourselves as agents of redemption in the built environment.

Perhaps our first impulse when thinking about ourselves as agents is to ask ourselves, "What can I do to help form or build up this community?" While it is commendable and important to ask such practical kinds of questions, we need to be sure that we don't unwittingly bring to that question an assumption of autonomous individualism. We discovered in chapter 3 that autonomous individualism poses a threat to every community.

While this autonomous-individual approach to personhood is pervasive in our culture, it is not a perspective that we find in the Bible. As mentioned above, the Bible shows us the maker and ruler of the universe exists eternally as three persons in mutually constitutive relationship. This perichoretic way of being, as we discovered in chapter 3, provides an important clue as to how we are to live. And it will also help us as we begin to think about agency.

As we read the Bible with our eyes open to the role of relationships and community in forming our identity and even our vocation, we can begin to see a more central role for some of the more communal dimensions of our existence. A good place to begin thinking about our identity in terms of the communities in which we exist is a context in which God's people were struggling mightily with their identity. During the time of exile, the Israelites had to answer the questions of who they were and what they were to do when they had been removed from the place they called home. The instructions that they were given at that pivotal time in their formation may prove useful to us as we struggle to figure out who we are and what we are to do in this in-between time.

Understanding the built environment involves learning to see and comprehend the space in between the buildings. However, there is another important in-betweenness that we need to be aware of if we are going to have meaningful interaction in the built environment. This is the concept of living faithfully in the already/not yet space of time in between the incarnation and the eschaton. The question of how to live in between where we've been and where we are going can be addressed from the vantage point of this in-between time for God's people. Having been removed from Jerusalem and relocated in Babylon put the Israelites in a very difficult situation.

The prophet Jeremiah had the unenviable task of announcing that their exile would not be coming to an end any time soon. They would be stuck in

Babylon for another seventy years. This was not the worst news they could have heard, but it was also not exactly what they wanted to hear. Jeremiah's message meant ultimate hope for their grandchildren and for the survival of the nation, but it was not a hope that would become realized in their lifetimes.

The instructions that Jeremiah gave for living in this in-between time were as follows:

> Thus says the LORD of hosts, the God of Israel, to all the exiles whom I have sent into exile from Jerusalem to Babylon: Build houses and live in them; plant gardens and eat what they produce. Take wives and have sons and daughters; take wives for your sons, and give your daughters in marriage, that they may bear sons and daughters; multiply there, and do not decrease. But seek the welfare of the city where I have sent you into exile, and pray to the LORD on its behalf, for in its welfare you will find your welfare.[1]

We can break Jeremiah's speech into two different parts. The first part of his instructions has to do with the domestic or private realm. The exiles are to build homes, take care of yards, and raise children. These simple instructions validate the work that we do to make our homes nurturing and hospitable environments for our families and close friends.

But Jeremiah doesn't end with the private realm. He asks his audience to take an imaginative turn at the thresholds of their homes and look to the vast world outside of their front doors. He has important instructions for them with regard to this public realm as well.

They are to seek the welfare of the city. The verb *seek* suggests intentional action. They leave their homes (as we do) by necessity. They leave to work and to procure services. These things will be done with or without a command from a prophet of the Lord. By instructing them to seek something, Jeremiah is telling them to enter the public realm with a sense of purpose.

The criterion that is to give shape to their intentionality is described by Jeremiah as welfare, or shalom. We've already been introduced to the term *shalom,* but now we see a bit more clearly here that it is a communal value. The Hebrew verb for "seek" (*dirshu*) is a plural command. Individual humans can't have shalom in the fullest sense of that word; only human communities can. Jeremiah didn't say to perform random (individual) acts of kindness or be a nice person; he said to seek shalom. Seeking shalom, then, necessarily means participating in one or more communities.

If we read Jeremiah 29 with our eyes open to communal aspects of our identity and vocation, we can see three distinct bodies (or communities) that are affected by Jeremiah's command.

- The first, of course is the *family unit*. This is the community of domestic life that operates in the private realm discussed above.
- Another community is constituted by the fellow denizens of the city of Babylon. I will refer to this community as the *polis* or politics. This community is found in the public realm. In many cases, the Israelites share little besides geographical proximity with this community. And yet this community inhabits the space in which shalom is to be sought.
- The third community is Jeremiah's audience. It is the gathered people of God. They may not be the only ones engaging in shalom-supportive activities in their communities, but they are the ones who have been explicitly commanded to do so. We might think of that particular community in our current context as the *church*.

Interestingly enough, when Alexis de Tocqueville visited the United States, he noted that the strength of this country was anchored in the family, the church, and the small town. These three areas of strength correspond roughly with the three communities that are described above. In the following three chapters, we explore how these three communities can act as agents of shalom in the built environment. In doing so, we can see how these communities shape and are shaped by the built environment.

5

Family

The Petersons

Jon and Marsha Peterson moved to the Houston area about twenty years ago. Marsha grew up in Florida, Jon in Colorado, and neither had previously lived in Houston. They met at the University of Florida, where Marsha studied business and Jon was finishing up an RN degree.

They got married soon after finishing their programs and moved to Pensacola, where Jon worked as a triage nurse and Marsha got an entry-level job with Sysco. They lived about an hour from Marsha's parents and two of her siblings and were able to remain fairly involved in their lives at this time. Jon's parents were a bit older and lived in a retirement home outside of Denver. His siblings were scattered around the country.

They moved to Houston when Marsha was offered an executive track position at Sysco's headquarters in Houston. There were a number of hospitals in Houston at which Jon could find work, and he had no problem finding a good job.

When deciding where to purchase a home, they looked for an area with the best schools. Although they didn't have children at the time, they knew that they wanted to start their family in the next few years and wanted to provide their children with the best opportunities.

They chose a spacious home in a residential subdivision about twenty minutes from the city center. Their home was in one of the better school districts in the area. The commute wasn't too bad. Marsha could get to work in about twenty-five minutes, depending on traffic, and Jon's commute was usually less than twenty. The closest grocery store was only three miles away, but the way that the roads were laid out made it more like a seven-mile trip. Within a fifteen-mile radius, they had a decent shopping mall, two movie theaters, and a number of restaurant options.

After living in Houston for about five years, they had their first child, and over the next eight years they had two more. The three now range from seven to fifteen years old and are in three different schools. Each day is pretty busy as they try to figure out how to get their kids to and from school, as well as get them to their various lessons and sporting events.

For fun the family likes to watch movies at home or have barbecues in the backyard. The children don't drive yet and need to be driven by their parents for most of their social activities. They like to have play dates arranged at their friends' homes or to go to the mall. Each child has her own room with a separate bathroom, and the older two spend quite a bit of time in their room texting their friends, on Facebook, or watching funny videos on the internet.

The family attends a large church about forty minutes away. The kids are involved in the youth group, and the parents are in a small group of peers. Through these programs, they have made some good friends, but since these friendships draw from a fairly large region, they have a hard time finding time to see one another outside of the program activities.

No one in the family spends much time outside within their own neighborhood. The youngest still likes to spend time on the swing set in the backyard. And the older two like to ride their bikes around. But besides the houses of a few friends from school, there aren't any destinations that they can get to on their own. And much of their free time during the day is spent being driven from one activity to the next.

The Petersons know the names of most of the neighbors that live on their cul-de-sac. Three of the families have kids the same age, and they talk with them the most. They also will occasionally have brief conversations over the fence in the backyard with the next-door neighbors. Beyond the cul-de-sac, their familiarity with neighbors drops considerably. Perhaps they know one or two other families within a five-mile radius. Occasionally the Petersons see a bus go by on the arterial near their house, but none of them has ever taken public transit.

The Petersons try to see both sets of parents at least once a year. It is a bit easier with Marsha's parents, since they can still travel to Houston. They can afford to fly to Denver more often than they do; the kids don't really enjoy spending more than an hour or two in the retirement community, and they aren't yet old enough to be left alone while Jon and Marsha leave town. They see their siblings on average about once every two years.

In short, the Petersons are a pretty normal American family living at the beginning of the twenty-first century. If we were to meet them at church, nothing about their family's story would stand out to us as unusual or remarkable. However, the way that the Petersons experience being a family is far from being the norm if we think about families throughout history or even within other cultures. We can use their story, therefore, to bring to light certain fundamental questions about the form, setting, and purpose of the family.

Key Questions

Scope of Family

There is much discussion today about the traditional versus the nontraditional family. Within the parameters of this debate, the traditional family is considered to be a husband and a wife and their natural children. The nontraditional family may be a single mom with her children, a homosexual couple with or without children, or a blended family that includes a husband and wife and their kids from previous marriages.

While we also see situations where grandparents end up raising kids because the biological parents are not able to raise their own children (often due to substance abuse or jail), what is most interesting about this discussion is that the "traditional family" is not usually assumed to include the extended members of the family, such as grandparents or aunts and uncles.

This is somewhat unusual when we look outside of a contemporary American context. In many cultures throughout the world, family is assumed to comprise all relatives, including grandparents, aunts, uncles, and first, second, and third cousins. A good case could be made that the extended family is more traditional than the nuclear family. Also, one's extended family is commonly considered to be a key aspect of one's identity.

This way of understanding personhood is not that unusual outside of a middle-class North American context. Roberto Goizueta sees this as a key distinctive of Hispanic American culture.

To be an isolated, autonomous individual is, literally, to have no humanity, no identity, no self, it is to be no-thing, a no-body. For, if personhood presupposes relationality, my humanity is defined by my relationships with others; I recognize myself as a self, as a person, only when I encounter—or, more accurately, am encountered by—another person. . . .

When two U.S. Hispanics meet each other, the initial discussion after the introductions will likely involve family and relationships: Who are your parents? What town is your family from? I knew your mother's second cousin twice removed! I had a friend who must have known your sister. It is thus quite disconcerting for Hispanics to meet an Anglo whose initial discussion will, instead, likely involve career and work: What do you do for a living? Oh, that must be very interesting work! Where did you do your training? These latter questions, reflecting an emphasis on individual, "achieved" and chosen identity over organic, received identity, are often perceived by U.S. Hispanics as insultingly dismissive of these relationships.[1]

The Mexican American communities that Goizueta describes understand family in a perichoretic way. That is to say, one's family is an inescapable aspect of our identity. Family, then, functions as a kind of askesis for them. I'm sure that some of those described by Goizueta sometimes wish that they could escape the baggage that comes with being a part of a large family. However, because they lack viable options, these families do stick together, and most of them do experience a richer sense of community and belonging than they would if they were more free to leave.

To be sure, there have been other contexts where people have moved away from extended family to pursue economic opportunities. This is often the impetus behind the various waves of immigration that we have seen throughout the past century or so. However, many immigrants from other contexts maintain connections with their extended family as they move to a new location. Often this is done for the explicit purpose of providing financial support for relatives back home. What is unusual about our context is the relative ease with which people cut their ties with family within the same country in order to pursue individual goals.

So the first question we need to pose when thinking about the family as an agent for redemption has to do with the scope and durability of the family. Is a family simply a set of parents and some children whose lives are closely intertwined while the children are minors? Or does family include the larger set of grandparents, aunts, uncles, and cousins? And does our larger family remain a key aspect of our identity throughout our lives?

Purpose of Family

A second question posed by the story of the Petersons has to do with the purpose of the family. We can begin with the institution of marriage. What is the purpose of a marriage? I think the popular perception is that the purpose of marriage is to provide a vehicle for two people to publicly recognize their love for and commitment to each other. And marriage formalizes the partnership between two people so that they can make joint financial and relational investments.

Jon and Marsha were living together during their last year of college and didn't feel that marriage was necessary to be sexually active. However, after living together for a year, they felt that their love for each other was strong enough that they could conclude that neither of them felt they were likely to find anyone else who could bring them more happiness.

In applying for a marriage license they were asking the state to help recognize the fact that their love was genuine. And they wanted the strength of a legal contract to protect each of them once they began to take risks together, such as purchasing a home and having children. From the Petersons' perspective, their marriage is fundamentally about providing a venue for them to pursue happiness and fulfillment. This is not to imply that Jon and Marsha are selfish. Jon is committed to Marsha's happiness, and likewise Marsha is committed to Jon's happiness. Both of them are committed to the happiness of their three children.

But recognizing the level of Jon and Marsha's commitment and encouraging the happiness of the five members of the Peterson family doesn't help explain why the state gets involved in marriages. If marriage is really about recognizing the intensity and strength of what is essentially a private relationship, why should the state care who gets married or help regulate the issues surrounding the dissolution of a marriage?

Historically, marriages were understood as essential political relationships. The government recognized that the strength and stability of a society depended on the strength and stability of marriages. Marriages not only stabilized the social order but also performed key functions (such as raising children and caring for indigent relatives) that the state couldn't afford to do on its own.

We could say that the state has a stake in marriages because a family provides the best institution for the raising up of children to repopulate the citizenry and ensure the viability of the republic. This definition helps to bring to light both the public and private roles of marriage and family. But this alone doesn't account for the full purpose of the family. The family is also a key context in which the Christian members of the family prepare and help fulfill the Great Commission as well as the cultural mandate.

Container for Family

Once we have considered the scope and purpose of the family we can begin to ask questions about the family and the built environment. What is the appropriate container for family life? While there are a great number of housing types that we could consider, for the purposes of this discussion, we consider just two. The pictures below show two common types of houses for a middle-class American family. The one on the left is a typical house in a pre-WWII neighborhood. And the one on the right is a typical house in an exurban subdivision. The type of home that the Petersons are likely to live in may look like the one on the right.

Typical Housing Types

We can note a couple of differences between these housing types. The first has to do with the larger context. Within the pedestrian shed (a quarter- to half-mile radius) for the house on the left, we can expect to find a coffee shop or a grocery store within three blocks, and perhaps an apartment building on the same block. Within that same radius for the house on the right, there will only be other detached single-family homes of roughly the same scale.

The house on the left is set in a simple grid of blocks. This grid allows one to choose multiple routes to get from one point to another. This means that the house on the left can expect people to walk or drive by on their way to other destinations. The road system that connects the house on the right to other destinations is a cul-de-sac/feeder road system. This system directs automobile traffic to major roads and prevents automobile and foot traffic from passing in front of this house on the way to somewhere else. The house on the right is characterized by less connectivity than the house on the left. In general, we can say that the house on the left is scaled to be accessed by pedestrians, and the one on the right is scaled for the automobile.

The next aspect we can examine has to do with town fabric. In chapter 2, we discovered that town fabric consisted in three functions: housing private needs, creating settings for monuments, and framing public space. We explored these functions with regard to commercial and civic buildings, but they pertain to residential buildings as well.

Setting aside the discussion of monuments, we can look at the differing ways these two houses connect interior space to the outside world and how they shape outdoor space. Both houses perform the primary function of defining interior space and sheltering the private needs of the families who live in them. But they are quite different in how they connect the interior space to the outside world. The primary threshold that allows passage from inside to outside for the house on the left is the front door. It is architecturally prominent and centrally located. For the house on the right, the primary threshold is the garage door. This door covers almost the entire front face of the house. The garage door is a distinct kind of threshold, because it allows passage from outside to inside but only for residents of the house.

The house on the left also has a liminal threshold in the front porch. This type of threshold encourages interaction between those on the outside and those on the inside of the house. For this house, the family invites interaction with neighbors as they sit on the porch in the evening. When we consider the grid layout of streets that allow pass-through traffic, we can see that the front porch also allows interactions with strangers.

For the house on the right, the front porch is gone, because there is no longer a need to sit outside to escape the heat of the house in the summer. Central air conditioning has made staying in the house more comfortable. And there is no need to relieve boredom by sitting outside and visiting with the passing parade. The television inside in the living room provides an even more colorful assortment of characters for their entertainment.

From the perspective of traditional residential architecture, it looks as if the house on the right is turned backward. The house isn't oriented for interaction with the public realm in front of it, but rather is oriented more to the back. We can't see it, but we can imagine that the house on the right has a spacious and well-appointed back deck and yard. In the backyard, the family can enjoy time together without being interrupted or watched by people passing by.

Next, we can consider how the two houses shape the public realm. We've already noted that the house on the left sits on a simple grid. So we can say that the street in front of the house forms a kind of outdoor hallway. This house sits on its lot so that the face is parallel to the street, which at least ties the house into the space in front. But it is too low and too far from the house on the other side of the street to really form any kind of streetwall, so the house itself doesn't create a strong sense of enclosure. However, the low fence in front helps provide a nice definition for the outdoor hallway.

The street in front of the house on the right is not straight but has a gentle curve. The house is sited on its property at an angle that doesn't line up with the neighbor's house. The landscaping does not relate to either the street or the neighboring houses. This combination of features doesn't form any kind of town fabric.

Themes

If you are an American citizen in the twenty-first century, it is likely that you wouldn't give the house on the right much thought if you were to visit a friend who lived there. Perhaps it looks much like the house that you grew up in or even the house you live in now. I think that it is fair to say that the house on the right represents a standard type of housing for the American middle class.

However, when we think about the form of houses as containers for family life in light of other questions about the scope and purpose of the family, we can begin to see some connections between these questions.

The house on the right is not scaled for the convenience of pedestrians. This not only affects how we experience this neighborhood, it also means that it is designed to function only when the head of the household is of driving age. Fortunately, this is a pretty wide net and includes a lot of households. But the population that is not included in this are those elderly who are too old to operate an automobile.

What is not shown in the house on the right are the retirement homes that had to be developed to provide a place for people to live after they became too old to drive and couldn't live in that kind of setting any more. We may not have noticed this, because, as we have noted, we tend to think of the traditional family as being a relatively short-term arrangement between parents and their minor children.

After the children grow up, we still consider these people to be family, but there is little expectation that we will be regularly involved in each other's lives after this phase is over. This short-term approach probably affects how we view not only the role of our own elderly parents but the elderly in our communities as well. It probably doesn't seem strange to live where there are very few elderly people.

The house on the left is set in a neighborhood where the elderly can still live. It may have an apartment building on the block that contains some elderly people who can no longer drive but can access their basic services on foot.

Another connection that can be made is between the form of the house and expectations concerning public interaction. The house on the right is oriented toward the interior and the backyard of the property. This is not accidental but reflects the fact that the family living in the house on the right probably sees the purpose of their family as primarily private. The fact that the house does not encourage or even really allow much interaction with the public outside of the house is not important, because that is not necessary for the family to fulfill its purpose. Now, to be fair, it is probably the case that the family living in the house on the left doesn't consider public interaction to be of primary importance. But whether they see it as integral to their family or not, their house is set up to allow and even encourage some interaction with the wider public.

It is important to note that this distinction applies to the adults and the children in these homes. The automobile orientation of the house on the right means that the adults will likely move between work and home without interacting with their neighbors. And it means that the settings in which they may have informal interactions (grocery store, coffee shop, church) may be scattered across a pretty wide territory. The children in this home will be socialized within the private realm of their friends' homes or at a shopping mall. And most of their interactions with people outside of their home will be mediated by the adults who have to make arrangements and drive them to various destinations. This observation about children will help lead us into the next section having to do with historical background.

Historical Background

Euclid *on Children*

In chapter 1, we were introduced to the landmark case of *Euclid v. Ambler Realty*. This case opened the door for exurban development patterns that were to dominate the twentieth century. Not only did this case establish the legal foundation for our most common residential pattern, it also reveals a number of attitudes and assumptions about home and family life.

The majority opinion was written by Justice Sutherland, and his comments provide a great deal of insight into prevailing attitudes about the built environment that shape our communities even today. The first thing that we observe in Sutherland's comments are embedded assumptions about children and families. Frequently, it is the well-being of children that is used as a justification for the need for functional zoning. This particular passage is one of many references to children: "Some of the grounds for this conclusion are promotion of the health and security from injury of children and others by separating dwelling houses from territory devoted to trade and industry."[2]

This tenet makes the most sense when we imagine the dangers of a particular kind of trade and industry. One could think of a slaughterhouse or a smelter. But to fully understand its implications, we need to think more broadly about trade and industry. What about a coffee shop or a corner grocery or a barbershop? Do children need protection from these kinds of places?

If we think about the broad scope of zoning regulation, we realize that what is intended here is to protect children not from butcher's knives and burning sulfur only, but rather from society at large. This law when implemented would in effect "protect" a ten-year-old boy from walking to a corner store to buy orange juice for his family or to the barbershop to deliver a message to his dad.

The implicit value expressed in this legislation with regard to children is a good example of what Dolores Hayden calls the "home as haven" model.[3] The home in this model is understood as a place where children are protected from the larger society. Children are kept in the home safe from society until they are old enough to form their own families, which in turn will be protected from public life.

This model of home life is based on a relatively recent understanding of the family. The term that Lawrence Stone uses to describe this new understanding of the family is a "closed domesticated nuclear family."[4] He tracks its development as it emerges among the bourgeoisie in England between the late seventeenth and mid-eighteenth century.

What is distinct about this understanding of the family is that members of the family become "the primary and overwhelming emotional focus of its members' lives."[5] Prior to this development, families were more "open," in the sense that the influence of neighbors, relatives, and members of one's guild were equally if not more important than those of one's nuclear family.

This is not to suggest that the case of *Euclid v. Ambler* created the home-as-haven model or the closed domesticated nuclear family, but rather shows that this view of family life became embedded institutionally early in the twentieth century and continues to perpetuate these assumptions about family life even today.

Evangelicals and the Prioritization of Home and Nature

The home-as-haven model is common in our culture regardless of one's religious commitments. If one sees increasing danger in society, and one's family as primarily a private affair, it makes a certain amount of sense to do everything possible to protect one's family from the dangers of society.

However, if one attempts to make sense of American attitudes and convictions "irrespective of religious commitments," one is likely to miss a number of key influences. This country has a strong tradition of being shaped by Christian and, especially, evangelical convictions. Evangelical conviction has influenced how we understand the built environment as well. We can see this in exploring the attitudes of one of the most influential evangelicals and his residential community. This section therefore includes an exploration of some of the ways that William Wilberforce and especially his Clapham community have shaped the ways Christians understand the family.

Wilberforce is probably best known for his heroic public service grounded on strong theological commitments, and he is looked at by evangelicals (as well as a great many others) as a role model for political engagement. He is credited with spearheading the successful campaign to abolish the slave trade throughout the British Empire. What is less well known is the role that Wilberforce's Clapham community played in segregating the domestic life of the family from the civic life of the wider community.

Wilberforce actually pursued two goals throughout his life. The first (and far better known) was the abolition of the slave trade. The second was the "reformation of manners." Robert Fishman clarifies that Wilberforce means by this term

> a broad attack on all forms of urban pleasures. He himself, a member of Parliament and wealthy heir of a distinguished mercantile family from Hull, resigned all his memberships in London clubs immediately after his conversion to the Evangelical cause in 1784. Attendance at the theater, he advised, was "most pernicious" and "directly contrary to the laws of God." As to "balls, concerts, cards, etc.," they might be tolerated "not as amusements to be enjoyed, but temptations to be undergone."[6]

Wilberforce made his home in Clapham, which was a village about five miles from London in the area of Surrey. It was no coincidence that Wilberforce made his home at Clapham, as this was where the most prominent leaders of the evangelical movement were to be found. In fact the evangelical resurgence of this time was popularly known as the Clapham sect.

Clapham consisted of a number of spacious residential estates arranged loosely around a commons. The men would commute to their offices in central London, while their wives and children remained at home. Prior to this early commuting pattern in Britain, only the aristocracy and farmers would have lived in the country, on large country estates surrounded by their landholdings.

Beginning in the early eighteenth century, members of the bourgeoisie in London began to use their growing wealth to imitate the aristocracy and build villas in the country. The key difference was that the bourgeoisie needed to stay connected with their businesses in London throughout the week, so they used these villas primarily as weekend retreats.

It is interesting to note during this time that there was very little of life that was exclusively part of the private realm even for the wealthy members of society:

> The typical merchant's townhouse, therefore, was surprisingly open to the city. Commercial life flowed in freely, so that virtually every room had some business as well as familial function. From the front parlor where customers were entertained and deals transacted, to the upper stories where the apprentices slept and the basement where goods were stored, there was little purely domestic space.[7]

The evangelical residents of Clapham initially followed the typical bourgeois pattern of maintaining a residence in London and a weekend retreat in Clapham. But over time, they gradually began to make Clapham their permanent home, and their townhouses became offices in the more modern sense of the word. The impetus that gave these evangelicals the nudge to exchange the benefit of being able to keep a close watch over their commercial and public pursuits for more time with the family was a growing conviction that domestic life and contact with nature were more spiritual than public life and the life of the city.

William Cowper exemplifies this perspective in his poem *The Task*:

> Domestic happiness, thou only bliss
> Of Paradise that has survived the fall![8]

> God made the country, and man made the town:
> What wonder then, that health and virtue, gifts
> That can alone make sweet the bitter draught
> That life holds out to all, should most abound
> And least be threaten'd in the fields and groves?
> Possess ye, therefore, . . . Your element.[9]

Time spent with the family and in direct contact with nature was understood as more spiritual than anything that could be offered in public.

Within the Clapham community, there was a clear place for vigorous involvement in politics for the reformation of society, but at the same time home was extolled as a more spiritual place, where women and children would be protected, and the necessary evil of public participation that the men endured could be washed away. Home and nature were understood as inherently spiritual and restorative places, whereas the cities and towns were literally irredeemable.

Evangelicals in Clapham turned their backs on the physical settings for sociality and conviviality in the cities and towns and sought to create settings for those kinds of experiences in the privacy of the home:

Participation

The library and the garden outside were the Evangelical substitute for all the plays, balls, visits, and coffee houses of London. Here the closed domesticated nuclear family became a reality. The social activities of London did not suddenly cease. Instead, the social graces were directed inward, toward the mutual education and moral betterment of the family itself.[10]

Consequently, the Clapham community is considered to be an early prototype for the creation idea that the suburbs (now exurbs) could function as a private retreat and an enclave for a like-minded community.

We might conclude that for all of the good they did in working to abolish slavery, the Clapham community also encouraged a distinct approach to dealing with the messiness of everyday life. They essentially dealt with the problem of the sinful city by making a strict division between public and private life. They sought to be agents of redemption in the governmental aspects of the public realm. But their hope for the private realm was marked by nostalgia. In extolling home and nature above all else, they were ultimately directing their hopes back toward the garden. While one cannot deny that they did a tremendous amount of good through their political efforts, their rejection of the actual city may have caused their model to be more problematic. While they were able to extol the spiritual superiority of the private realm and invest themselves in the public realm, their successors were less capable of holding these things in tension.

In subsequent generations, the evangelical community continued to focus on the private realm while growing less and less interested in the public realm as a place for meaningful Christian investment. This tendency, while understandable, fails to deal meaningfully with an important biblical theme of seeking shalom within the context of even sinful cities.

The Evolution of the Suburban House

As the attitudes about home and family life from the Clapham community were saturating the mores of "decent society" in Britain and the United States, the housing type that would serve as the best container for this approach to family life was being developed. We can see a progression of housing types in the image below.

The typical home for a bourgeoisie Londoner in the eighteenth century was a townhouse that shared a wall with the other townhouses on the block. From a built environment perspective, we can see that this design not only met the needs of the homeowner in terms of interior space but also did a nice job of defining the streetwall and contributing to the town fabric.

By the beginning of the nineteenth century, we begin to see "suburbs" springing up that are not unlike the Clapham model. They represent a transitional step. Like the row houses that preceded them, these houses were placed along straight streets or were arranged to define the space of a square or other geometrical design. The credit for this housing design is often given to John Shaw's plan for St. John's Wood. Fishman describes its distinction.

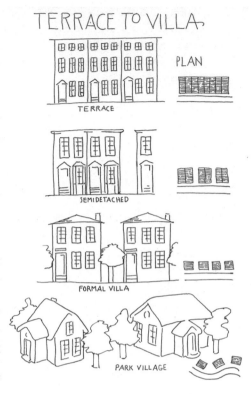

TERRACE TO VILLA

TERRACE

PLAN

SEMIDETACHED

FORMAL VILLA

PARK VILLAGE

> The houses are semidetached, that is, each freestanding unit comprises two houses joined by a party wall. Long, narrow gardens of one to three acres stand to the side of and behind each house. The solid urban row or terrace of houses is thus broken up to give a semisuburban sense of greenery and openness.[11]

The third picture in this sequence is the formal villa, the detached single-family house. This aspect of what would become the suburban idea is based on the classical villa. As Fishman explains,

> Indeed there was some real connection between the villae suburbanae that ringed ancient Rome as early as the first century B.C. and the eighteenth-century London villas. The Romans had established the pattern of a wealthy urban elite building opulent pleasure houses set in gardens in the picturesque countryside outside the city.[12]

And then finally, the most important step toward the suburban ideal may be attributed to John Nash and his Park Village development:

> The name Park Village has become a favorite cliché, but for Nash it had a precise meaning in delineating the two major influences that went into the design. It was a synthesis of the picturesque landscaped park with the picturesque village. Nash had grasped the basic idea of Clapham and the other early suburbs: they

were houses in a park. As his first (and most original) drawings for Park Village shows, he completely avoided the formal language of eighteenth-century urban design. Instead, the houses are set within a picturesque landscape with its characteristic curving paths, scattered plantings, and even ornamental water conveniently provided by the Regent's Canal, which wound around the edge of the park.[13]

In addition to ignoring traditional urbanism in the layout of the street and the siting of the houses on the property, Park Village reflected a new trend toward naturalistic landscaping:

Nash understood how to create a picturesque landscape out of individual house lots. He paid particular attention to the use of trees and shrubs both to define the private property around each house and to contribute to the total park effect. "The plantations," he writes, "are to screen the more offensive parts of the cottages, separate then from each other and give intricacy to the scenery; the division between the ground of the several cottages are to be live hedges and ironware fences." Natural intricacy, not formal clarity, had become the basic design principle.[14]

As the concept of the suburban home as retreat took hold, such naturalistic landscaping was soon accompanied by historicist architectural styles. Historicist architecture represents a freedom to choose from a variety of historically rooted styles and even to combine them to create pleasing associations for the owner over and above any connection with the traditions normally associated with such styles.

In this picturesque world of associationism the old criteria of formal unity and consistency no longer applied. Gothic, Italianate, or Old English all signified much the same emotional message of retreat, contentment, and duration over time; hence there was no real inconsistency in mixing them together on the same street or in the same house.[15]

This last observation has less to do with the suburban house as container for the family as we have come to understand it, but it does show how houses have become detached from history and place. In chapter 4 we considered how, especially in the vernacular tradition, the style and construction of a building reflected the accumulated wisdom of constructing buildings within a particular climate and the tastes and practices of a local population. The historicist variety of architecture that became common in the late nineteenth and twentieth centuries reinforces the notion that the house is being seen more and more as a setting for individual nuclear families to enjoy the benefits of middle-class life.

As the suburban housing type made its way across the Atlantic to American shores, there was one more significant step in its development. Frank Lloyd Wright was one of the most influential American architects of the twentieth century. His designs are characterized by a strong sense of connection to and harmony with the natural environment. However, despite this wonderful sense for connection with the natural environment, Wright was not at all interested in connections among people within the broader society. He felt strongly that the nuclear family should be allowed and encouraged to have complete autonomy.

Wright's societal vision was called Broadacre City, and in it there was no central city or town, but rather a minimum of one acre for every family. Families, then, would be relieved of the burden of being forced to interact with other people. Individuals could use communication and transportation technology to keep up whatever connection to others that they might require. Despite the fact that many features of Wright's vision have become part of our everyday life, Broadacre City was not given much attention during his lifetime. However, the houses that Wright envisioned for Broadacre City did become popular. As Witold Rybczynski explains:

> In 1936, shortly after he unveiled the model of his proposed city, Wright began building the first in a series of houses that he called Usonians, the sort of small, affordable homes that were the staple of Broadacre City. He published the designs in popular magazines such as *House and Home* and *House Beautiful,* and the houses' distinctive features—one-story layouts, low roofs, carports, kitchens overlooking living areas, and rough stone fireplaces—soon showed up in so-called ranch houses built by ordinary builders. Between 1935 and his death in 1959, Wright built more than 150 Usonians, and his idea of living in houses in a countrylike setting, which is, after all, the mainstay of Broadacre City, took hold in the American popular imagination.[16]

Family as Agent of Redemption

As was mentioned in the introduction to this section, the prophet Jeremiah expects families to be critical agents in the command to "seek the welfare of the city." Therefore, when thinking about the prospects and possibilities for families within the built environment, we need to be careful not to limit our thinking to just what seems normal within our current culture. We need to think seriously about the possibility that whether or not we recognize it, we are part of extended families. We need to be open to the possibilities that our families may be called into being not only to be settings for the cultivation of our own happiness, but also to be agents of redemption. The rest of this chapter is devoted to exploring a few ideas to get us pointed in this direction.

House as Connecting Point

We can begin by rethinking the home-as-haven model. Instead of thinking about our homes as places where we protect our children from exposure to the wider society, we could begin to think about the ways our homes can provide a safe setting for ourselves and our children to participate in the larger society.

As Christians, we can influence our society for the good not only through holding public office or by supporting good legislation. We also can work for the good of society in more informal ways by building positive relationships with our neighbors and others who happen to pass through our neighborhoods.

This shift in perspective may be for societal good, but it may be beneficial for our families as well. Richard Sennett claims that this approach to family and society strengthens family life. Sennett understands families to grow stronger through engagement with the outside world:

> The more the primacy of the family is challenged by multiple points of social contact, the stronger the family will become. This strength will occur not as a resistance to the outside, but as the very result of being limited by a complex outer world.[17]

Hospitality

Another way to approach this issue is to think about our homes as settings for hospitality. Hospitality usually means welcoming others as guests into your home for a meal or for a bed. It has been understood as an important virtue in numerous cultures throughout history.

In many cultures, including the classical tradition, there has been a decidedly opportunistic aspect to the understanding of hospitality. One was encouraged to extend hospitality to someone from whom one could expect to derive some kind of benefit. Having the boss over for dinner might increase your chances for promotion.

According to Christine Pohl, one of the ways that the Judeo-Christian tradition of hospitality has been distinct is in encouraging the extension of hospitality to those who cannot reciprocate.[18] This is due to the fact that hospitality in this tradition is rooted in God's character. The most basic definition of hospitality is to make room for another. In this regard, God's work in creation can be considered an act of hospitality. In this act, God makes room for a creation that is distinctively other than God.

In the Old Testament, God's people were commanded to practice hospitality, but it was usually to foreigners and strangers that such hospitality was to be extended. The New Testament picks up this theme and commands Christians to extend hospitality to strangers:

> Do not neglect to show hospitality to strangers, for by doing that some have entertained angels without knowing it.[19]

The early church also picked up this tradition and made hospitality a fundamental aspect of Christian discipleship. Part of this was to serve the growing community, as travel was dangerous, and evangelists and church leaders depended on the hospitality of brothers and sisters in the faith to provide safe and economical lodging. The early church also continued the tradition of offering hospitality to strangers and other vulnerable groups.

If we think about our homes in terms of hospitality, we don't have to think only about welcoming guests in for a meal or to sleep at our houses. We can begin by thinking about our houses in terms of how they serve to make room for the others who may pass by our homes. Such making room can even begin by helping people to feel comfortable in the public space in front of our homes.

James Rojas provides an interesting case study in this kind of hospitality from the residential neighborhoods of East LA.[20] Rojas begins by observing how intimidating the typical middle-class front door can be for a stranger. First, one has to have the intentionality or boldness to enter into someone's private realm by crossing a moat of manicured front lawn to reach the threshold of the front door. When the bell is rung and the owner opens the door, there is a loaded moment when the owner has to decide whether the person at the door is a friend or a stranger. If she is a friend, she will probably be invited in for a visit. If she is a stranger, there will be a very short period in which the visitor has to provide a justification for being there. Most likely the justification won't be acceptable, and the door will be closed on the visitor. The typical middle-class home is set up to keep strangers out and allow friends in, but not to encourage the formation of new relationships.

Rojas contrasts this with the way that Mexican American residents of East LA have adapted this basic style of house and yard to create a more social (read: hospitable) space. These residents have amended their front yards by adding a fence (either chain link or wrought iron) and a front gate. While one might think of a fence as being an antisocial move, in fact it has had an opposite effect.

The fence and front gate have essentially pushed the threshold of the home all the way out to the sidewalk, so that those passing by can more easily engage in conversation with the homeowner. The fence creates what Rojas calls "defensible space," by which he means space that is clearly demarcated as private space, which allows the owner greater freedom in spending time in that space. Rojas claims that such front yards even have a distinct name (*la yarda*) and that they are treated very differently by the Mexican American community.

The middle-class American front yard is usually a well-tended space that sends a message to the community of social stability and "playing by the rules," but not an invitation to interaction. *La yarda*, by way of contrast, tends to be a highly personalized space. It will include toys for the kids, artwork, and even a religious shrine. Because of the fence, the resident can spend time in the front yard feeling perfectly safe and in control of the social setting. If she wants to visit with neighbors, she can position herself near one of her two side fences. If she is feeling more open to new relationships, she can lean on the front gate. Here she can exchange informal conversation with people passing by, with little social pressure. Rojas claims that this is such a comfortable setting that two relative strangers can be standing within a few feet of each other without either of them feeling pressure to make conversation.

Family as Extended

It may or may not be realistic for us to experience the reality of extended family within our own cultural context in quite the same way that it exists in other cultures. However, thinking about the value of extended family can lead us to value intergenerational interaction within our neighborhoods and in the public spaces of our cities and towns. We can allow our imaginations to be enriched by a picture of *eschatological* hope provided by Zechariah:

> Thus says the LORD of hosts: Old men and old women shall again sit in the streets of Jerusalem, each with staff in hand because of their great age. And the streets of the city shall be full of boys and girls playing in its streets.[21]

Here we have both young and old interacting, not in private households, but in the streets or the common spaces of the city. And it is a good thing.

The architect Christopher Alexander shows a keen sensitivity to this kind of mix in his coauthored book of architectural design principles. In a chapter entitled "Old People Everywhere," Alexander expresses his conviction that every community ought to have a certain percentage of old people, so that we can all benefit from their wisdom and experience.

There is a natural tendency for old people to gather together in clusters or communities. But when these elderly communities are too isolated or too large, they damage young and old alike. The young in other parts of town have no chance of the benefit of older company, and the old people themselves are far too isolated.[22]

Home as Preparatory

By highlighting some of the ways that our homes should connect us with others who are not family and who may be demographically different, I am in no way completely rejecting the home-as-haven model. Our homes as primary settings for our experience of the private realm should be places of refuge for our family. Our homes should be places where we feel safe, not only physically but emotionally as well. Our homes should be places where we can let our guard down, be goofy, and experience tenderness with those we love.

However, even as our homes are providing refuge from the outer society, we can be thinking about our contribution to that society. Our experience with our own families can be an important training ground for dealing with people who are different from us or even annoying to us.

Richard Mouw holds that this kind of training can best happen at the family dinner table.[23] This is the place where our children can learn and practice the virtue of civility. For this to happen, it is important that we make every effort to eat together as a family as often as possible. And it is important to teach our families to stay at the table even when we are finished, and especially not to leave just because a family member is bothering us. To stay at the table even when we disagree with what is being said there or even when we find it annoying is to practice civility.

The Orange Juice Test

Do you live in a place where you could send your eleven-year-old son or daughter out on his or her own to purchase a carton of orange juice? This question, known as the "orange juice test," reveals much about the kind of neighborhood your home is in, as well as your understanding of family. On the one hand, to pass the orange juice test your home needs to be located in a somewhat mixed-use neighborhood. If there are only other single-family homes for a mile in every direction, sending your child out for orange juice would be a fool's errand. The orange juice test assumes some kind of corner store that is within walking distance.

The other side of the orange juice test has to do with your comfort level in sending older children outside of your home unsupervised. When many of us were growing up, it was perfectly acceptable for children to play and wander throughout the neighborhood during daylight hours with little or no supervision. For many families that is no longer an acceptable practice. Concerns about an increased risk of accidents and abductions have prevented most parents from letting their children be unsupervised outside of the home.

While this hesitancy may simply be a logical extension of the home-as-haven model, in its current manifestation it is based largely on misinformation. According to Lenore Skenazy,

> Violent crime in America has been falling since it peaked in the early nineties. That includes sex crimes against kids. . . . [A]lthough perhaps the streets were somewhat safer in the fifties, children today are statistically as safe from violent crime as we parents were, growing up in the seventies, eighties, and nineties.[24]

Because of rising divorce rates and messy custody battles, we have seen higher rates of abduction of children by a relative, but stranger abduction is as rare now as it ever was.

Our fears about accidents and abduction have been largely fueled by the unrelenting demand for exciting content by cable news networks that have to fill twenty-four hours each day with programming. Between the over-the-top reporting on extremely rare (but true) tragic events and increasingly graphic police dramas, we see an astounding number of frightening images every day. And our fears have been reinforced by our imaginations and the rumor mill. Skenazy notes that despite all of our concerns about poisoned Halloween candy and razor blades in apples, since 1958 there have been zero cases of any child being poisoned or hurt by tampering with Halloween candy.[25]

The orange juice test is a relatively simple way to evaluate how our children can participate in the life of our neighborhoods. One can devise any number of similar tests to examine how well our neighborhoods work for a broad span of the human community. One might think about a "salon test" or a "prescription test" to find out if an elderly individual could get her hair done or pick up a prescription without depending on someone else for transportation. This test would reveal whether the products and services that an older person requires are available within walking distance, but it also may show how well suited the neighborhood is for pedestrians—short crossing distances and curbs that are not too high. These kinds of tests can help us to think about how our extended families and our neighborhoods can be used as agents of redemption.

For Further Reading

Childress, Herb. *Landscapes of Betrayal, Landscapes of Joy: Curtisville in the Lives of Its Teenagers.* SUNY Series in Environmental and Architectural Phenomenology. Albany: State University of New York Press, 2000.

Clapp, Rodney. *Families at the Crossroads: Beyond Traditional & Modern Options.* Downers Grove, IL: InterVarsity Press, 1993.

Fishman, Robert. *Bourgeois Utopias: The Rise and Fall of Suburbia.* New York: Basic Books, 1987.

Hayden, Dolores. *Redesigning the American Dream: Gender, Housing, and Family Life.* New York: W. W. Norton, 2002.

Pohl, Christine D. *Making Room: Recovering Hospitality as a Christian Tradition.* Grand Rapids: Eerdmans, 1999.

Rybczynski, Witold. *Home: A Short History of an Idea.* New York: Penguin Books, 1986.

Sennett, Richard. *The Uses of Disorder: Personal Identity & City Life.* New York: W. W. Norton, 1992.

Skenazy, Leonard. *Free Range Kids: Giving Our Children the Freedom We Had without Going Nuts with Worry.* San Francisco: Jossey-Bass. 2010.

6

Politics

Kinds of Power

On April 10, 1968, the New York State Transportation Department called a public discussion of the proposed Lower Manhattan Expressway. This project was intended to alleviate traffic by running an elevated ten-lane high-speed road to help automobiles get quickly from Long Island to New Jersey. This project, if completed, would end up destroying four hundred buildings, force eight hundred businesses to move, and evict 2,200 families.

The purported reason for the meeting was to hear public response to the plan, but really the officials planning it were just going through the motions to fulfill a particular requirement for these kinds of projects. Proof of "public testimony" would actually help expedite their plans to get this project built.

In fact, the officials at the meeting were not even the players who had any say about how the project would be carried out. The real power behind the Lower Manhattan Expressway was Robert Moses, whose official title was Chairman of the Triborough Bridge and Tunnel Authority and who was arguably one of the most powerful persons in New York, although he'd never been elected to office. Robert Moses was responsible for hundreds of public works projects in New York City and beyond. He was not used to having anyone stand in his way.

But that night Jane Jacobs would stand in his way. As she approached the microphone and pointed out the sham of this meeting, she declared:

What kind of administration could even consider destroying the homes of two thousand families at a time like this? With the amount of unemployment in the city, who would think of wiping out thousands of minority jobs? They must be insane.[1]

Jacobs then led the crowd in a parade across the stage, where they ended up destroying the stenographer's tape so that there would be no public record of the meeting, which would thus slow the project down. Jacobs was arrested that night, but her arrest ended up pushing enough public sentiment against the project that eventually it was shelved and never got built.

This was not the first time that Jacobs played a key role in defeating Robert Moses. She had helped prevent him from building a roadway through Washington Square Park. And she helped to organize the group that kept Greenwich Village from undergoing "urban renewal." The story of Jane Jacobs taking on Robert Moses is truly a modern version of David and Goliath.

Moses, while not ever in an elected position, was an influential political figure. He did legitimately represent the institutional power of the state. But Jacobs's ability to take him on and win demonstrates that there is more to political power than simply the institutional power wielded by elected officials and government appointees.

Perhaps the word *polis* is sufficiently wide to capture the power wielded by Robert Moses as well as by Jane Jacobs. *Polis* can refer to the many ways that we pursue collective ends and organize our common life together. Polis recognizes that institutional politics represents only one aspect of political power in our communities.

As we move from a consideration of the role of family in the built environment to the realm of politics, this story provides an interesting transition point. In many ways, the power that Jacobs was able to wield at that meeting on April 10 was partially based on her ability to represent the perspective of the families who would be affected by this project. As a wife and mother raising two boys in New York City, she could understand and identify with the perspectives of ordinary families.

Strengthening the Polis

Civic Virtue

If the power to influence resource allocation or collective action includes both institutional and informal power, we can begin our exploration by thinking about the sources of these various forms of power. Although Robert Moses was a charismatic personality and a shrewd manipulator of systems, ultimately his formal power was granted to him by the governor of New York state.

Jane Jacobs's source of power was more self-generating. We can describe her ability to mobilize power and frustrate the plans of someone as powerful as Robert Moses in terms of civic virtue. Civic virtue can be thought of as a measure of a person's care for the public realm combined with the local knowledge, organizational skills, and courage necessary to effect positive change in that realm.

Richard Sennett explores the idea that civic virtue is more than a kind of power that is expressed outside of formal institutional power, it also often grows best in the absence of institutional power. Sennett believes that civic virtue is necessary to the strength and well-being of our communities, and also that we need to be careful of inhibiting its development by too much reliance on institutional power.

Sennett believes that we should not look to formal institutions to solve all of our community problems but should encourage citizens to work out problems on their own. For instance, if a bar in a largely residential neighborhood is too loud late at night, the last thing residents should do is call the police. They should approach the bar owner and seek a solution to the problem. If he or she is uncooperative, then they should organize with other residents and picket the bar. They can continue to think of creative ways to increase the pressure until the bar owner agrees to cooperate.

The quality of common life is improved when neighbors work together to solve problems; moreover, particular neighbors gain practical experience in and skills for working within the polis. That is to say, civic virtue is developed. Instead of trying to set the goal of planning as the avoidance of problems, therefore, Sennett suggests that planning should focus on enlarging the forum for experience and exploration.

> This, I believe, is the true task of planning modern cities. The ills of the city are not mechanical ones of better transport, better financing, and the like; they are the human ones of providing a place where men can grow into adults, and where adults can continue to engage in truly social existence.[2]

Sennett believes that as much as possible people should be encouraged to work out their problems and relationships at a person-to-person and local level. This is the only way that human beings will develop into maturity and cities will grow into civilized environments. And Sennett believes, as does

Daniel Solomon, that one of the main purposes of the physical spaces of our community is to provide settings for such interaction:

> Once preplanned city space is removed, the actual use of the space becomes much more important in the lives of its users. For when predetermined use through zoning is eliminated, the character of a neighborhood will depend on the specific bonds and alliances of the people within it: its nature will be determined by social acts and the burden of those acts over time as a community's history.[3]

What is gained in these kinds of scenarios is not only a more pleasant environment, but also the strengthening of relational bonds among residents and others who work within the neighborhood. With this in mind, we can think of two ways that the residents of Lower Manhattan benefited from Jacobs's civic virtue. They avoided a public works project that would have sapped the vitality from their neighborhood by cutting it in half, and they experienced a strengthening of their relational bonds by working together on a common project.

Social Capital

The strength of the relational bonds that are built up when neighbors work on a common project can be described as social capital. Robert Bellah contends that like resource capital and human capital, social capital can be considered to be an economic good.[4] Strong social capital brings less need not only for police intervention but also for formal contracts and lawyers. This makes things less costly and more enjoyable for everybody.

While social capital is usually increased when neighbors work together to pursue a common project, social capital is also strengthened by ordinary interaction among neighbors in day-to-day life. In the previous chapter we looked at how spending time on a front porch or yard and living in a place where one can walk to destinations create opportunities for neighbors to talk to one another. Now we have a term to use to describe the strengthening of such relational connections.

Common Grace

Once we put terms such as *civic virtue* and *social capital* on our radar, we need to account for them theologically, because one of the things we are bound to discover is that these goods don't emerge exclusively out of the Christian community. In fact, one could claim that in our current context, civic virtue is more likely to be found outside of the Christian community and that there are certain neighborhoods that have more social capital than do many churches.

How do we account for the fact that we are sometimes surprised by the good things that we find outside the Christian community? If all people are infected with sin, why is it that people outside the Christian community experience what appear to be blessings from God or do things that seem to further God's ends on the earth? Some helpful answers to these kinds of questions can be understood in terms of common grace. *Common grace* refers to nonsalvific blessings from God that may be bestowed upon both Christians and non-Christians. Like saving grace, common grace is a gift from God; but unlike saving grace, it does not save a person from his or her sins.

Common grace has at least three major forms. The first has to do with natural blessings: "for he makes his sun rise on the evil and on the good, and sends rain on the righteous and on the unrighteous."[5] When favorable weather leads to a good harvest, the benefit is shared by believers and nonbelievers alike. The second form of common grace has to do with the restraint of evil. People are sinful, but it isn't too hard to imagine people acting worse than they actually do. What causes people who don't believe in a higher authority to resist an evil act for which they would not be punished? Common grace.

Acts of civic righteousness are the final form of common grace. This is a rather large category. A soldier falling on a grenade for a comrade is an example of this concept. Even an artist doing great works of art might be considered an expression of civic righteousness. Civic righteousness is the form of common grace that will be most helpful in our exploration of the polis.

An understanding of common grace allows us to see differently each person that we encounter. Instead of seeing others as just under God's judgment, we can look expectantly for ways that God is already blessing their lives and affirm them in those areas. Common grace also gives us permission to see all forms of culture as potentially good, regardless of their origin.

This may be a different way of thinking for evangelical Christians. Typically, if there is a cultural form that we find attractive, we have often felt the need to reinvent it as a more explicitly "Christian" product. If we are a Christian and happen to like heavy metal music, there are many who would point us to a Christian band that plays songs about Christian themes in a heavy metal style.[6]

We tend to be somewhat selective when we do this, however. We seem to accept a cultural form such as medical technology without thinking to inquire about its Christian association. If we have a kidney problem and need to be hooked up to a dialysis machine twice a week, we don't generally ask whether it is a "Christian" dialysis machine. That is to say, we don't feel the need to know whether this medical technology was invented by a Christian or is being used by a Christian technician to understand its obvious utility for us.

In the same way, common grace allows us to applaud the work of Jane Jacobs and even recognize God's hand in the ways she blessed her neighbors by leveraging her civic virtue and developing social capital regardless of whether she felt her actions were motivated by Christian conviction.[7]

Top-Down versus Bottom-Up

In many ways the development of cities and towns in the twentieth century can be seen as a struggle among the various forms of power in the polis. The legendary battles between Robert Moses and Jane Jacobs are representative of a common struggle between those who wanted to see cities and neighborhoods develop organically from the bottom up and those who wanted to see development from the top down. For most of the twentieth century, the top-down approach predominated, with a few notable exceptions (e.g., Jane Jacobs), but in the last quarter of the century, many of the "successes" of the top-down approach were being called into question. In these early years of the twenty-first century, we are witnessing a reappraisal of both the process and content of development.

Zoning as a whole can be seen as a top-down rationalizing of the complex process known as the city. However, zoning involves a lot more than just separating housing from commercial so as to make the development of these building types more efficient. Zoning also breaks out other systems, such as traffic control and emergency response systems, to make them more efficient. As we have noted, an important legacy of *CIAM* was an expert culture that rejected common sense in favor of the insights of various "experts." When considering a particular instance of streetground, the last person that a planner would want to weigh in on the question of how wide a street should be would be a resident who lives on that street. Expert culture looks to traffic engineers to provide a technical answer to the question using projected vehicle loads, and fire marshals to dictate street-width minimums for their trucks to get through, in order for this decision to be made.

Modern Rational Urban Planning

While top-down urban planning could be understood to be as old as cities, the form that it took in the twentieth century can best be described as modern rationalistic urban planning. While it is easy to critique this approach in retrospect, to be perfectly fair we do need to acknowledge that the nineteenth century was a difficult time for large cities in the United States and around the world. Robert Fishman describes some of the changes that were happening:

> In the first half of the nineteenth century the great European cities had overflowed their historic walls and fortifications. (The American cities, of course, never knew such limits.) Now boundless, the great cities expanded into the surrounding countryside with reckless speed, losing the coherent structure of a healthy organism. London grew in the nineteenth century from 900,000 to 4.5 million inhabitants; Paris in the same period quintupled its population, from 500,000 to 2.5 million residents. Berlin went from 190,000 to over 2 million, New York from 60,000 to 3.4 million. Chicago, a village in 1840, reached 1.7 million by the turn of the century.[8]

Certainly the pace of the growth of cities and the myriad social problems that were accompanying this growth undercut any confidence in the status quo. It seemed to many as if the challenges brought on by such forces as the Industrial Revolution were too voluminous to be contained by the outdated models of traditional neighborhood and organic city. Such unique challenges called for unique solutions. The two most notable of these solutions were functional zoning and urban renewal.

Functional Zoning

Functional zoning ordinances were made permissible by *Euclid v. Ambler,* but that case did not cause the widespread adoption of this regulative tool during the postwar years. Part of the popularity of zoning can also be explained by material and institutional factors, but there were forces at play in the polis as well. When a city adopts a zoning ordinance, it becomes necessary to create governmental agencies that can enforce the stipulations of the law. Once these new agencies become embedded in the institutional structure of the municipality, they tend to become rather intractable, regardless of their usefulness to the larger goals of the city or neighborhood.

This dynamic seems to have been anticipated in *Euclid v. Ambler.* Even proponents of zoning will readily admit that sometimes zoning prohibits the development of a business that is likely to be beneficial to a neighborhood. If one is not too afraid of strangers, a locally owned coffee shop on a corner might be a good thing. However, from a zoning perspective, it isn't feasible to differentiate between a good building (coffee shop) and a bad building (slaughterhouse): "in some fields, the bad fades into the good by such insensible degrees that the two are not capable of being readily distinguished and separated in terms of legislation."[9] The substantial issue here isn't the relative differences between good and bad businesses, but rather the assumption that everything must be accomplished by top-down legislation. As we saw in chapter 1, "solving" problems from a godlike, top-down perspective often leads to outcomes that do not work well for residents of a local area.

It is not very hard to tell the difference between a neighborhood-enhancing and a neighborhood-harming business if you are living or working in the neighborhood. So in using this as a reason for justifying zoning, the justices are deliberately tipping the balance of power away from neighborhood stakeholders and toward municipal government. Specifically, the city government is given the power to regulate land uses in a particular neighborhood over and above private homeowners, nonprofits, or property owners who intend to develop a parcel of land for commercial use.

The fact that one cannot tell the difference between a slaughterhouse and a coffee shop from a zoning map could really be used in two different ways: either to justify the prohibition of coffee houses and slaughterhouses in a particular neighborhood, or to call into question the appropriateness of using zoning as a tool for regulating the kinds of activity that can go on in the buildings of a neighborhood. Because of a prior commitment to expert culture, zoning as a planning tool became almost universal, and coffee shops in neighborhoods became scarce.

Urban Renewal

Urban renewal is a term used to describe a phase of planning history in the 1950s and 1960s that involved large-scale projects for clearing swaths of neighborhood stock (described as slums) to make way for public works projects (expressways and bridges) and public housing. Urban renewal gained traction in the United States through the passage of federal funding programs such as the Housing Act in 1954 and the Federal Highway Act in 1956, as well as through gaining legal justification in the landmark case of *Berman v. Parker* in 1954.

However, the principles and priorities of urban renewal were really established earlier in the twentieth century in the work of the *CIAM*, introduced in chapter 4. In many ways, the project undertaken by *CIAM* can be considered to be a rational rethinking of the entire form of the city.

One of the leading figures of *CIAM* and the publisher of the conclusions of the Athens Charter was an individual by the name of Le Corbusier. Le Corbusier was highly skeptical of the ability of an organic process to devise workable solutions to complex modern problems and thought not only that strict rationality is the thing that sets humans apart from animals but that it would be our only hope of surviving the current crisis.

> The pack-donkey meanders along, meditates a little in his scatter-brained and distracted fashion, he zigzags in order to avoid the larger stones, or to ease the climb . . . he takes the line of least resistance. But man governs his feelings by his reason.[10]

Part of Le Corbusier's lack of confidence in organic processes was the experience of watching his hometown and the vocation of his father become obsolete. Le Corbusier (then, Charles-Edouard Jeanneret) was born in the city of La Chaux-de-Fonds, which was home to a community of makers of handcrafted watches. During his formative years, he saw his community go through a crisis as mass-produced watches from Germany began to flood the market, thus decimating the handcrafted-watch market.

Le Corbusier sensed that the traditional city (like traditional watchmaking) was facing a significant crisis. He felt that the quaint premodern town could not compete with the brutal and powerful industrial city. Le Corbusier felt that wedding artistic vision with technology and statistics would yield a new and exciting day for the modern city. One aspect of his vision was cities with densities as high as 1,200 persons per acre. The incredible height of his skyscrapers would provide dramatic settings for residents, while allowing up to 85 percent of the surface area to be unoccupied by buildings.

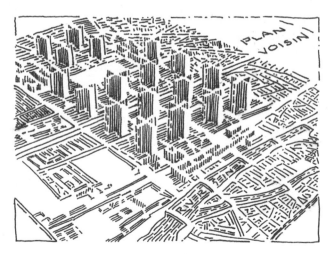

Le Corbusier's *Plan Voisin*

Le Corbusier called his urban vision "Radiant City." It was part of Le Corbusier's vision that his scheme must be applied in the center of existing cities.

Politics

He considered the congested character of these cities the embodiment of the problem with the industrial city. One of his first articulations of this vision was his *Plan Voisin*, which involved tearing down a ten-block section of old Paris and replacing it with a number of cruciform-plan high-rise skyscrapers placed four hundred meters apart.

The skyscrapers thus placed were to give the sense of a parklike setting with lots of green space and the skyscrapers "growing" in even rows. Le Corbusier's reason for attacking the congested city was to provide maximum mobility and speed to the modern urban dweller. His scheme is linked by private automobiles traveling uninterrupted on superhighways. "The city built for speed is the city built for success," Le Corbusier famously claimed.[11]

Although Le Corbusier's fellow Parisians were too smart to accept his rational rethinking of the city, his ideas were readily picked up in the United States. His vision of the generic skyscraper and high-speed thoroughfare was articulated and popularized by General Motors' Futurama exhibit at the 1938 World's Fair in New York City.

While Le Corbusier's *Plan Voisin* was intended for numerous socioeconomic classes, in this country, the projects that reflected his vision were largely focused on housing projects for the poor. From the mid-1950s through the 1960s, a number of neighborhoods were razed and replaced by large housing projects that looked very much like Le Corbusier's Radiant City.

Some of the neighborhoods that were razed were falling apart and experiencing significant problems. However, a number of vibrant and functional neighborhoods also were included on the list for removal. Part of the problem was that the definition of "slum" used in urban renewal schemes was often based on abstract statistical measures such as density of population or age of the buildings, and there was no attempt to assess whether the neighborhood in question was actually working.

We can say, then, that the phase of planning in the United States known as urban renewal represented a prioritization of "rational" analysis over any attempt to account for what had indeed been working in the actual history of a place. This was Le Corbusier's basic framework for understanding urban issues, and, as we shall see, it didn't work very well.

The Day Modernist Architecture Died

We've already noted through the pizza analogy in chapter 1 that many people are beginning to question the wisdom of functional zoning. With regard to urban renewal, however, enthusiasm for the program ended more abruptly.

Pruitt-Igoe was an urban renewal housing project in St. Louis that was completed in 1954. It consisted of thirty-three high-rise buildings of eleven stories each. The project provided 2,870 units of low-income housing to St. Louis residents. It was designed by Minoru Yamasaki, who was also the architect for the World Trade Center towers. Yamasaki's proposal was declared "the best high apartment" of the year in 1951. The total cost of the project came to 36 million dollars.

Like most of the other high-rise housing projects of that era, Pruitt-Igoe created more problems than it solved. Almost immediately, the complex became riddled with crime and filth. In this case, the situation became so bad that they began destruction of the buildings in 1972, just sixteen years after the project was completed.

Images of the demolition of Pruitt-Igoe have become iconic of the failure of urban renewal and, to some extent, modernist rational planning in general. Architectural historian Charles Jencks declared the demolition of Pruitt-Igoe "the day Modern architecture died."[12]

What Lessons Were Learned?

There is widespread consensus among the planning community that the unquestioning confidence that was placed in modern rationalist planning during the twentieth century was a mistake. Pruitt-Igoe was the most dramatic, but by no means the only, failure of a project based on these principles. The question that is still being debated, however, is, What lessons were learned? We know that large-scale high-rise projects are not the best way to house the poor, and we also know that strict functional zoning is probably unsustainable. But what is still not clear is whether we need to rethink some of the specific proposals that came out of the modern rational planning movement or whether the real problem has to do with fundamental assumptions of that movement that continue to be influential today. To answer this question, we can turn to Jane Jacobs, who was one of the few critics who saw problems with the modern rational planning movement well before 1972.

The Kind of Problem a City Is

It is not uncommon to hear a pretty broad spectrum of planners praise Jacobs's *Death and Life of Great American Cities* and claim that they have been positively influenced by her ideas. It would be hard not to appreciate the wisdom of this outsider to the field, who as early as 1956 was expressing grave concern over the strategies of urban renewal that were enthusiastically supported by planning experts. A number of concepts and terms from that book, including "mixed-use" and "eyes on the street," have become enshrined in the contemporary planner's lexicon.

However, in some ways, it is Jacobs's insights from chapter 19, on what kind of problem the city presents, that levy the strongest critique of the planning community and may be most instructive in helping us forge a way forward. In this chapter, Jacobs asks her readers to pause before suggesting solutions to the problems posed by the city, in order to ask what kind of a problem the city is. She claims that answers provided by planners and visionaries throughout history have been wrong because they were answers to the wrong questions. The first thing we need to do, Jacobs asserts, is make sure that we have the question right.[13]

Problem of Simplicity

Jacobs believes that there are three basic kinds of problems for which solutions are required. The first she calls the problem of simplicity. These were the kinds of problems tackled by science from the seventeenth to the nineteenth centuries. In these kinds of problems, two or perhaps three variables were studied to better understand their relationship. The relationship between gas pressure and volume provides one example.

Early attempts at city planning, such as Ebenezer Howard's Garden City, represented an attempt to fix the complex issues facing London as a problem of simplicity. Howard thought that if he could provide the right balance of jobs, housing, and recreation, he could lure people out of London to live in his smaller-scale communities. The problem with this model lies in trying to provide the right job, the right housing, and the right recreational opportunities to each individual in the city.

Garden City

Jacobs preferred the natural complexity of real urban life to Howard's paternalistic and reductionistic Garden Cities. Howard's vision, while it looked good on paper, ultimately suppressed the creative initiative of individuals and local communities; "as in all Utopias, the right to have plans of any significance belonged only to the planners in charge," Jacobs complained.[14] Howard had abstracted the city to a simple problem of jobs, housing, "recreation," and access to nature, and the result was nothing like the cities that Jacobs loved. Rather, these Garden Cities embodied "the dishonest mask of pretended order, achieved by ignoring or suppressing the real order that is struggling to exist and to be served."[15]

Problem of Disorganized Complexity

The second kind of problem is that of disorganized complexity. As science at the beginning of the twentieth century began to face more complicated issues, it found that for many problems it could not account for each of the factors one by one. One could study the behavior of three billiard balls on a table as a problem of simplicity, but the behavior of a million billiard balls on a table would be impossible to predict using such tools. For more complex issues such as these, we use statistics to help us find patterns of behavior.

Jacobs saw urban visionaries of the early twentieth century such as Le Corbusier dealing with the city as a problem of disorganized complexity. Le Corbusier's Radiant City is based on the notion that technology applied to good statistical data could solve the problem of the city. Jacobs thought that Le Corbusier's plans for saving the city would kill it with sterility. Even though the Radiant City model has been deemed a failure, many planners continue to follow Le Corbusier's model of treating the city as a problem of disorganized complexity by an overreliance on statistics to lead us to fail-proof solutions.

Problem of Organized Complexity

The third kind of problem is that of organized complexity. Starting in about the 1930s, the life sciences began to make significant strides by recognizing that organic systems involve issues of organized complexity. Biological systems include a large number of complex factors that are "interrelated into an organic whole."[16]

Jacobs believes that cities are more like biological systems than anything else and need to be recognized as such to be properly understood. Jacobs sees cities as living organisms, and sees the key to understanding them in paying close attention to how they actually function in everyday life. Jacobs believes that cities, like other organic systems, have the "marvelous innate abilities for understanding, communicating, contriving, and inventing what is required to combat their difficulties."[17]

Jacobs's insight that cities and neighborhoods function as systems of organized complexity is a compelling one and has important implications for the way that we seek positive change in the built environment. However, Jacobs's insight represents one of two fundamental ways that have been proposed to correct the mistakes of modern rationalistic city planning.

Alternative Responses

Ultimately, Jacobs's critique of modern rationalist planning comes down to her belief that this approach failed to see the city as working like a living body. As noted above, many planners today have failed to appreciate that insight and continue to treat the city as a problem of simplicity (for which we need to find the right mix of jobs or housing) or a problem of disorganized complexity (for which we need to find the right statistical analyses). However, there are other strong critiques of modern rationalist planning that do not share Jacobs's conviction that the city functions like a body. Comparing Jacobs's approach to these alternative responses will bring to light some fundamental questions that face us in our current situation.

Two Visions of Urban Life

I think that the most compelling and influential voice representing this alternative critique of modern rationalist planning is the Dutch architect Rem Koolhaas. Koolhaas is one of the twenty-first century's leading architects and the winner of the coveted Pritzker Prize. From the CCTV building we saw during the 2008 Olympics in China, to Seattle's public library, to Prada in Beverly Hills, a Koolhaas project lends instant credibility to a city, country, or corporation that wants to establish a certain panache.

Although Koolhaas and Jacobs have both been critical of modern rationalist planning, the kinds of urban environments that Jacobs and Koolhaas have championed are radically different. Jacobs loves the intimacy and complexity of her beloved Hudson Street neighborhood. While it can be a bit difficult to pin Koolhaas down, we do get some sense of his urban sensibilities when we look at the Seattle Public Library that he designed.

Right photo by Embry Owen

Two Visions of Urban Life

Clearly, these are very different images of urban life, but what I want to demonstrate is that these divergent pictures represent more than just differing aesthetic tastes. Jacobs and Koolhaas represent two very different understandings of what cities are and how they should be put together. And we can begin to tease out the difference by looking at the way they critiqued modern rationalistic planning.

Root Metaphors

It is often thought that the construction of metaphors is sort of a secondary act. First we conceive of an idea or observe a thing, and then we employ a metaphor as a communication strategy. However, it has recently been suggested that metaphors may be more primary to our way of thinking and may, in fact, reveal our understanding of reality.[18] When we examine our words carefully, we see that our language is saturated with metaphors at every turn. We "grasp a point," we "conquer a fear," we "grow in our faith," we "drop the ball," or we "catch our stride." Each of these metaphors conveys not only a particular event but also a perspective on those events. Sometimes it can be helpful to look for root metaphors that reveal overarching themes in those who generate interesting ideas.

In their efforts to propose an alternative approach to that of modern rationalistic planning, both Jacobs and Koolhaas employ telling metaphors. Jacobs, in *Death and Life of Great American Cities*, compares modernist planners to bloodletters: "As in the pseudoscience of bloodletting, just so in the pseudoscience of city rebuilding and planning, years of learning and a plethora of subtle and complicated dogma have arisen on a foundation of nonsense."[19] Koolhaas in his essay "Whatever Became of Urbanism?" makes reference to such planners as alchemists: "Modernism's alchemistic promise—to transform quantity into quality through abstraction and repetition—has been a failure, a hoax: magic that didn't work."[20]

Both Jacobs and Koolhaas use pseudoscientific metaphors to critique modernist planning. Jacobs likens modernist planning to the "science" of bloodletting, which weakens or kills the patient in an attempt to cure him. Koolhaas likens such planners to alchemists, who attempt to transform lead into gold.

These divergent images can be taken as root metaphors that reveal how Koolhaas and Jacobs understand the city. The most telling difference has to do not with the metaphors themselves, but rather with the implied object of each metaphor. It is here that we begin to see how each of these critiques implies a vision not only of the city, but also of its prospects for transformation. For Jacobs, the city is a living body that can be hurt by well-meaning but deluded saviors. For Koolhaas, the city is an inert, malleable substance that can't change grim economic realities like scarcity and uneven distributions of power, but it can keep us distracted for some time.

We next unpack these root metaphors a bit to see how they help make sense of some of Jacobs's and Koolhaas's distinct takes on how we can impact the city. In particular, we look at three aspects of city life: how cities experience change, how cities affect public relationships, and how cities provide settings for human expression.

For Jacobs, then, change in the city functions like transformation in living organisms such as the human body. There are a number of implications of Jacobs's use of this metaphor. We examine three below.

City as Body

Self-Repair

The first is that cities should develop according to patterns set forth in their organic form. When we think of repair or improvement of human bodies, we think either of a restoration to health after a bout of sickness or of an attempt to augment certain desirable features through diet or exercise.

What we don't normally think of is a radical reconstruction of the human form or the addition of completely novel features (such as wings). There is an implicit conservatism, therefore, in Jacobs's body metaphor—bodies are generally restored to health. Another implication has to do with the process of transformation. Human beings (and other organisms) contain the ability to self-repair without invasive intervention. While we do sometimes have to employ chemotherapy to attack cancerous cells, by far the more typical pattern is to see head colds cured and minor cuts repaired without any medical intervention at all.

This tells us much about how Jacobs understands transformation to take place among people and practices in the city. She sees in ordinary cities a form that is basically good and assumes the ability of residents to enact a kind of self-repair. The city and its neighborhoods occasionally need outside intervention to fulfill this potential, but for the most part what they need is less rather than more government intervention.

Engagement

We will next examine how Jacobs understands how cities affect the way that we relate to one another in public. The term that I use for this concept is *engagement*. For Jacobs, the locus for participation in the city is the sidewalks. There are three aspects of engagement in her opening chapters on the uses on sidewalks in *Death and Life*. The first use of sidewalks is public safety. Jacobs sees vibrant streets combined with people's natural inclination toward watching other people to be the key to public safety. A functioning city street, then, should police itself if its denizens are participating: "No amount of police can enforce civilization where the normal, casual enforcement of it has broken down."[21]

The second aspect of engagement is the bond of trust formed by ordinary and frequent social contact among people in the city.

> The sum of such casual, public contact at a local level—most of it fortuitous, most of it associated with errands, all of it metered by the person concerned and not thrust upon him by anyone—is a feeling for the public identity of people, a web of public respect and trust, and a resource in time of personal or neighborhood need.[22]

This bond of trust is what we identified earlier in this chapter as social capital. Social capital is a measure for the quality of relational life in a particular area.

The third aspect of engagement has to do with the assimilation of children. However, one can see in Jacobs's reasoning that she is not only concerned with the well-being of children. Children in the city provide a venue as well as a reason to take responsibility for one another.

> In real life, only from the ordinary adults of the city sidewalks do children learn—if they learn it at all—the first fundamental of successful city life: People must take a modicum of public responsibility for each other even if they have no ties to each other. This is a lesson that nobody learns by being told. It is learned from the experience of having other people without ties of kinship or close friendship or formal responsibility to you take a modicum of public responsibility for you.[23]

One can see in this quotation Jacobs's understanding of an implicit covenant that exists among people who live in proximity to one another. We will return to the concept of engagement in part III.

Enactment

Last, we examine how Jacobs understands the city as a setting for human expression. The term that I use to describe this aspect of her work is *enactment*. As noted in the introduction, it is imperative that we think of the built environment not just as a static entity, but rather as enacted space.

For Jacobs, enactment in the city is like a loosely choreographed dance. One small section from Jacobs's lengthy description of "the sidewalk ballet" on Hudson Street exemplifies her perspective.

> When I get home after work, the ballet is reaching its crescendo. This is the time of roller skates and stilts and tricycles, and games in the lee of the stoop with bottletops and plastic cowboys; this is the time of bundles and packages, zigzagging from the drug store to the fruit stand and back over to the butcher's; this is the time when teenagers, all dressed up, are pausing to ask if their slips

show or their collars look right; this is the time when beautiful girls get out of MG's; this is the time when the fire engines go through; this is the time when anybody you know around Hudson Street will go by.[24]

Behind this ballet imagery, then, we can see Jacobs's notion of enactment as involving a kind of rhythmic cooperation among the residents of a particular neighborhood. Just as the components of our bodies can respond in a coordinated way in response to something like music, so also the people of a neighborhood find their lives spontaneously coordinated by the various rhythms of the neighborhood.

City as Lead

Rem Koolhaas, by way of contrast, does not see the city as a living body, which means that he does not see cities or neighborhoods as having the ability to self-repair. He does not look for the building up of social capital on the sidewalks. And he certainly doesn't expect to witness anything so coherent as a ballet taking place on his streets.

To be quite honest, Koolhaas's root metaphor, if it can be counted as such at all, isn't nearly as well developed as Jacobs's. He calls rationalistic planners (like Le Corbusier) alchemists, which implies that he sees cities as lead, subject to someone's dubious aspiration to transform them into gold. Not much to build our analysis on, but it does fit in with many other things that he has said about the city, as well as the projects in which he has been involved. For Koolhaas, the city, like lead, is inert and somewhat malleable and, perhaps most important, can be taken as a kind of abstract medium for the working out of power relationships.

Transgression

I begin unpacking this metaphor by exploring the way that Koolhaas understands transformation to take place in the city. As to the means for carrying out his vision for the city, Koolhaas is neither naive nor idealistic. He understands that he needs access to power to get his buildings built and seems to have few qualms about the source of this power. One of his most prominent recent projects is the headquarters of the Chinese government's CCTV. You may have seen pictures of it during the 2008 summer Olympics. He has been critiqued for his contribution to what is essentially a vehicle of propaganda for a closed and repressive government. Koolhaas defends his action by elliptically claiming that his participation in this project might somehow contribute to the transformation of China's closed system. For Koolhaas, transformation takes place through transgressive artistic acts.

Koolhaas also seems quite content to be working for major capitalist players as well. He has designed two emporiums for Prada in Manhattan and Beverly Hills, for instance. Again, Koolhaas defends his alliances with capitalist power as potentially transgressive. He thinks that it is foolish to try to change the direction of the capitalist system initially, but rather recommends to would-be revolutionaries that "the best they can do is master surfing and exploit the force of capital."[25]

This notion of mastering surfing and exploiting the forces of capital as a strategy for transforming the city resonates with Koolhaas's alchemist metaphor. Unlike Jacobs, Koolhaas sees no normative form to limit or shape the process of transformation. He also doesn't see the possibility of local communities performing self-repair. Koolhaas sees at work global forces that, like the ocean, cannot ultimately be controlled. The best that one can hope to do is to harness these forces for fun or exhibition (hence, surfing).

The surfing metaphor breaks down a bit when we try to include in it Koolhaas's transgressive aspirations. Koolhaas is not just surfing for fun and exhibition; he wants (I think) to undermine the totalizing forces of state-controlled communism and the equally oppressive private force of corporate capitalism by deliberately failing to provide his clients with soothing and stabilizing images in the buildings he designs for them. If Prada and the Chinese government are this generation's alchemists, who are bolstering the status quo by holding out the false hope of gold for the masses, Koolhaas is the rabble-rouser who exposes the spurious nature of this project.

Voyeurism

Koolhaas believes that public life has largely been replaced by private consumption in semipublic places. We enter the public realm to go shopping or perhaps to get something to eat. Therefore, it is not that surprising that the public places formed by his projects are not particularly inspiring. As Sarah Goldhagen notes, his buildings strive to embody his particular vision of contemporary life. This vision does not glorify public life—he provides no grand plazas for human interaction. The only outdoor public space in his Eurolille project is the mall, which is a "flat, monotonous, interiorized steel-and-glass beached whale, stretched along 1,100 feet of a multi-lane road."[26]

He seems concerned that his public spaces don't portray false and romantic notions of community life that no longer apply. As he confessed in a recent interview, he wants "to understand the city no longer as a tissue but more as a 'mere' coexistence."[27] Koolhaas does not want his public places to be too grand, because of his acknowledgment that much of life is lived in the private realm.

Participation

But Koolhaas isn't particularly interested in letting people rest comfortably in their insular private lives. One of his transgressive actions is to force some kind of public interaction on an unsuspecting populace. The ramps and oddly carved voids of his buildings create events where users unexpectedly find themselves both looking at others and being looked at. One reviewer described the design of a private home as voyeuristic. The reviewer concludes with a chilling summary: "In the Koolhaasian city people are never really alone, but neither are they really together."[28]

Again this can be compared with Jacobs's notion of engagement. Jacobs saw engagement in the city as having to do with the self-policing of the residents, the building of bonds of trust with one another, and the taking of responsibility for one another. Koolhaas, not seeing any of these aspects of city life being viable, promotes a kind of unsettling voyeurism among people in the city as a way of reminding us that such connective tissue no longer exists.

Amplification

In terms of the city as a venue for human expression, there are two sides to Koolhaas's approach. As an architect, Koolhaas seems to understand the city as a kind of canvas for artistic expression. When Koolhaas's firm, OMA, was given the commission from the Chinese government discussed above, the team came up with a skyscraper that bent in the middle, allowing the top to come down and meet the bottom in a kind of loop.

Koolhaas, fascinated by the concept, was hesitant, because Peter Eisenman had once proposed a looping building. Koolhaas agreed to go forward only when he was reminded by a member of his staff that he had suggested the idea in an earlier proposal. In this, we see that artistic originality is a key value for Koolhaas. The city, for Koolhaas, provides a kind of canvas for the expression of his artistic impulses.

This said, it should be pointed out that Koolhaas is deeply critical of architects who assert their artistic impulse to the point of killing a particular place's aura. Koolhaas's attention to the particular aura of places leads him to find pleasure in some pretty surprising places, however. He has written appreciatively of computer-generated high-rises in the Pearl River delta of China, for instance. As a student, he studied constructivist and Stalinist buildings and affectionately noted "a bleak row of dilapidated concrete apartment towers" in St. Petersburg for their "heartbreaking delicateness."[29] He was distraught when the porn shops were removed from Times Square in New York City. The offices for OMA are in Rotterdam, a city in Holland that was largely destroyed during the war and rebuilt in 1960s and 1970s architectural motifs.

He greatly prefers this setting to the quaintness found in the beloved houses and canals of Amsterdam.

Part of this contrarian aesthetic can be traced back to Koolhaas's childhood, four years of which were spent in Jakarta. When he returned to the Netherlands at age twelve, the contrast between the vibrant chaos of Indonesia and the tame environment at home was a shock to his system; "the Netherlands seemed to him a living museum, all artificiality and cultivated tulips." "I was stunned by how boring and conventional and tidy everything was," Koolhaas recounts.[30]

This helps explain some of Koolhaas's unusual tastes but also helps refine what he means by a place's aura. The aura of a place is important to Koolhaas, but he is also vehemently opposed to nostalgia or contrivance. His appreciation for Rotterdam has nothing to do with the "soul" of Rotterdam, but rather comes from its honest expression of banality and globalism. What Koolhaas seems to be looking for in the built environment are settings that "lay bare the psychic conditions of modernity."[31] He sees the modern city in its more unsettling forms to be the locus for this kind of experience.

As a designer and builder of buildings, however, Koolhaas wants more than just to appreciate places that embody this kind of rawness; he also wants his work to make a contribution. A word that frequently gets used to describe what Koolhaas's buildings do to the existing conditions of the urban environment is *amplify*.

Evaluating the Options

As we think about Jacobs's and Koolhaas's understandings of how cities work, two very different conceptions emerge to correspond with the two literal pictures with which we began. When it comes to transformation, Jacobs understands the city as having the organized complexity of a biological system and expects natural development as well as self-repair. Koolhaas sees transformation as being a function of unsettling images produced by transgressive artists. Engagement for Jacobs is a building up of networks of trust through neighborhood interaction. For Koolhaas engagement is a kind of voyeurism that is forced on an unsuspecting public. And last, for Jacobs, enactment is the rhythmic coordination of informal rituals such as the ballet of street life. For Koolhaas enactment involves an amplification of the "psychic conditions of modernity."

Tradition versus Avant-Garde

Coming back to the question posed at the beginning of the chapter, we can say that both Jacobs and Koolhaas are critical of the top-down approach to urban planning that held sway in the era of modern rationalistic planning. Jacobs's bottom-up approach is founded on her basic assumption that the city or neighborhood has a kind of implicit organization to it that naturally emerges when humans live in proximity to one another over time. Koolhaas is more skeptical. He sees Le Corbusier's analysis as being overly rationalistic, but he doesn't accept the notion that there is any implicit organization at work at the local level either.

Koolhaas seems to think that we need to avoid the artificiality of pretend order, whether it comes from the top down as in modern rationalist planning or from the bottom up in overly nostalgic visions of common life at the neighborhood level. He appreciates things that emerge from the bottom up, but only when they express a certain "honesty" about the inherent conflicts and ugliness of contemporary life. Because people would rather ignore such grim realities and cover them up with artificiality, Koolhaas sees the job of the architect or planner to be an agent of transgression who continually challenges our attempts to find meaning and order in our lives.

Interestingly enough, whatever else we would say about the merits of this approach, in practice it tends to lead back to a top-down approach to planning. Because popular taste tends toward the nostalgic and pretty, in Koolhaas's approach an elite cadre of enlightened artists is needed to challenge us and bring us back to a more "honest" understanding of our condition. Koolhaas provides one example of this notion of the architect as transgressive vanguard, but he is really representative of a fairly common understanding of the role of the architect today. Koolhaas represents the avant-garde approach to architecture.

Neighborhood as Order of Creation

It is interesting to evaluate Jacobs's and the avant-garde's approach from an eschatological perspective. Implicit behind Jacobs's confidence in the city and neighborhood to function coherently is some sense of structure and order that emerges when people live in proximity to one another. There may be a number of ways to account for this implicit structuring and ordering, but one coherent way to think about it is to envision a gracious and sovereign God who both created humanity in his image and is drawing the human creation toward a communal experience of wholeness and harmony.

From this perspective, we could think of human cities and neighborhoods not as accidents of history, but rather as orders of creation that God is using to prepare people for the life of shalom that we are to experience in the eschaton. Koolhaas doesn't see any structure or order emerging when humans live in proximity to one another. Likewise, it would be hard to find in Koolhaas ·

any sense of humanity being led in any particular direction by a gracious and sovereign God.

This seems to raise a fundamental question that needs to be addressed when thinking about the built environment. If we feel that the top-down, overly rationalistic approach of modern planning was misguided, we need to think seriously about the viability of alternative approaches. If there is an implicit order and rightness of form that comes about when humans live in proximity, we can place more confidence in insights that emerge from the people who actually are living in a particular place in history. But if there is no order or right form for human community, we need to weigh the costs and benefits to accepting an avant-garde kind of anarchy and disruption in our common life versus the compromise of seeking some kind of pretend order through top-down planning or capitulating to popular tastes.

Participation in the Polis

Looking at these two influential visionaries from an eschatological perspective raises the stakes of our potential participation in the common life of our cities and neighborhoods. One could make a case for building social capital and cultivating civic virtue from a purely self-interested perspective. It is more enjoyable and meaningful, not to mention much safer, to live in a community that is high in social capital. And the cultivation of civic virtue within yourself and among as many of your neighbors as possible is the surest route to social capital as well as to the kinds of structural changes that will make your community life better.

However, it could be that civic virtue and social capital are not only important to maximizing your experience of everyday life in your community but are also key elements of God's plan of redemption for your neighborhood and city. If this is the case, we can presume that God is likely already at work drawing us and our neighbors into organically ordered patterns of more social cohesion and harmony. Our work is to discover where God is at work in the polis and figure out where we can help out.

For Further Reading

Block, Peter. *Community: The Structure of Belonging*. San Francisco: Berrett-Koehler, 2008.
Fergusson, David. *Church, State and Civil Society*. Cambridge: Cambridge University Press, 2004.
Fishman, Robert. *Urban Utopias in the Twentieth Century: Ebenezer Howard, Frank Lloyd Wright, and Le Corbusier*. Cambridge: MIT Press, 1982.

Participation

Flint, Anthony. *Wrestling with Moses: How Jane Jacobs Took on New York's Master Builder and Transformed the American City*. New York: Random House, 2009.

Forrester, Duncan B. *Truthful Action: Explorations in Practical Theology*. Edinburgh: T&T Clark, 2000.

Jacobs, Jane. *The Death and Life of Great American Cities*. New York: Vintage, 1961.

Kemmis, Daniel. *The Good City and the Good Life*. Boston: Houghton Mifflin, 1995.

Lakoff, George, and Mark Johnson. *Metaphors We Live By*. Chicago: University of Chicago Press, 2003.

McKnight, John, and Peter Block. *The Abundant Community: Awakening the Power of Families and Neighborhoods*. San Francisco: Berrett-Koehler, 2010.

Putnam, Robert D. *Bowling Alone: The Collapse and Revival of American Community*. New York: Simon and Schuster, 2000.

Sennett, Richard. *The Uses of Disorder: Personal Identity & City Life*. New York: W. W. Norton, 1992.

Von Hoffman, Alexander. *House by House, Block by Block: The Rebirth of America's Urban Neighborhoods*. Oxford: Oxford University Press, 2003.

7

Church

Cadence

In the previous chapter, we were introduced to Jane Jacobs's beloved "sidewalk ballet." This simple description captures well the informal coherence that is so often found in lively neighborhoods. Jacobs noted the kind of ballet that is found on Hudson Street at 5:00 PM on a weekday, but we could locate any number of "ballets" being enacted at other times in other neighborhoods.

When we are attuned to these kinds of rhythms of the public realm, we can begin to think about the origin of these various movements. In Jacobs's "ballet" many of the rhythms were tied in with economic systems (people getting off work, shopping, deliveries being made) as well as other rhythms tied to social rituals (dating) and childhood practices (play).

But clearly numerous other rhythms are behind the "dancers" performing in these various ballets. We explored a number of such possible rhythms in chapter 4. You may recall that many of the rhythms that we discovered were connected to life passages and liturgical traditions. This suggests that faith communities may have a significant role in "counting the cadence" in some of the ballets that are taking place in various neighborhoods.

In this chapter we explore the diverse ways that churches interact within, are shaped by, and possibly shape the built environment. But we will begin our exploration by looking at a faith community that is outside of the Christian faith.

Eruv Lines and the Driving Teshuvah

In a great many residential urban neighborhoods, it is common to see Orthodox Jews walking alone or together on Saturday mornings about the same time to synagogue for Sabbath (or Shabbat) observance. It is not only their distinctive clothing that makes them stand out from the other residents of the neighborhood. It is also the fact that one group of people who live in separate homes are walking together to the same place at the same time. Try to think of another community (or even activity) that similarly walks together. This doesn't happen in very many churches anymore, nor does it happen for baseball games or grade school. Occasionally a neighborhood might have its own Fourth of July parade where people walk the streets together, but that's only once a year.

It is not just a demographic fluke that causes the Orthodox to present themselves to the community in this way. Nor does this practice represent a small minority of the Orthodox who just happen to be visible to us because of their practice. Orthodox rabbis have determined that it is unlawful to operate an automobile on the Sabbath, even for the purpose of attending Sabbath services.[1] To maintain the integrity of the Sabbath law that prohibits both operating an automobile and walking a great distance on the Sabbath, the Orthodox have placed an *eruv line* around their various synagogues.

An eruv line defines the space within which a faithful Orthodox Jew can set up his home. This line functions to prevent the individual from violating the Sabbath but also encourages the formation of strong Jewish neighborhoods around Orthodox synagogues. This is an interesting aspect of the Orthodox communities in the United States. This has not been characteristic of Conservative Jews in the second half of the twentieth century, however, because of the way that they have interpreted the Sabbath regulations.

In 1950, six rabbis from the Committee on Jewish Laws and Standards (CJLS) met to offer an opinion on the legality of operating an automobile for the purpose of attending Shabbat services at one's synagogue.[2] At this time, many Jews were living in the exurbs and could not easily walk to synagogue; consequently, Shabbat observance was seen to be in serious decline. Eventually, three of the rabbis were able to author a consensus statement conceding that walking is the recommended means of traveling on the Sabbath but that if the decision is between driving to attend Shabbat and not attending Shabbat, Conservative Jews would be permitted to drive. This document actually described a more comprehensive program for revitalization of Sabbath observance; however, it is more widely known as the *driving teshuvah* for its allowance of driving on the Sabbath. A general impression among Conservative Jews is that this teshuvah legalized driving on the Sabbath, and as such it has had a significant impact on Conservative Jewish practice.

This debate among the Conservative Jewish rabbis reveals a number of interesting ways that faith communities experience as well as shape the built environment. The experience of the Conservative Jewish community following the driving teshuvah is less interesting for our purposes, due to the fact that this decision allowed them to behave much like Christian faith communities in the postwar era. What is more interesting to note is how the arguments levied against this decision reveal interesting aspects of the intersection between faith communities and the built environment that have not been seriously considered for some time.

Tehumin

Rabbi Ben Zion Bokser, who authored the minority report that opposed driving on the Sabbath, explains his view of the purpose and basis of the driving prohibition: "The prohibition of travel on the Sabbath was a vital contribution to preparing the day for its mission to sanctify life. The basis of this prohibition is the verse in Exodus 16:29, 'Abide ye every man in his place; let no man go out of his place in the seventh day.'"[3]

This general understanding of the purpose of the Sabbath can been broken down into a variety of considerations. The first is that of *tehumin*, which has to do with "fixing one's domicile in a particular place, and then limiting one's motions within a prescribed radius of that place." Or, as Rabbi Novak puts it, "the intention of the law is to keep one in the vicinity of his or her own neighborhood—'neighborhood' being the area of normal walking distance."[4] The concept of tehumin is a kind of voluntary limitation, much like the concept of askesis that we introduced in chapter 2.

The driving teshuvah claims that the notion of tehumin has become outdated under the conditions of suburbanization and with the introduction of automobile travel. Rabbi Bokser takes just the opposite approach and sees tehumin to be even more important under contemporary conditions:

The complexities of large city life which have diversified the interests and occupations of individual members of the family and have subjected them to different time schedules has proven a serious menace to the stability of the family. The Sabbath as a sanctifying influence on the lives of people depends on its being set within a fixed home and on uniting the entire family for the Sabbath experience. If on the Sabbath, too, members of the family will each go his way and pursue a private schedule of social or recreational life, the Sabbath experience will drop out of our lives altogether. . . . If we want to preserve the Sabbath, then we must create fixed home experiences and limit movement away from home, in order that the family be kept together. There can be no Sabbath atmosphere, none of its sanctifying or relaxing elements, without the rejection of the things that undermine the home's fixity and threaten the stability of the family as an integrated unit of human life.[5]

Rabbi Bokser here raises an important point about freedom and choice. The promise of the automobile as well as postwar exurban development have to do with absolute freedom to do whatever we want whenever we want. But Bokser reminds us that in certain areas, true freedom can be found only when we learn to say no to lesser freedoms (such as mobility) in order to gain some greater freedoms (such as a harmonious family life).

Shevut

A second aspect of Sabbath observance is the *shevut* (or rabbinic prohibition) of *uvdin d'hol* (or weekday things). This has to do with the Sabbath being distinct from the other days of the week. As Rabbi David Golinkin, in his decision on the Masori movement in Israel, puts it, "In other words, Shabbat should not look and feel like a weekday. There is nothing more weekday-like than driving a car."[6]

It is fairly common among Christians to be critical of some of the Sabbath prohibitions within the Jewish community as being legalistic or obscure. And certainly some of the rationale for not driving a car on the Sabbath might be subject to that kind of critique. Much of the discussion on the driving teshuvah had to do with specific work prohibitions, such as whether or not the workings of a combustion engine constitute the lighting of a fire or whether the possibility of a breakdown might force someone to work to remedy the situation.

However, Rabbi Bokser demonstrates that what sounds obscure and petty to our ears may also provide fresh avenues to countercultural insights concerning practices that have been unquestioningly adopted by the wider culture. In attempting to preserve the integrity of the Sabbath, Rabbi Bokser finds a platform for critiquing the experience of driving an automobile that is unusual in the 1950s. He maintains that the very act of operating an

Participation

automobile constitutes a subtle but significant form of work directly for the driver.

> The tension of driving in traffic, of pressing against crowds, of being subject to noise, of waiting in line—all these are extremely exerting to the nerves of people. They make any trip a tiring experience. The Sabbath is meant to free us not only from the work that tires the body but from the experiences which tire and weary our nervous system.[7]

Rabbi Bokser helps us to see that while the automobile offers some relief from physical exertion, driving a car can wear on us in a number of other ways.

Kehillot

As we consider the implications of the driving teshuvah, we should note that, unlike the historical Christian practice of gathering for worship, the act of gathering for public worship is of secondary importance for Jews. What is of primary importance is the observance of the Sabbath in one's home with one's family. The decision to widen the circle of Sabbath observance to the rest of the neighborhood came later as a way to supplement and reinforce what was happening in the home. Public Sabbath observance is very important to many Jews and considered to be essential to the preservation of Jewish life, but its secondary status does play a role in how the debates are construed.

This prioritization of home Sabbath observance has allowed some Jewish commentators to see more clearly the way religious practices impact the neighborhood as a whole. Note how this author mentions the importance of Jews living close to *one another* before mentioning their proximity to the *synagogue*: "It has been my experience that one potentially important component of [Jewish] communities is geographical, namely, living within walking distance of one another and the synagogue."[8]

And Rabbi Golinkin underscores this notion:

> The Masori movement wishes to create kehillot (communities), not just synagogues. It is impossible to create a community when every family lives a great distance from every other family, and in order to create a community which observes the Shabbat together, its members must live in close proximity to each other.[9]

Rabbi Golinkin's advocacy of the *kehillot* emphasizes the importance of the relationship that Jews have to one another as having some bearing on the quality of community life.

Worship, Home, and Fundamental Ethical Choices

As this debate is played out among the rabbis, it becomes clear that an underlying issue has to do with the prioritization of religious life among Jewish households. The driving teshuvah was meant as a concession to provide an opportunity for those Jews who were living beyond walking distance to the synagogue to attend Shabbat services without breaking the law. In effect, however, the teshuvah fueled its own necessity as many Jews took it as wholesale permission to purchase homes beyond walking distance to the synagogue. At the same time, it allowed countless synagogues to relocate to areas to which most of the members would have to drive to attend.

This apparently inevitable cycle presumes, according to some of the rabbis, that the practice of Sabbath observance and the mode of getting to the synagogue are of secondary consideration. Rabbi Bokser challenges the notion that the choice of where to purchase one's home is outside the realm of moral choice: "The decision rests on subjective factors over which the individual involved alone is sovereign. He, alone, can decide that he had no other alternative as to where to make his home and that the distance involved is his capacity to walk."[10]

Rabbi Bokser also challenges some of the reigning assumptions about how far one is able to walk: "Our problem has become acute because, with the prevalence of the automobile, the art of walking has simply disappeared from many people and they use their cars for the shortest distances."[11] Rabbi Bokser here raises an important question about cause and effect. Certainly due to postwar development patterns, many places we need to get to have become too far to access on foot. However, at the same time, we have largely lost the cultural practice of walking, so that we no longer think of walking as a viable method of transportation even when the distance isn't great.

In ethics, we can distinguish between ad hoc and fundamental ethical decisions. Ad hoc decisions are those that are relatively isolated and contained within a relatively short time span. A cashier gives us too much change back after our purchase. Do we keep the extra change as a "bonus," or do we alert the cashier to the error and return the extra change? That is an ad hoc ethical choice.

Fundamental ethical choices involve longer time spans because they shape and constrain other choices. As Rabbi Bokser indicates, the decision of where to purchase a home is a fundamental ethical choice. If a Conservative Jew purchases a home that is fifteen miles away from the synagogue, then that choice becomes multiplied many times over each time she finds that she has to drive to synagogue or as she finds that she cannot see other members of her synagogue as often as she'd like to because of how far their homes are from her own.

Where we purchase our home with regard to where our church is located is a fundamental ethical choice. And the location, siting, and style of church that we construct for worship are all fundamental ethical choices as well. In this chapter, we explore some of these issues as we consider the role of churches as agents of redemption.

Church Types

"So, what kind of church do you belong to?"

There are a number of different ways that we could answer this question. Most likely, our first impulse would be to answer in terms of what makes our church distinct from other churches. We would most likely think of some common delimiters between church communities: Protestant or Catholic; mainline or evangelical; traditional worship or contemporary; liberal or conservative; perhaps even exurban, urban, or rural. But it is unlikely that our answer would be construed in terms of how the church relates to the built environment.

And yet the way that churches relate to the built environment has changed radically over the past few generations, and we now have very different models for this. These differences have significant implications for how the church worships, forms disciples, and engages the world. In this section, we explore some of the implications of these important distinctions.

As with many other aspects of the built environment, we can note the difference between churches that were constructed before and after World War II.

Typical Church Types

The church on the left is a traditional church built prior to the Second World War. I call this kind of church *embedded*. The church on the right was built after World War II. I call this church *insular*.

Embedded Church

Churches built prior to the Second World War can be called *embedded* churches because they facilitate direct connections between the interior space of the church building and the public space of the wider society outside. These churches usually come right up to the sidewalk and often have either a very small parking lot or no parking lot at all. The buildings of these embedded churches tend to stand out in the neighborhood by being taller or more grandiose in style than the rest of the buildings on the block.

Insular Church

Churches that began to be built after the Second World War tended to look different from the ones built prior to this time. These can be called *insular* churches because they are insulated from direct contact with the community that surrounds them. These churches tend to include a large parking lot that acts as a buffer between the space inside the church building and the space of the world outside the church property. These churches tend to sit on lots that are ten acres or more.

The insular church is not set up to attract (or even communicate with) the pedestrian on the street, because the layout of the property doesn't encourage pedestrian traffic.[12] The church is oriented toward people driving cars. The church visually relates to the neighborhood through its large sign(s) directed toward the street. The architecture of the building is most likely to be utilitarian.

Churches and Town Fabric

As we did when looking at housing types, we can examine these various church types in terms of how they interact with the town fabric as defined by Solomon. In this section, we look at the thresholds of churches, the ways that churches help form shared public space, and how churches function as monuments.

Thresholds

The distinction between the embedded and the insular church can be discerned readily by their doors. Embedded churches tend to have elaborate and symbolically rich doors that communicate something of the ethos of the church to those not associated with it who pass by on the sidewalk. And they help people coming to church make the transition between life outside and life inside the church. Insular churches tend to have generic and utilitarian doors, not unlike the doors one finds in postwar retail shops and office buildings.

With regard to the various rhythms of public life, the embedded church can probably have the greatest impact. As the community gathers for worship on foot, it bears witness to the reality of its commitment to a common life and the priority of worship for its families. Insular churches certainly have members who are equally committed to common life and to worship, but as they approach the church driving their cars, they are not likely to be noticed by the rest of the community.

The question of thresholds brings to our attention the odd case of churches that were built before the Second World War but were later modified to accommodate automobile travel. We can describe these churches as *adapted*. In these churches, one sometimes finds both kinds of doors in place. There are the more elaborate and symbolically rich doors that are never or rarely used, because people have changed the way that they access these churches. There is often an alternative set of generic and utilitarian doors that are meant to correspond with the new routes to church from the parking lot.

What is unfortunate about the adapted church is how unsatisfying it can be to access for worship. In a typical case, the front doors are used only infrequently, and most people enter through a very generic and utilitarian door that is set closest to the parking lot, and then they have to take a circuitous route through the church to find the sanctuary.

Shaping Space

Obviously, the embedded church is better suited to the task of shaping space than is the insular church. The embedded church defines the streetwall by coming right up to its property line. And this kind of church often will anchor a corner of a block, lending a sense of presence and stability. Many embedded churches also include courtyards that can be accessed by the public throughout the week, and which create delightful outdoor rooms that enhance the community.

Because of the need to accommodate a large number of automobiles, insular churches do not generally do a good job of shaping public space in the community. In this, most contemporary churches are no different from any other kind of building; from fast-food restaurants to shopping malls and office parks, most contemporary buildings consist of a single structure in the middle of a property, surrounded by an ocean of parking.

In most cases, the church alone probably cannot improve the situation greatly. The shaping of public space is almost always accomplished by at least two (and usually many more) adjacent buildings. Even if an insular church decided to rebuild its sanctuary right up to the property line, it most likely couldn't create a sense of enclosure, since there wouldn't be any streetwall on the opposite side of the street.

However, insular churches can potentially tie into the efforts of other entities in their communities that are thinking about these issues. A number of shopping malls, for instance, have begun rethinking their space in such a way that they tie back into the built environment. They have done this by surrounding the perimeter of their property with mid-rise apartment complexes in order to create a sense of enclosure and make better connections with the street network outside of the mall. Any insular church within a couple of blocks of such a project could probably help jump-start the public life of that community by making similar moves on its property.

Monument

As we have noted, most structures within the built environment must play the role of fabric buildings in order to help set apart the monuments. This has not been the case with church buildings. Historically, church buildings have been allowed and even encouraged to function as key monuments within communities. Even today, with a heightened sensitivity to the separation of church and state, there seems to be an acceptance of churches continuing to play monumental roles in the community. This presents a unique opportunity for churches to have a public witness.

Churches can play into this monumental status in two ways. In the first case, they can demonstrate their special status through height and mass and through a more grandiose architectural vocabulary. In addition to these aspects of their construction, they may also be placed in such a way as to line up with any axial lines (intended or not) that exist in the surrounding community.

In most cases, embedded churches are surrounded by the kind of town fabric that may contain axial lines and can benefit from this kind of placement. But, depending on the way the streets are laid out in the community, there may be opportunities for insular churches to locate on certain axes as well.

Since monuments normally represent the shared values of a particular community, churches should think carefully about how they want to express their monumental status. There are numerous resources available to help churches think through how they want to present themselves to the community through the design of their church building.

Church as Parish

Throughout this book we have been considering the implications of the fact that as Christians we live our lives not as individuals, but rather as faithful participants in perichoretic community. In light of this discussion, it should not be surprising to discover that we need to widen our consideration of the scope and purpose of the church as well. The Christian church was never intended to be an isolated autonomous entity, but rather was meant to be an agent of redemption in the community. The concept of church as parish will help us to remember this important consideration.

The Missional Church

Over the past decade or so, the missional church movement has provided a helpful stimulus for rethinking the role of the church in the world.[13] This movement challenges what has become the dominant way that the church thinks about mission. The current understanding is linear in its progression. God calls the church into existence, and then out of obedience to God's command, the church launches particular initiatives and programs under the heading of mission. The result of this kind of thinking is a minimization of the role of mission in the life of the church. A church might have a mission budget representing 10 percent of the total budget, and perhaps a mission committee to oversee that budget. And if the church is really motivated, it may support one or more missionaries. In this case, mission is a secondary concern, and institutional survival is the primary concern.

The missional church movement proposes an alternative way of thinking about missions. It begins with God, who has a missional heart for the created world. God's missional heart is what motivates him to send Jesus into the world, and the church is first and foremost an expression of this missional heart: "As the Father has sent me, so I send you."[14]

From this perspective, mission isn't one of the many activities that the church undertakes; the church itself is an expression of God's missional heart. The church's entire reason for existence is to be a faithful expression of God's missional purpose. This rethinking has two immediate implications. First, it challenges the institutional survival mind-set of the church. If the church isn't participating in mission, then why is its survival even important? Second, it causes the church to see its work in the context of the larger story of how God's missional heart is being expressed.

This second point has important implications for the built environment. One of the key questions that begins to flesh out this second implication is,

"What is God doing in the neighborhood?"[15] This question is meant to get the church thinking outside of its internal programs and survival and to consider the missional possibilities going on right outside of its doors. In asking the question of what God is doing in the neighborhood, we stumble into the ancient and widespread understanding of church as parish.

Historical Models

One of the most obvious places to go for thinking about Christian engagement in the actual public places of the city is the *parish* model. This model is most commonly found within the Catholic, Orthodox, and Anglican traditions, although it is found in other national Protestant churches as well.

A parish is a territorial unit that constitutes the jurisdiction of one particular church, over which one priest exercises spiritual authority. *Parish* can also refer to the active congregation of a particular church, but in many cases the geographical aspect of this term is quite strong. A resident of a particular parish may think of herself as connected to the parish church even though she doesn't attend worship services there. Likewise, many parish priests and congregants think about the needs and concerns of the people living within their parish regardless of whether they come to church or not.

I think that a church leader with a missional perspective might view the historical parish model with some ambivalence. On the one hand, to think of your church in terms of parish is to think of what God is doing in the neighborhood. On the other hand, church as parish usually implies a fairly high degree of cultural buy-in to the church as a central institution for the lives of the residents of a particular neighborhood. The missional church movement has been inspired to a large degree by the observation that strong cultural buy-in for the church is no longer central to people's lives. I do not think that a reconsideration of the parish model is likely to lead to any kind of wholesale recovery of this model; however, I do think that this model can open up our imaginations to new possibilities for the church.

An enticing example of the parish model in practice is the ancient tradition of *beating the bounds*. On Ascension Day, the parish priest and other leaders would lead a group of boys around the boundaries of the parish and beat out the boundary markers with boughs. Prior to modern surveying methods, this was an important way to prevent neighboring parishes from encroaching on territory. It was also important for the young boys to be involved so that the boundaries of the parish could be preserved from generation to generation.

The beating of the bounds perhaps suggests the fundamental contribution that the parish model could make to the local church. I think that it would be a highly productive exercise for a church to make a regular practice of defining its geographical footprint and then doing strategic thinking in terms of the needs and opportunities presented within that footprint. Such a practice would be more accurate and helpful the more it was informed by hands-on local knowledge. That is to say, the more that church members and leadership actually spent time within the footprint talking to people and observing with all of their senses, the greater would be their understanding of where God is at work in their parish.

Parish and Church Type

Obviously, the siting and layout of the embedded church offer many advantages for the church-as-parish model. However, it should be noted that church form alone does not correlate directly with parish thinking among the leaders or members of a church, nor must it constrain possibilities. That is to say, in our current climate it is often the embedded churches that have adopted a fortress mentality for their church and have made decisions that have created distance between the church and the parish. And, while many insular churches are geographically insulated from their surrounding community, some of the churches that are doing the most creative thinking about how to engage their neighborhoods are insular in their layout.

Church and Home as Parish

Again, given the various cultural forces at work, it is unlikely that the parish model as such will see widespread adoption by churches in the United States. That is to say, I don't expect to see very many churches draw the majority of their congregations from those who live within walking distance. However, I do believe that most churches and members of churches could benefit from learning to think in terms of parish.

As we've noted above, parish thinking in a very general sense has to do with accepting geography as a significant factor in faithfulness to God's call on our lives. A church can do this even if the majority of its members live more than a mile or two from the church building. It is, of course, extremely helpful if some members (and leaders) live within a mile or two of the church building. A church can identify those members and leaders and see them as key ambassadors for the church in the neighborhood. Insights from those neighborhood members can be especially valued when doing strategic planning. And the homes of those members can be used creatively as footholds to get members of the church who don't live in the neighborhood to experience the neighborhood on the ground.

I believe that another way the parish model can be meaningfully employed is to encourage people to think of their homes in terms of parish. Just as the church might regularly think about its mission in terms of the geographic footprint of the church building, so also can church members think about the geographic footprint of their homes as pertinent to their family's calling to be ambassadors in the neighborhood. In this sense, the church thinks and acts in terms of parish as a constant reminder and a training ground for every member to bring this kind of thinking back to his or her home and neighborhood.

Church and Civic Virtue

One of the most important contributions of the missional church movement and the historic parish model is to help churches overcome institutional myopia and to see the wider world as the setting for our calling as Christians. With regard to the built environment, this involves taking our geographic setting more seriously. However, we can consider the various ways the church can encourage care for the wider community in areas that are beyond the scope of the programs of the church. We can begin this exploration by revisiting the concept of civic virtue.

Schools of Civic Virtue

Once we begin thinking about the church as a model and training ground for a recovery of parish thinking among our members, we can widen our scope a bit and think about the church as a model and training ground for civic virtue in general. Ronald Thiemann makes this point persuasively in his book *Constructing a Public Theology*:

> Churches and synagogues have in the past helped to foster those "habits of the heart" that allowed for the development of a civic-minded, public-spirited citizenry. We can do so again if we develop a new vision of how excellence and compassion, self-interest and virtue, private gain and public good can once again be brought together. If churches can once again become "schools of public virtue," communities that seek to form the kind of character necessary for public life, then they can play an essential role in helping to forge a more compassionate but no less excellent vision of the American dream.[16]

Thiemann's instructive book explores the various ways that the preaching of the church as well as its liturgy can help to inspire and inculcate civic virtues among its members. While I agree with Thiemann's overall thesis, I also find him deficient in considering the ways that such an approach can be greatly enhanced through a more thoughtful engagement with the built environment.

One way to draw this insight out a bit is to expand our understanding of liturgy to include actions and practices that happen outside of the church walls. We can begin by thinking about the kinds of secular liturgies that are performed outside of the physical structure of the church and, in fact, completely independent of and often contrary to the mission of the church.

Secular Liturgies

We tend to think of *liturgy* as a very churchy word. And if we are evangelicals, we see it as a *high*-churchy word for a certain kind of Christian activity. And yet a case can be made that liturgy plays a much more important role in all of our lives than we may realize. In a recent book, James K. A. Smith argues that much of our identity and many of our core beliefs are formed less by our formal education than by the various liturgies in which we participate.

If we think of *liturgy* in the traditional sense of the term, this may be a very hard assertion for us to swallow. However, the liturgies to which Smith refers do not include the liturgy associated with Christian worship. Rather, Smith is speaking of the various secular liturgies that we encounter in everyday life. These liturgies include things like the shopping mall and the sporting event.[17]

The liturgy of the shopping mall teaches us about the importance of consumption to "solve" the problem of our imperfections as well as about the disposable character of the material world. We may recoil intellectually against the content of such "lessons," but if Smith is correct, the truths conveyed by these liturgies settle deep into our identity. Even good teaching, if it is restricted to the intellectual sphere, will not be able to counteract the impact of these societal lessons.

Smith proposes that if we are to have any hope of counteracting such falsehoods, it will be found in paying close attention to practices. Secular liturgies shape us because they are a kind of widespread cultural practice with a high degree of buy-in. If the church hopes to provide a viable alternative to these liturgies and their effects, perhaps the place to explore is within the realm of the church's liturgies. However, it is my conviction that such exploration needs to be expanded to the public spaces outside of the church proper.

Worship in the Built Environment

One way to connect the church liturgy to aspects of the built environment that exist outside of the reach of church programs is to focus our attention on the elements that are part of the worship event that do not remain in the church building throughout the week. With respect to these things, I will either ask, "How did they get here?" or "How will they leave this place?" The three practices that are revealed by this line of inquiry are the call to worship, the invitation to the table, and the dismissal. This way of thinking provides a helpful development of Lash's notion of performing the Scriptures that was introduced in chapter 2.

Call to Worship

The call to worship is understood as the beginning of the Protestant service of worship. Some churches will place announcements before the call to worship or practice new hymns or songs at this time, so as to bracket the service of worship and to indicate to the congregation an expectation of heightened attentiveness to the presence of God among the gathered community. It is understood that what happens between this call to worship and the end of the service does not contain the whole of one's experience of worship in any given week, but it does bracket our gathered worship in an important way.

While this is a useful way to focus the congregation's attention, it is also possible to think of the call to worship as actually happening earlier in the day. Many people either sleep in on Sunday morning or perhaps participate in alternative activities such as sports. In this cultural context, the committed member of the worshiping community gets up before a specific time and chooses particular clothes in light of the fact that he or she is being called to worship at a particular time and place.

Because this aspect of the call to worship is fixed by tradition, there is no need for any particular prompt to indicate the call. I know that worship begins at 10:30, so I plan to be ready and out the door by 10:00 every Sunday. But there are other traditions of calling to worship (both within and outside of the Christian community) that are more explicit. One can look to the tradition of church bells—or even to the use of the *adahn,* used in the Muslim community to call the faithful to *salah* (ritual prayer)—as a more tangible example of a call that extends all the way out to a person's home. If one thinks of literally being called to worship within earshot, it is reasonable to look at the route that the worshiper takes in response to the call as part of the gathered worship experience.

We noted in chapter 4 that the rhythm of weekly worship provides a regular reminder that time is a gift and that the cadence of our lives grows out of a fundamental relationship with our Creator. Such grounding in God's gracious invitation and the rhythmic conceptualization of time is more clearly proclaimed in churches that are embedded in the neighborhood. Persons walking to church *enact* the call to worship in the public space of the sidewalks leading up to the church according to specific rhythms of the ecclesial week as well as seasons of the ecclesial year. While it is very difficult to ascertain the destination of a car passing by on a freeway, people can give off a variety of clues to indicate that they are going to worship (note the example of Orthodox Jews). For this reason, I contend that the practice of walking to church can be a kind of bodily public proclamation of the faith.

This form of communication is not simply a unidirectional discourse, however. It is not simply a matter of Christians proclaiming something about what they believe. People walking to church also *engage* the other people and things that they encounter differently than they would while driving or riding in an automobile. This is significant when we consider Wolterstorff's contention that Christian worship represents a unique kind of gathering that invites rather than excludes interaction with one's life outside of worship: "Not much of the Christian liturgy would be left if we did in fact leave life in the world behind when we crossed the threshold into the place of the liturgy."[18]

What this means with respect to the call to worship is that when Christians respond to God's invitation to worship within the weekly rhythm, they not only gather disconnected bodies and minds but also bring into worship elements of the world outside of the church.

This observation is typically applied to the kinds of experiences that one has during the week preceding Sunday worship. One brings to worship concerns about one's family, one's coworkers, and the world at large. However, I contend that the practice of walking to worship potentially broadens the kinds of things and experiences that we can bring to worship. In a context for which weekly activities are often shaped by a person's social location (where he works, who his friends and family are, what he reads), and where the exposure a person has to the natural world is often buffered by modern technology (heating, air-conditioning, shelter), the corridor leading to church can expose that person to a wider world.

The worshiper who walks to worship greatly expands the kinds of impressions that can be brought into worship. The ambulatory worshiper picks up hundreds of visceral clues indicating that she is passing through a distressed neighborhood near the church. Or she notices that spring is on its way, with the appearance of tiny buds on the trees that line the streets, eluding the eyes seeing the trees at thirty miles per hour through tempered glass. All of these observations provide grist for a person's prayers and perhaps impetus for more robust singing of God's praises in the context of gathered worship.

Invitation to the Table

The experience of the Lord's Supper involves the conflation of three essential elements. There must be the elements of bread and wine, faithful congregants at the table, and the risen Lord made present through the Holy Spirit. To see this sacred event in terms of enacted space, we can talk about the church as the place where the event happens. The elements, the congregants, and the Lord are the props and people, respectively. And then we need to think about how these things move in time.

With each of the elements, we can ask, "How did they get here?" Although all three elements are essential, a case could be made that the risen Lord is the most significant of all the elements required for a celebration of the Lord's Supper. Certainly it is the one that has received the most theological attention over the past two millennia. However, the question of how (and in what form) the risen Lord is made present at the Lord's Supper is less instructive for our present consideration of the built environment.

When I ask the question, "How did they get here?" in reference to the congregation and the communion elements, it at first appears that I am repeating the question posed regarding the call to worship. However, upon further reflection, it can be asserted that relating this question to the sacrament brings out significantly different aspects of the question.

The question of the distribution of the elements, in the first place, involves another moment of physical (or at least volitional) locomotion. Within traditions where congregants come forward to receive the elements, this movement is a bit easier to see; however, even the more subdued experience of taking the elements from a tray and ingesting them involves one's making a decision to move from passive observation to appropriation. In both cases, one's posture, one's interaction with others sharing the experience, and the attitude of one's heart toward God indicate the manner by which this movement is being conducted.

A separate but related question has to do with how each participant in the sacrament "got here." We can think of this first in terms of salvation, in the sense of getting to a place of contrition for one's sins and faith in the lavish promises of the gospel. It is possible that for some participants the act of volition in coming forward to take and ingest the elements and the movement of affirming the claims of the gospel on one's life are one and the same motion—that is to say, in some cases the sacrament functions as a converting ordinance.

However, we can assume that for most participants, these movements have been separated both spatially and chronologically. I accepted Christ on July

8, 1978, and I receive the communion elements on Oct. 4, 2011. The question of "how I got here" is as much wrapped up with what happened in 1978 at it is with what happened in 2011. This gets at the larger story of each person's life. How did each one hear, see, and experience the message of the gospel in such a way that they were willing to accept its implications for their lives? Whether such implications have been fully realized or not, each person who appropriates the gospel story into his or her life gives assent that their primary identity is in the reconciling power of Jesus Christ. Other communally or biologically derived aspects of identity (race, gender, sexuality, regional characteristics) are important but secondary, and many achievement aspects of their identity (social status, career, external beauty) carry little or no ultimate significance in comparison.

Insofar as this is realized in the life of the individual, it may have some implications for the manner by which one gets to the Lord's table. Since one's primary identity is in Christ, one has to accept the fact that there are no hierarchies surrounding the table. Unlike the boarding of an airplane, where people are called forth according to the price category of their tickets, everyone who comes to the table is of equal status before God. Everyone who has accepted Christ should be invited to the table regardless of socioeconomic status or other external considerations.

A celebration of the Lord's Supper, therefore, almost always begins with an "invitation to the table." In my tradition, we make a special point to ensure that we recognize the breadth of that invitation by informing those gathered that one doesn't need to be a formal member of this church, but all who trust in Christ as their Savior are welcome around this table. This is a gracious statement, but it could lead to some more substantial issues if the sentiment behind such words were extended into the neighborhood.

Do all those who trust in Christ within the context of our geographic footprint truly feel welcomed, even invited, to this table? To hear the gracious words of invitation, they must first feel comfortable enough to come onto the church property and walk through the doors that separate the inside from the outside. To ask this question is to raise issues about the way the thresholds of our churches intersect with the neighborhoods as well as to ask about our role in building up the social capital in our neighborhoods.

As we have already noted with regard to one's home, there are relatively clear boundaries guarding access—if one is a member of the family, one can walk in at will; if one is not a member of the family, one must be especially invited. As we have noted in this context, a front porch or a low fence and a front gate can help reduce some of the barriers to entry. We could think about ways that the church could make itself more inviting. While maintaining this attitude may sound impossibly idealistic, such matters were of ultimate importance to Paul when he upbraided the Corinthian church for its practices of making social distinctions in the context of communally celebrating the Lord's Supper.[19]

The final question of locomotion that I will look at is that of how the elements get to the table. In my church, this responsibility is assigned to the deacons, who take turns bringing the bread to church. Typically, whoever has been given this responsibility on a given week will pick up the bread from a grocery store and bring it to church on Sunday morning. Because the juice or wine keeps longer, there is often a stock of this element kept at the church. So the bread, we can assume, follows the same route as the person responsible for bringing it as he or she responds to the call to worship on that day.

However, for both the bread and the wine, it is interesting to ask how they came to be at the grocery store. Most likely they arrived by truck from large processing plants outside of the region, while the grapes and the wheat arrived at the plants by way of truck from even farther away. In any case, the question of "how they got here" with regard to the bread and the wine most likely involves participation in and implicit consent to a set of labor practices and a transportation infrastructure that may or may not reinforce the claims of the gospel.

This might seem the most obscure of the three questions we have been asking about the communion elements, but it may lead to some interesting connections in certain neighborhoods. Within certain demographic groups, the local-food movement has gained popularity. This movement is very interested in local food networks and rethinking the routes that food takes from the farmer to the table of the consumers of the food. For a church to think about the food network of even the communion elements might help build a deeper connection to those who live in their general vicinity. However, irrespective of how such explorations may connect us to this community, I do think that local food networks provide lots of interesting possibilities for expanding social capital in our neighborhoods.

Dismissal

The final implied movement practice that I consider is the dismissal. The dismissal is typically understood as the end of the service of gathered worship. Some churches do follow the dismissal with a musical postlude, but the dismissal is where the gathered time of worship is considered to be officially ended. A common dismissal involves the pastor saying, "Go in peace and serve the Lord."

While there will be aspects that overlap, the dismissal should not be thought of simply as a reversal of the activities that together constitute a response to the call to worship. First, one hears the dismissal in a different communal context than one "hears" the call to worship. Thinking of church practices as extending beyond the realm of the church, one typically "hears" the call to worship at home and either alone or with one's family.

In contrast, one hears the dismissal more directly and in the midst of the covenant community. Second, if one allows for the possibility that one is changed by a fresh encounter with God's Word or with the sacraments, then one goes home a different person (or with a renewed understanding of the person one is in Christ) than the one who came to church. These two distinctions open up a number of possibilities as we consider the options for how a particular community might "go," how "in peace" could inform their movement, and what it means to "serve the Lord."

The first thing to notice is that the *go* is not qualified by a time reference. It is not "go tomorrow morning into the world," but simply *go*. The other thing to notice is that it is not an individualized command, but a communal injunction. There are different ways that we might think about what going into the world means to us as individuals versus what it means to members of a specific community.

The *direction* of the sending is more clear. Those who have heard and tasted the Word in worship are supposed to then go into the world in response to this experience. The Greek word for *world* in the New Testament can have a number of different connotations. It can refer to the entirety of creation, or it can refer to those people who are estranged from God. In either case, seen from the perspective of the Christian community, the world is more in the public realm of society than in the public realm of the church or in the private realm of the Christian family and friends. Again, this liturgical moment looks different when seen from the perspective of the built environment.

It would seem to comport with the scope, immediacy, and direction of the dismissal if the congregation collectively left the church building and immediately stepped into the public realm of the sidewalk in front of the church. If one supposes, further, that many of them are walking to their homes, one can imagine large clumps of congregants going in either direction and then fragmenting into smaller clumps with the passing of each block.

Compare this scenario with the more typical pattern in the insular church, where the congregants leave by way of a set of utilitarian doors facing the parking lot and remain on the church property until they reach the private sphere of their individual automobiles. In the parking lot, each individual or family unit is immediately separated from all other family units and individuals. The automobile shields the congregants from the public realm until they arrive safely at home. If the dismissal charge is remembered at all, it comes into play on Monday morning as the adults head off to work and the children to school.

Perhaps it is in the dismissal that the disconnect between the liturgy and the practices of the church is most glaring. Francis Mannion makes just this claim from a Catholic perspective:

> We need to take seriously one of the most neglected rites of all, the dismissal rite—which sends us on a sanctifying mission into the city. If we do not take the dismissal seriously in this respect, then the liturgy becomes, as the Old Testament prophets never tired of saying, false worship.[20]

Church as Agent of Redemption

This simple clarification of the connection between the dismissal and the actual world as it exists outside the doors of the church allows us to recover the original sense of liturgy as public work.

> Liturgy must be public rather than private, civic rather than domestic, cosmic and not merely psychological, natural and not simply spiritual. The Church and its liturgy do not exist in a place apart from the human city but as institutions in the midst of the city gracefully transfusing and redeeming its life. The liturgy is the unification of the New Jerusalem and the human city, so that in the process everything human is redeemed.[21]

If the church hopes to be an agent of redemption in the built environment, it needs to think more carefully about the various ways its members interact, not only within the walls of the church or in their private homes, but with the world that exists right outside of the church's doors.

For Further Reading

Bess, Philip. *Till We Have Built Jerusalem: Architecture, Urbanism, and the Sacred*. Wilmington, DE: ISI Books, 2006.

Cavanaugh, William T. "The World in a Wafer: A Geography of the Eucharist as Resistance to Globalization." *Modern Theology* 15, no. 2 (1999): 181–97.

Frazee, Randy. *The Connecting Church: Beyond Small Groups to Authentic Community*. Grand Rapids: Zondervan, 2001.

Guder, Darrell L., and Lois Barrett. *Missional Church: A Vision for the Sending of the Church in North America*. The Gospel and Our Culture series. Grand Rapids: Eerdmans, 1998.

Participation

Kieckhefer, Richard. *Theology in Stone: Church Architecture from Byzantium to Berkeley*. New York: Oxford University Press, 2004.

Kilde, Jeanne Halgren. *When Church Became Theatre: The Transformation of Evangelical Architecture and Worship in Nineteenth-Century America*. Oxford: Oxford University Press, 2002.

Loveland, Anne C., and Otis B. Wheeler. *From Meetinghouse to Megachurch: A Material and Cultural History*. Columbia: University of Missouri Press, 2004.

Rasmussen, Larry L. *Moral Fragments and Moral Community: A Proposal for Church in Society*. Minneapolis: Fortress Press, 1993.

Roxburgh, Alan J. *Missional: Joining God in the Neighborhood*. Grand Rapids: Baker Books, 2011.

Smith, James K. A. *Desiring the Kingdom: Worship, Worldview, and Cultural Formation*. Cultural Liturgies. Grand Rapids: Baker Academic, 2009.

Thiemann, Ronald F. *Constructing a Public Theology: The Church in a Pluralistic Culture*. Louisville: Westminster John Knox, 1991.

Turner, Harold W. *From Temple to Meeting House: The Phenomenology and Theology of Places of Worship, Religion and Society*. The Hague: Mouton, 1979.

Part III

Engagement

Not too long ago, a coalition of evangelical Christian leaders received quite a bit of media attention simply by raising the question, "What Would Jesus Drive?" in a number of popular periodicals. This campaign was intended as a moral challenge to the recent influx of SUVs on the streets of North America. The fact that this coalition included some fairly conservative Christian groups made this statement stand out among a growing chorus of voices concerned about the environmental impact of rampant petroleum use.

While I was (and am) largely in agreement with the instigators of the "What Would Jesus Drive?" campaign, I also see significant limitations to the approach taken by this movement. Yes, SUVs appear to be clear examples of poor stewardship of limited natural resources. And yes, Christians who wish to be good stewards of the earth should probably think about choosing a vehicle that uses resources more economically.

However, approaching the problem of the overuse of fossil fuels from the perspective of individual consumer choices (such as what kind of car one should purchase) seems to be a misdirection of our attention. If we are going to imagine Jesus in the twenty-first century and then think about what kind of car he might choose, we should at least be willing to take this logic a bit further. We may want to ask why in the United States we have built a world where Jesus would have to drive an automobile to participate in daily life at all. As we noted in chapter 1, the exurban development patterns that we have followed for the past half-century have, in most cases, made driving an absolute necessity for participation in everyday life. It's worth our asking the question of why this is so and whether this represents the kind of life Christ calls us to live.

If Jesus's "dwelling among us" means that he lives as we typically do, he would most likely be living in a subdivision at least a few miles from where he might interact with people in a quasi public setting—like a shopping mall or a grocery store. In this case, Jesus would need to own and operate some kind of automobile simply to have the kind of diverse interaction with people that we see him having in the Gospels.

This strikes me as a little odd. Rather than seeing this thought experiment as a critique of the private consumption choices of Christians, I tend to see it as a critique of the public choices of countries like the United States. Rather than asking, "What would Jesus drive?" I want to ask, "Why must Jesus drive?" Or, more to the point, what would Jesus think of the automobile-dependent lifestyle that we have spent the past half-century constructing?

The ability to shift our perspective from the narrow question, "What would Jesus drive?" to the broader, "Why must Jesus drive?" requires us to understand a bit more about the kinds of cultural critique in which we can raise such questions. In this introduction to the final section, we explore two common approaches to cultural critique in order to highlight the advantages of the approach we will employ to think about engagement with culture.

The two most common strategies for cultural critique are known as *applicationist* and *correlationist* approaches.[1] They can both be considered linear and unidirectional because they typically move in only one direction. The applicationist moves from Scripture to the world and the correlationist moves from the world to Scripture. As we shall see, neither of these approaches does an adequate job of helping us to think about engagement in the built environment.

Gordon Lynch provides a useful framework for evaluating methodologies that will help navigate some of the questions posed in the section above. Lynch begins by elucidating the applicationist model. When Christians comment on some cultural thing, either to praise or to critique it, they are most likely to use an applicationist approach.

The *applicationist* approach begins with a fixed schema of theological orthodoxy based on normative texts and (sometimes implicitly) received traditions for interpreting those normative texts. A cultural expression, then, is evaluated on the basis of whether it reinforces or contradicts theological orthodoxy. For instance, I believe that God values the institution of marriage and doesn't want to see covenant vows broken. On that basis, I might conclude that *The Horse Whisperer* is a bad book, because it downplays the broad range of consequences that normally accompany an extramarital affair.

The "What Would Jesus Drive?" campaign can be seen as an applicationist critique of culture. Within the broader evangelical community there is renewed interest in the stewardship of creation as a faithful expression of Christian discipleship. Since fossil fuels are a nonrenewable energy source, and because they may also play a significant role in global warming, evangelicals have become increasingly aware of consumer products that encourage heavy use of fossil fuels, and they can be critical of the users of those products.

Engagement

This is not an unfair criticism—SUVs do burn more fossil fuels than compacts. However, that SUVs are popular with the American consumer does not fundamentally explain why our per capita use of fossil fuels is so much higher than it is for people in almost every other country in the world. We can frame the issue this way. Imagine a citizen in Denmark who owns an SUV but who buys groceries at various neighborhood shops and takes the train to work. Now imagine an American who drives a Prius but lives in a subdivision that is forty miles from where she works and fifteen miles from the closest grocery store. In this scenario, the American will most likely burn a significantly greater amount of fossil fuels even though she may have purchased the high-efficiency car. In light of this scenario, we see that the question of what Jesus would drive doesn't allow us to get at the heart of the issue.

Of course, there are greater and lesser degrees of sophistication that can accompany the applicationist approach, but one persistent problem with this approach is that the relevant cultural expression is not often heard on its own terms before the critique is offered. In the case just examined, we know that there is a connection between our driving habits and our energy use; we just haven't done enough careful thinking about the specific conditions that contribute to our driving habits.

Another kind of weakness is that such a unidirectional approach doesn't allow the canon of theological orthodoxy to be examined for the cultural baggage that may be implicit in its own formulation. For instance, much theological orthodoxy in the West reflects some of the same cultural bias as does our culture as a whole. As we discovered in chapter 3, our perspective tends to be marked by a strong bias toward the decisions and actions of the autonomous individual when thinking about questions of theological ethics. This is why the "solution" to various environmental problems involves changes only at the level of individual consumer choice.

What it means to be an environmentally responsible American, from this perspective, is that you will purchase a Prius rather than purchase an SUV. To ask why we need to purchase a car at all is nonsensical, because it leads us toward community-level solutions. To choose to live without a car within your current context would also involve the availability of walkable communities and a good public transit system. Neither of these can be boiled down to a consumer choice for the individual. For these reasons, the possibility of living without a car rarely is entertained when Christians discuss ethical choices.

An alternative methodology for the purpose of cultural critique is the *correlationist* approach. This approach, popularized by Paul Tillich in his *Systematic Theology*, begins with a particular cultural phenomenon and seeks to identify the deep questions of existence inherent within it.[2] These questions then can be taken to the normative texts and traditions of a particular religious community for the purpose of seeking answers.

One place we tend to see the correlationist approach at work is in the context of youth talks. Typically, in an attempt to connect with her or his audience, a youth pastor will take some popular cultural artifact (a recent movie or song) and use it to raise a question for which an answer can be found in the Bible. The youth pastor understands the popularity of the movie or song with young people as an indicator that it expresses something that resonates with their thoughts and feelings.

As opposed to the applicationist approach, the correlationist approach requires the inquirer to "hear" the cultural expression on its own terms without too quickly imposing alien theological categories on it. The correlationist model has been criticized, however, as restricting the kinds of questions that we ask about various cultural phenomena. Correlationist questions tend to reflect the perspectives and biases of the social groups that ask them.

With respect to the questions pertinent to the built environment, a user of the correlationist model may ask: (1) what is the ideal environment for family life, and (2) what is the most convenient way for my family and me to meet our needs for employment, entertainment, socializing, and wellness? These may very well be the kinds of questions the Petersons from chapter 5 ask when considering a home purchase. While these questions represent heartfelt issues that many American families face, they also imply a particular approach to home and family life that may be challenged or reconsidered on the basis of an encounter with Scripture.

As we have seen, the form that these questions take reflects what Dolores Hayden would call the home-as-haven model. Within this model, the home is seen as a place where children are protected from society rather than as a setting from which children are prepared to engage and participate in society. This perspective prioritizes private life as well as the primacy of convenience in our everyday decisions. As we have noted, the question of the public significance of family life is notable more for its not being asked than for how it is implicitly answered for most American families. And to attempt to generate theological answers about home and neighborhood through this particular lens is already to narrow the kinds of answers that we might generate.

As unidirectional approaches, both the applicationist and the correlationist models for critiquing culture have significant limitations. The applicationist model allows one's particular theological framework to have too strong a voice and often doesn't adequately "hear" the cultural expression it is trying to critique or reflect critically on the cultural embeddedness of its understanding of orthodoxy. The correlationist model gives the values of a particular community such a dominant voice that it drowns out the witness of that community's authoritative texts.

Of more use to us as we consider engagement in the built environment is the *critical correlational model* developed by David Tracy, Don Browning, and others. The critical correlational model is useful here because it allows for the Christian community and the wider society to engage in a mutually critical conversation that can bring to light insights as well as limitations that are part of each tradition.[3]

The critical correlational model has four steps. The first step (called descriptive theology) begins with a "thick" description of a particular problem. We take time in this step to examine a cultural phenomenon in all of its complexity. The second step (or historical theology) takes soundings in relevant normative traditions for a particular community. We make sure we allow Scripture to address the questions that have emerged as well as the questions that haven't. The third step (or systematic theology) involves a mutually critical conversation between these two distinct realms. We should find in this step things to affirm and critique in both the cultural form and the ways that Scripture has been previously applied. The fourth step is to make recommendations based on the mutually critical conversation and to emerge with fresh questions to bring to the realm of church and society. These questions, then, provide another starting point to begin this process again.

What is most important about the critical correlational model is not necessarily following the steps in their exact order, but rather to understand the process of exploring various issues as a dynamic and dialogical process rather than a linear one. To avoid the shortcomings of the unidirectional approaches, one must be prepared to both listen to a particular question and examine the question that is being asked.

With regard to the built environment, we will discover that simply including things like town fabric or social capital in our thinking shifts the kinds of questions we ask and brings to light new insights as well as new questions. Hopefully, the other discovery that we will make is that our understanding of the built environment becomes more rich and nuanced as we put our books down and actually get out into our communities with our eyes and ears open. The critical correlational model does a particularly good job of recognizing the role of tacit knowledge in making sense of the built environment.

Ultimately, we employ the critical correlational model, not in order to gain a clearer understanding, but to be more faithful in our engagement with the built environment. Engagement has to do with our taking responsibility for the built environment within the context of the communities in which we participate. Engagement picks up the cultural-mandate thread described in the introduction, and it takes seriously our situation of already and not yet as we attempt to remain faithful while waiting for the coming eschaton.

As creatures who bear the image of God, we have been given special responsibilities in the created order. The built environment in which we live, work, worship, and play is not just a given; it is what it is partially as a result of decisions that we've made along the way. In this final section, we look at five lines of inquiry that will open up key areas where a built-environment perspective can be most helpful.

The exploration of engagement is spread out over two chapters. The first has to do with the "productive" work that goes on in the built environment. In this chapter, we explore issues of money, resources, and housing. The second chapter has to do with the "lighter" work that goes on in the built environment. In this section, we explore beauty and friendship in the built environment.

8

The Sustainable Environment

Sustainability

Sustainability is hot right now. Every conceivable product or service offered can instantly boost its public image by claiming the "sustainable" moniker. Not only is sustainability a significant issue in obvious realms, like agriculture, one doesn't have to look too hard to find it touted in everything from business practices to clothing. Even some cruise lines are claiming to be sustainable.

This growing interest in sustainability probably reflects some anxiety over the impact that humanity has had on the planet over the past few millennia. There is a concern that our use of resources has been accelerating to the point that we may be facing a severe shortage of key resources in the near future. Similarly, people are worried that we may exceed the planet's capacity to absorb the waste that is generated by the lifestyle to which we have grown accustomed.

Support for sustainability is a no-brainer. Who in their right mind would be opposed to sustainability? Is it even coherent to argue for unsustainability? Sustainability gets a bit more complicated, however, when you begin to think through the details.

In the first place, sustainability implies purpose. For instance, if preserving the earth's natural resources and minimizing waste were really the only goals, it would be perfectly coherent to adopt some kind of phase-out program for the human species. This would be easy enough to implement. It would involve no more than sterilizing all women of childbearing age for a generation or two. But I suspect that such an initiative would generate quite a lot of resistance.

Such a thought experiment reveals that as important a goal as it is, the sustainability of the earth in and of itself is not the only goal. Because the earth has been created by a God who created humans in God's image, gave them a special role among creation, and cares deeply for the human race, any realistic talk of sustainability will have to involve sustainability for current and future use and enjoyment by humans.

Another issue has to do with implementation. It wouldn't be too hard to devise a plan that would reduce the use of resources and minimize waste for the entire human species. The problem would lie in getting everybody to accept the plan and to adjust their lives according to its stipulations. There will always be a very small sector of the population concerned enough and motivated enough to voluntarily adjust its lifestyle to live more sustainably. But such actions by a small minority will not ultimately significantly reduce the impact the human species as a whole is having on the planet.

A final issue has to do with social stability. There are a number of ways to lessen humanity's impact on the planet that would involve minimizing social mobility. If we could just freeze people in their current socioeconomic status and do everything possible to maintain the status quo, we would probably end up using fewer resources and generating less waste than in the current system, where those who are lower on the socioeconomic ladder aspire to live like those who are higher on the ladder than they are and possibly to join the ranks of a higher class. But any such system would generate a great deal of disaffection and probably lead to violent upheavals among those stuck in the lower classes.

For these kinds of reasons, sustainability cannot realistically be pursued solely as a negative goal. That is to say, we aren't likely to succeed if we think of sustainability in terms of ceasing certain behaviors and placing limits on our lifestyles. True sustainability therefore must involve some accounting for what we *can do* and articulation of a lifestyle for the human species that is both responsible *and* not too distasteful. That is to say, we must be at least as articulate about what we are for as we are about what we are against.

This kind of thinking brings us back to the garden where humanity got its start. As we noted in the introduction, humans were placed in a garden and instructed to cultivate the land. In this setting, sustainability meant tilling the soil. It meant gathering and planting seeds. And it meant harvesting and processing crops. This was what shalom looked like when the human species got its start.

As we also noted, humanity didn't remain in the garden, but rather was removed from that setting and placed on a trajectory toward a different kind of environment. The ultimate destination of this trajectory was described, not as a garden, but as a city. Shalom in the sense of living in harmony with our God, with one another, and with the rest of creation would still be a viable concept. But the setting for shalom is now en route from a garden to a city.

The difference between the setting of the garden and the setting of the city involves more complex social structures, more sophisticated expressions of culture, and the development of a built environment as a setting for human thriving. As we move along this trajectory, cultivation looks different than it did in the garden. On this trajectory, faithful cultivation involves setting up rules and developing institutions for production, distribution, and enjoyment of the world's resources.

And it involves taking responsibility for the physical settings in which production, distribution, and enjoyment will take place. That is to say, it involves working with and contributing to the built environment. There is a lot that we don't know about what God intends for the ultimate future of creation. What we do know is that the ultimate setting for human thriving will at least include the cultural artifact that we know as the city. We do not need to assume that the city will be the only setting for human thriving (I, for one, envision a continued place for shalom in rural and wilderness settings), but we cannot ignore the city or see it as antithetical to God's purposes for humanity.

Therefore, we need to continue to explore the possibilities and prospects for shalom in the context of the built environment. And in doing so, we need to pay special attention to the role of the city in this pursuit. What we are to discover is that true sustainability is really another way of saying, "Seek the shalom of the city." In this chapter, therefore, we explore the idea of sustainability from three different angles: human thriving, environmental stewardship, and justice in the context of the city.

Human Thriving

Bike Lanes

The meeting had been called by the department of public works to provide details to the public concerning a massive roadway repair and improvement project in the neighborhood, as well as to solicit feedback from residents, business owners, and other interested parties. The roadway under consideration was the major route between the freeway and the east end of the city. It served as a convenient, if uninspiring, route. The road itself was too wide and pocked with potholes, but the more pressing issue was that the foundation that had held it up for over fifty years was giving way. The entire stretch of road was going to have to be completely rebuilt.

The city officials had decided to use this crisis as an opportunity to pursue a broader set of goals they had been developing for the built environment. They had spent the past few years sketching out plans and applying for grants and now had put together funding for an even more ambitious project. The current plan had ample sidewalks lined with trees and historic lampposts. It designated bike lanes on both sides of the road. And the planners had left room for tying into a light rail system if the city later could find the money to extend the current system.

The whole project was going to cost just under ten million dollars. It was an ambitious but exciting plan, and one could hear the enthusiasm in the planners' voices as they presented the details. However, the first person to ask questions of the plan was notably less enthusiastic.

"Have you collected any data on how many bicyclists travel this road?" was the first question from the public.

"No, sir, we don't have that data right before us."

"Well, I live on Sycamore Street, just across town. There are designated bike lanes on that street, and I've counted maybe five bicyclists on a good day."

"Thank you for sharing that with us. We will do our best to find out the answer to your question as we implement this project."

"That's fine, but what I'm getting at is whether it is worth all the added expense of including these bike lanes and lampposts. I'd wager that more than a couple of million dollars of this project is tied up in these doodads, and frankly I don't think that it is worth it. No one walks on this road, no one bikes on this road, and because of our climate, I don't think that people are going to—no matter how nice your bike lanes are. I think that you are just wasting the taxpayers' money."

It was probably not what the planners wanted to hear as the first question of the day, and, to be fair, it didn't represent the tenor of the meeting as a whole. But this gentleman (we'll call him Bill) was most likely not the only person holding this point of view. There were probably a great number of people in the community who felt that building things like bike lanes was a waste of money that could have been better spent elsewhere. Everyone in the community could benefit from jobs, road maintenance, and police services; only a very small minority of bicyclists benefit from bike lanes. Shouldn't government spending be focused on the more broadly shared needs?

The Purpose of a City

Let's begin by unpacking the question about bike lanes a bit further. Let's assume that Bill was not a libertarian or an anarchist and saw value in the city in which he lived and a legitimate purpose for the municipal government that oversees the operations of the city. Let's assume further that Bill accepted taxation as a legitimate way for the government to pay for certain goods that benefit the citizens of the city. In the example, we noted job creation, infrastructure, and police services as legitimate expenses.

We could infer from this brief list that Bill sees the city in which he lives as a setting for human thriving. Perhaps he moved to this city because of a job that he had been offered, and he remains in the city in his retirement because it provides access to the things and services that he and his wife require for the lifestyle that they enjoy, and it offers police and fire protection against the things that threaten that lifestyle.

His understanding of the purpose of the city is pretty straightforward. The city as an institution exists to mitigate risk by using resources to prevent and respond to fire and crime. Most of the other benefits of the city come from the private sector. Businesses provide jobs that provide the income that people need to live. And businesses provide the goods and services for which people can spend their income. Bill and his wife enjoy the variety of restaurants in their city as well as the good medical facilities. The government can best support the private sector by offering tax and other incentives to businesses as well as by maintaining the transportation infrastructure that businesses need to survive.

We can call this perspective minimalist, because it sees a fairly minimal role for municipal government. The government is needed to do a few things, and bike lanes are not legitimate uses of government time or taxpayer expense.

Thriving and the City

There is much that we can affirm about Bill's point of view. As we saw in chapter 4, one of the benefits of wisdom is human thriving. It is not hard to see how human thriving might involve at least some degree of material prosperity as well as protection from loss. This perspective offers some legitimacy of the role of municipal government to encourage economic growth and to provide various protections from loss.

From a built-environment perspective, this point of view also lends support to the city as a specific kind of setting for human dwelling and thriving. Harvard economist Edward Glaeser, in his book *The Triumph of the City*, argues that the city is humanity's greatest invention and is key to its present and future thriving.

> Cities, the dense agglomerations that dot the globe, have been engines of innovation since Plato and Socrates bickered in an Athenian marketplace. The

streets of Florence gave us the Renaissance, and the streets of Birmingham gave us the Industrial Revolution. The great prosperity of contemporary London and Bangalore and Tokyo comes from their ability to produce new thinking. Wandering these cities—whether down cobblestone sidewalks or grid-cutting cross streets, around roundabouts or under freeways—is to study nothing less than human progress.

In the richer countries of the West, cities have survived the tumultuous end of the industrial age and are now wealthier, healthier, and more alluring than ever. In the world's poorer places, cities are expanding enormously because urban density provides the clearest path from poverty to prosperity. Despite the technological breakthroughs that have caused the death of distance, it turns out that the world isn't flat; it's paved.[1]

So far, the insights provided by Glaeser could be seen to lend support to Bill's point of view. He too sees benefit in the city as a specific setting for human dwelling; that is why he has chosen to live in one. His perspective may, however, be challenged in two directions. The first is with regard to some of the specific ways that cities encourage prosperity. The second has to do with a more comprehensive understanding of human prosperity.

The Creative Class

Since the Industrial Revolution, economic growth in a region has largely been seen as a function of the discovery, extraction, and processing of various natural resources. In this view, corporations that perform these functions have been seen as important engines of economic growth. Cities that support the work of such corporations through tax incentives and relaxed environmental laws have been understood to be pro-business and therefore pro-growth.

Even though today, especially in the developed world, much economic growth does not involve the processing of raw natural resources, this perspective continues to predominate. Cities that make all kinds of concessions to large corporations continue to be thought of as pro-growth and encouraging of job creation. This perspective is often set in opposition to "tree huggers" and other elitist groups (such as bike commuters), who are seen to be blocking corporate interests and economic growth.

Richard Florida contends that this perspective is outdated and even potentially inhibiting to economic growth.[2] Florida believes that in the information age, the real engine of economic growth is not the extraction of natural resources or even large corporations per se. Florida argues, rather, that what is needed for economic growth is the highly skilled work force that he calls the creative class. Successful companies are interested in locating in places that have a good supply of creative-class workers, even in places to which creative-class workers would be willing to relocate:

> It's often been said that in this age of high technology, "geography is dead" and place doesn't matter any more. Nothing could be further from the truth: Witness how high-tech firms themselves concentrate in specific places like the San Francisco Bay Area or Austin or Seattle. Place has become the central organizing unit of our time, taking on many of the functions that used to be played by firms and other organizations. Corporations have historically played a key economic role in matching people to jobs, particularly given the long-term employment system of the post–World War II era. But today corporations are far less committed to their employees, and people change jobs frequently, making the employment contract more contingent. In this environment, it is geographic place rather than the corporation that provides the organizational matrix for matching people and jobs. Access to talented and creative people is to modern business what access to coal and iron ore was to steelmaking. It determines where companies will choose to locate and grow, and this in turn changes the way cities must compete. As Hewlett-Packard CEO Carly Fiorina once told this nation's governors, "Keep your tax incentives and highway interchanges; we will go where the highly skilled people are."[3]

We discovered in chapter 2 that place is an important aspect of a meaningful human life; here we find out that place may play a role in material prosperity. This perspective on what is known as "the new economy" leads Florida to ask what kinds of places are attracting the creative class. And what he is finding is that the creative class is attracted to cities that are vibrant and interesting, places where they can enjoy free time with friends and family in attractive settings.

Therefore, a city that encourages development by relaxing its environmental laws to the extent that there are no longer any attractive wilderness areas for its citizens to explore may be supporting one kind of economic growth while inhibiting another, more important kind of growth. Similarly, a city that fails to spend money on bike lanes and other urban amenities, in order to maximize the tax breaks it can give to corporations, may be preventing other corporations from relocating to their area.

Thriving Health and Safety

Another way that Bill's perspective can be challenged has to do with adopting a broader definition of human thriving. As we have seen, if Bill thinks about human thriving as a metric for evaluating the purpose of the city, he does so in a minimalist way. Thriving, from his perspective, has to do with how much money one has to buy goods and services (good salary and low taxes) and how protected one is against loss (police, fire, and medical facilities).

However, one can think about thriving as more than just money in one's pocket and mitigating the risk of loss. We can begin expanding our thinking by considering the case of health. One could think of an area in which good health will be preserved as a place with good medical facilities. However, another way to think about health is to consider the ways that the places we live encourage healthy practices.

There has been a great deal of research done in the past decade on the connection between the built environment and public health. It turns out that automobile-dependent development correlates strongly with obesity, diabetes, and depression. Denser development that encourages a full range of transportation options (such as bike lanes) correlates with significantly better health.

In a similar vein, one could think about bodily protection, not just in terms of how equipped the police are to respond to violent crime and the fire department to residential fire, but in terms of how likely we are to be injured or killed in an automobile accident. As noted in chapter 1, what poses the greatest possibility of injury and death is not fire or violent crime, but rather accidents involving automobiles.

This observation leads to a careful consideration of the two fundamentally different kinds of street layouts that we have seen in the past century. In turns out that the traditional grid is a great deal safer than the exurban cul-de-sac and arterial pattern. This makes sense, since the gentle curves of the exurban model allow faster automobile travel, and the wider roads put pedestrians in harm's way for a greater distance.

One discovery that is less intuitive, however, has to do with bike lanes. It probably won't surprise anyone to discover that bike lanes make it safer to ride a bicycle in a particular area. It may not even be a total surprise to discover that the more bicycles there are in a particular area, the safer it is for all bicyclists. Drivers who expect to encounter bicyclists on the road tend to pose less of a risk to the bicyclists that they cannot see.

What is surprising is that the more bicyclists there are in a particular area, the safer it is for everyone, whether or not they happen to be riding a bicycle.[4] Drivers tend to drive slower and be more attentive to what is going on in the street when they see bicycles around. Areas with higher bicycle use see fewer accidents involving cars hitting bicycles, fewer accidents involving cars hitting pedestrians, and fewer accidents involving cars hitting other cars. This research suggests that Bill may stand to benefit from living in a more bike-friendly community than he ever supposed.

Environmental Stewardship

Common Perceptions

The staff retreat for a national environmental advocacy group had just gotten started. "Let's begin by getting together a few sketches to help us visualize our target," the consultant suggested. "We'll start by trying to get a lock on the population with whom we can most easily partner. Where do they live?"

"Vermont."

"OK. What are their houses like?"

"That would be a LEED-certified house constructed from straw bales and fully loaded with high-tech conservation equipment."

"What other things do we see around the house that demonstrates their care for the environment?"

"They have a Prius in the driveway . . . no, two Priuses."

"Their Priuses are in the driveway because the whole garage is dedicated to recycling-sorting bins."

"What do these people do in their spare time?"

"They listen to NPR and they go on long walks in the wilderness preserve behind their house."

"Great, this is the face of our donor base. Now, who are we trying to reach? Where do they live?"

"New York City."

"What evidence do we have that they care about the environment?"

"Almost none. Most of their time is spent on and surrounded by concrete. They rarely spend time enjoying nature. They live in a very old building with an outdated furnace. And they don't think to look for a recycling bin before they throw an aluminum can away."

The Greenest Place in America

The case study above betrays a deep-seated bias within mainstream environmentalism as well as within the wider culture. It is thought that cities and urban life represent the greatest threat to the environment and, further, that what it means to be environmentally responsible is to live as far (geographically and culturally) from the city as possible. David Owen asserts that this bias is not only unfair, but also patently untrue.

Using New York City as his case study, Owen shows that this teeming agglomeration of humanity is by far America's greenest city. To be sure, New York City uses a tremendous amount of resources and generates a lot of waste.

However, what is less often considered is that New York is home to eight million people, which is about thirteen times as many people in the entire state of Vermont.

Looking at resource use from a per capita basis, Owen makes some surprising discoveries:

> Most Americans, including most New Yorkers, think of New York as an ecological nightmare, a wasteland of concrete and garbage and diesel fumes and traffic jams, but in comparison with the rest of America it's a model of environmental responsibility. In fact, by the most significant measures, New York is the greenest community in the United States. The most devastating damage that humans have done to the environment has arisen from the burning of fossil fuels, a category in which New Yorkers are practically prehistoric by comparison with other Americans, including people who live in rural areas or in such putatively eco-friendly cities as Portland, Oregon, and Boulder, Colorado. The average Manhattanite consumes gasoline at a rate that the country as a whole hasn't matched since the mid-1920s, when the most widely owned car in the United States was the Ford Model T. Thanks to New York City, the average resident of New York state uses less gasoline than the average resident of any other state, and uses less than half as much as the average resident of Wyoming. Eighty-two percent of employed Manhattan residents travel to work by public transit, by bicycle, or on foot. That's ten times the rate for Americans in general, and eight times the rate for workers in Los Angeles County. New York City is more populous than all but eleven states; if it were granted statehood, it would rank fifty-first in per-capita energy use, not only because New Yorkers drive less but because city dwellings are smaller that other American dwellings and are less likely to contain a superfluity of large appliances. The average New Yorker (if one takes into consideration all five boroughs of the city) annually generates 7.1 metric tons of greenhouse gases, a lower rate than any other American city, and less than 30 percent of the national average, which is 24.5 metric tons; Manhattanites generate even less.[5]

What is especially interesting about the case of New York City is not just that its environmental record comes as such a surprise, but what it says about the role of the built environment versus individual choice in environmental sustainability. New Yorkers, for the most part, don't seem to care about the environment particularly, and yet they happen to live in a setting that has evolved historically into an environment particularly well suited for human habitation. We explore the implications of these observations after a brief excursus establishing the scriptural basis for environmental concern.

Biblical Stewardship

As noted in the introduction, the third creation mandate from Genesis 1:28 involves stewardship of the earth and its creatures: "have dominion over the fish of the sea and over the birds of the air and over every living thing that moves upon the earth." Although there have been times in human history when "exercising dominion" over creation involved little more than the careless exploitation of the natural world, now it is more clearly understood that dominion involves the careful use, cultivation, and protection of the world and the rest of the created order.

The word that is most commonly used to describe what dominion looks like in action is *stewardship*. A steward is someone who takes care of and manages something that doesn't belong to him or her. A steward is accountable to the owner of the resource and is likely to be called to give an accounting for how well the resource has been managed. Such an accounting will not involve how closely the steward's actions conformed to her or his own values and standards, but rather how the steward's actions conformed to the values and standards of the owner.

The Bible provides a firm foundation for environmental stewardship. In Psalm 24:1, we are reminded that the creation belongs not to ourselves but to God: "the earth is the Lord's and all that is in it." We are to tenderly care for creation as the Lord tenderly cares for creation:

> You make springs gush forth in the valleys;
>   they flow between the hills,
> giving drink to every wild animal;
>   the wild asses quench their thirst.
> By the streams the birds of the air have their habitation;
>   they sing among the branches.
> From your lofty abode you water the mountains;
>   the earth is satisfied with the fruit of your work.[6]

As disciples of Jesus Christ, Christians have additional reasons to care for creation. Our Lord participated in the creation of the world, died to reconcile creation to the Creator, and helps hold all of creation together:

> He is the image of the invisible God, the firstborn of all creation; for in him all things in heaven and on earth were created, things visible and invisible, whether thrones or dominions or rulers or powers—all things have been created through him and for him. He himself is before all things, and in him all things hold together. He is the head of the body, the church; he is the beginning, the

firstborn from the dead, so that he might come to have first place in everything. For in him all the fullness of God was pleased to dwell, and through him God was pleased to reconcile to himself all things, whether on earth or in heaven, by making peace through the blood of his cross.[7]

Just as we look forward to experiencing the fullness of the redemption purchased by Christ on the cross, so also the creation looks forward to being redeemed.

For the creation waits with eager longing for the revealing of the children of God; for the creation was subjected to futility, not of its own will but by the will of the one who subjected it, in hope that the creation itself will be set free from its bondage to decay and will obtain the freedom of the glory of the children of God. We know that the whole creation has been groaning in labor pains until now.[8]

While this is clearly implied in the verse above, as we consider the implications of this journey from the garden to the city, it is important to realize that the nonhuman creation (plants and animals) has a place not only in the garden but also in the city.

Then I saw a new heaven and a new earth; for the first heaven and the first earth had passed away, and the sea was no more.[9]

On either side of the river is the tree of life with its twelve kinds of fruit, producing its fruit each month; and the leaves of the tree are for the healing of the nations.[10]

American Environmentalism

Having established environmental stewardship as an important part of our vocation as human creatures with a special responsibility for the rest of creation, we can return to the example of New York City. The question that we need to ask now is not why New York City is the greenest community in America, but why it is so hard for us to see the environmental benefits of New York, and why it will be difficult to get people to see it as a model of environmental efficiency.

Antiurbanism

The first answer to this question has to do with a decidedly antiurban bias in the American psyche. Thomas Jefferson famously dismissed cities as injurious to our well-being:

I view great cities as pestilential to the morals, the health and the liberties of man. True, they nourish some of the elegant arts, but the useful ones can thrive elsewhere, and less perfection in the others, with more health, virtue and freedom, would be my choice.[11]

Engagement

Similarly, we look to Henry David Thoreau and his Walden Pond experience as the quintessential morality tale. To escape the filth and crowds of the city for the pure setting of the wilderness is spiritually cleansing.

Rather than accepting the possibility that the city, as a human artifact, represents a great deal of wisdom concerning how people can live together efficiently, we have prejudged it as a place of decadence, evil, and waste. Such an antiurban bias may also represent a rejection of the unique role that humans play within the created order. We seem to think that what it means for humans to live more harmoniously in creation is to disguise the fact that we adapt nature for our purposes, and rather attempt to imitate the nonhuman creation as much as possible. As Daniel Lazare observes,

> Green ideology is a rural agrarian ideology. It seeks to integrate man into nature in a very kind of direct, simplistic way—scattering people among the squirrels and the trees and the deer. To me that seems mistaken, and it doesn't really understand the proper relationship between man and nature. Cities are much more efficient, economically, and also much more benign, environmentally, because when you concentrate human activities in confined spaces you reduce the human footprint, as it were.[12]

From this observation we can assert the importance of not overinterpreting all that dominion implies, but not underinterpreting it, either. To be good stewards of the earth and the rest of creation, we need to accept the fact of human intervention and imprint on the natural world.

Individualism

A second reason that Americans have a hard time accepting New York as a model of environmental stewardship is that it doesn't fit very well with our deep commitment to individualism. Most of the efficiencies of New York City have to do with the way that the form of the city shapes the coordinated activities of its residents. The density of living conditions makes walking to many destinations feasible, because when there are 67,000 people living within one square mile, it is likely that the good or service that you need will be provided within a few blocks. Similarly, that many people living in close proximity means that a good public transit system and an army of taxis can be provided and used throughout the day. Electricity use is low because, as Owen observes about his life in New York, "heat escaping from our apartment helped to heat the apartment above ours."[13]

This type of collective solution is problematic for Americans on a couple of levels. We tend to resent anything that appears to restrict the individual choices that we may want to make at any particular time. Skeptics might point out that if more places became like New York, many Americans would be virtually denied their right to an automobile and a backyard.

But even within the logic of this way of thinking, it is not entirely clear how best to maximize one's freedom. As Charles Komanoff points out, "New Yorkers trade the supposed convenience of the automobile for the true convenience of proximity."[14] An automobile does offer a certain kind of freedom, but it can also be a burden to be constantly responsible for a couple of tons of steel that needs to be maintained and safely parked at all times. Some of my greatest experiences of freedom of mobility have been when spending time in a city with a good public transit system. I can move easily from one part of the city without getting lost and can change my mind on a whim without worrying about parking or finding a gas station.

In any case, even if there were universal recognition of the environmental benefits of a place like New York, it is unlikely that this model would be universally adopted. What would be beneficial is if more cities were to unapologetically embrace their high-density urbanism so that the option of living in that way would be viable for more Americans.

What is problematic for Americans about extolling the urban way of life in New York City as a possible solution to the environmental problem is that it confronts us with the uncomfortable reality that we cannot have it all. We cannot have maximum freedom for automobile travel *and* have a decent public transit system at the same time. We cannot have space for every possible thing our heart desires *and* keep our energy use at a worldwide sustainable level. Rather than face these hard choices head-on, many of us would rather have our environmental responsibility packaged as a consumer good. It's more convenient to have the large house that is far away from everything and to then drive a Prius to assuage our guilt. Even better is to do something really wasteful like fly a private jet and then offset the waste by purchasing carbon credits. If we really care about environmental stewardship, we need to be prepared to take the role of the built environment in general and cities in particular seriously as an important component of managing precious resources wisely.

Justice in the City

Displacement

Kimberly and Robert Lawrence met during their third year at a Christian college. They got married soon after graduation and were praying about where to set up their new life together. They felt a strong calling to make a difference in a disinvested neighborhood in an inner city, and when they shared this idea with their small group, they found that two other couples strongly resonated with their sense of call.

Within a few months, the group had pinpointed the neighborhood to which they would commit their energy, and each couple had found a reasonably priced home on the same block. This wasn't hard to do, since about 40 percent of the houses in the neighborhood were vacant. Each of the houses needed a lot of work, but they were all beautifully designed and well constructed. In time, the couples had managed to restore the architectural dignity to each house. They also fixed up their yards and maintained vibrant flower beds throughout the summer.

The couples were financially supported by donations from friends and family, so they were able to spend a lot of time helping to keep the neighborhood clean, setting up a block watch program, and starting an after-school tutoring program in their homes. In time, the tutoring program led to them advocating for a charter school in the neighborhood, which got started just as they began to have children of their own.

Over time, one saw evidence of change in the neighborhood. Vacancy rates had dropped dramatically, and more and more lawns were well kept and flower beds tended. As might be expected, rents in the neighborhood started going up, as did property taxes for homeowners. It wasn't long before two of the apartment buildings were sold and the new owners converted them into condominiums.

Brian Lees, an elderly gentleman who lived in one of those buildings, couldn't find a new rental in his price range so he had to move to another neighborhood seven miles away. He had lived in his former neighborhood for over fifty years and had lots of friends and relations within walking distance there. In his new neighborhood he was a stranger. He had met the Lawrence family a few times and thought that they seemed like nice people. But he wished that they'd never moved into his neighborhood.

Gentrification is the popular name given to this increasingly common pattern. More and more people of means are choosing to live in urban neighborhoods. Some, like the Lawrences, have ministry motivations, others simply like the character of the houses and lifestyle of the older urban neighborhoods, and still others can tell a good investment when they see one. But, in many cases, the impact appears to be the same. People without means have their lives disrupted as they are displaced to the next place where no one wants to live.

At some level, this seems to be a question of justice. We recognize that people with more financial means are able to purchase fancier things than those of lesser means. Because the Lawrences were born into families of a higher socioeconomic class than Brian Lees, does that then mean that he doesn't get to feel settled in his home when he follows all the rules and never even is late with his rent? It doesn't seem just.

We explore questions that arise from this case study as well as other issues involving justice in the built environment after a brief sketch of a biblical perspective on justice.

A Theology of Justice

The term *justice* has seen better days. There is a clothing store by that name that targets the preteen set and that represents the first couple of hits when one performs a web search for the term. The fact that a clothing store with no apparent commitment to the concept of justice could get away with claiming this name may signal that this word has become, for all intents and purposes, meaningless within our popular culture.

However, in the witness of Scripture, justice is upheld as a rich and highly significant concept. It is, first of all, a characteristic of the God we worship.

> The LORD is king! Let the earth rejoice;
>   let the many coastlands be glad!
> Clouds and thick darkness are all around him;
>   righteousness and justice are the foundations of his throne.[15]

This text also demonstrates a second important aspect of biblical justice: justice is associated with righteousness and truth. That is to say, justice has a specific content. It is very common in our culture to think of justice solely in terms of fairness. If there is a "level playing field" and an "open and transparent" process, we tend to think that justice has been done regardless of the outcome.

But this is not, apparently, God's way of seeing things. God is interested in people getting what they deserve—or at least getting enough to maintain dignity and well-being: "learn to do good; seek justice, rescue the oppressed, defend the orphan, plead for the widow."[16]

God calls us to pursue justice especially for the poor and most vulnerable members of our society. This mandate for justice even extends to how we use our land and build our homes:

> Ah, you who join house to house, who add field to field, until there is room for
> no one but you, and you are left to live alone in the midst of the land![17]

From this brief sketch, we can draw a couple of preliminary conclusions about justice in the built environment. Because God is a just God, he cares not only that humanity in general has a place in which to thrive but also that all people have the opportunity to find a good place in which to live in the land. God does not approve of those who have the power or the means to maximize the space for their dwelling to such a point that it prevents others from finding a decent place to live. This is true regardless of the legal or political rationale the wealthy and powerful can marshal to justify their action.

Gentrification

Euclid on the Poor

Before we can really address the question of the justice of gentrification, we need to recognize that questions of justice in the American neighborhood didn't begin with the gentrification debates of the past couple of decades. A closer reading of *Euclid v. Ambler* gives us an interesting glimpse into the moral foundations of the American neighborhood. And it is especially interesting to note these foundations in light of what we know about God's commitment to justice.

As you may recall from chapter 1, one of the driving forces behind the *Euclid* decision was the well-being of children. A closer reading reveals that perhaps only children of a certain socioeconomic class are considered. In explaining why it is acceptable to prohibit apartment buildings from existing on the same block as detached single-family homes, Justice Sutherland provides the following rationale:

> Very often the apartment house is a mere parasite, constructed in order to take advantage of the open spaces and attractive surroundings created by the residential character of the district. Moreover, the coming of one apartment house is followed by others, interfering by their height and bulk with the free circulation of air and monopolizing the rays of the sun which otherwise would fall upon the smaller homes.[18]

Given all of the other language about protecting children, one commentator quipped, "one wonders, given the omission, whether Justice Sutherland knew children were raised in apartment buildings."[19]

Frankly, I'm not sure that he did. However, the point of this justification comes across loud and clear. Zoning, from its inception, can be seen as a tool for protecting the home as a setting for private consumption for middle- and upper-income members of the community.

Income Segregation

One of the first things that this look at *Euclid v. Ambler* (as well as the gentrification issue) brings to mind is that the question of neighborhood may be as significant to one's experience of home as one's individual dwelling unit. We see in *Euclid v. Ambler* that one concern behind the decision to allow zoning wasn't simply to protect certain neighborhoods from urban ills such as industrial enterprise, but also to protect middle-class families from poor families.

It took some time for this to get comprehensively worked out at the policy level. The zoning code adopted in *Euclid* disallowed apartment buildings to be built in the same neighborhoods as single-family residences. This helped to ensure that families of very different means wouldn't live on the same block. Over time, however, such income segregation would become quite pronounced. We have come to expect strict income segregation in every exurban neighborhood. By using tools such as low-density zones that require one house per five acres, developers now build housing units for fine gradations of income level. It is interesting how appalled we are to discover how recently certain neighborhoods were racially segregated yet see no particular issue with the income segregation that has become a standard feature of American life.

Before considering the current issue of gentrification, we must realize how entrenched income segregation has become in our understanding of how neighborhoods function. For most of the twentieth century, we have allowed or encouraged the practice of cordoning off the poor to less desirable neighborhoods. From the 1960s through the 1990s, this often meant that the poor had to remain in crumbling urban areas (or dysfunctional urban renewal projects), while the middle class and wealthy fled to the exurbs. Now that cities are becoming popular again, this same story seems to be playing out in a different context. Those with means now want to live in the city, and those without are being relegated to the exurbs.

Gentrification Reconsidered

While it is true that many people from the middle and upper classes are now choosing to live in urban neighborhoods, and that many people from the lower class are finding their most economical housing option in the crumbling first-rung exurbs, the story is not as straightforward as it may seem. The popular understanding of gentrification is that there are these very stable urban neighborhoods of renters and owners who have lived there for a long time. When these neighborhoods start to become fashionable and wealthier people begin to purchase homes there, home values go up, rents go up, apartments get converted to condominiums, and all of the people who were living in the neighborhood are forced by economic reasons to relocate.

While there is no shortage of anecdotal evidence to back up this narrative, this story does not hold up to more careful analysis. Lance Freeman, a professor of urban planning at Columbia University, recently conducted a major study that challenges the details of this story.[20] In the first place, he notes, older urban neighborhoods are not as stable as we think. There is a lot of transition in urban neighborhoods even before gentrification rears its ugly head. In the second place, while gentrification does cause displacement for some residents, gentrifying neighborhoods in general become more stable than they were before. That is to say, residents who lived in the neighborhood before gentrification tend to remain in the neighborhood longer as it gentrifies.

The issue, it seems, is that many people don't really want to live in a blighted neighborhood. People are always looking for opportunities to move to a slightly less blighted neighborhood, and when they find a good deal somewhere else or get a promotion at work, they jump at the opportunity to move. When a neighborhood begins to experience new investment, residents who have already been living in the neighborhood have an incentive to stay, and they often can find creative ways to do so.

When thinking about gentrification, we also need to consider the alternatives. In some ways the logic behind the anti-gentrification argument is disturbing. The argument seems to be that we should keep certain neighborhoods dangerous, dirty, and ill maintained so that no one who has the means to live anywhere else would choose to live there. If this is the best way to achieve stability for certain neighborhoods, then this is indeed a sad state of affairs.

If we define gentrification simply as investment, then I think that it is not helpful to simply be against gentrification. If our concern has to do with the displacement of people who want neighborhood stability, it seems to make more sense to be opposed. There may be a number of ways that don't involve forbidding new investment to give residents an opportunity to stay in a neighborhood.

Part of what makes us suspicious of gentrification is our recent history with "urban renewal." Because ample funding was available and legal precedent in place, many cities declared neighborhoods to be "blighted" when they weren't. At that time a neighborhood could be slated for destruction because of density of population or the age of the buildings. This clearly was a mistaken and harmful initiative.

This recent history causes us to be skeptical of claims of blight as well as a bit romantic about the kinds of neighborhoods that are now being gentrified. Because of economic shifts and ill-conceived policies, we now have a number of urban neighborhoods that really are in need of new investment. And we have protections in place now that did not exist during the period of urban renewal. The historic preservation movement has helped us to see the value of old buildings in a neighborhood, and the New Urbanist movement has helped us see that density is not necessarily a bad thing. This means that charming apartment buildings, houses, and public spaces are no longer being wantonly destroyed.

Another issue to consider is how the current movement of the middle and upper classes into urban neighborhoods is not exactly the same story as when people of means moved out of those neighborhoods from the sixties through the nineties. When the middle and upper classes moved into the exurbs, they were moving into areas that structurally required income segregation. All the houses in the neighborhood were invariably of similar scale and price range.

As the middle and upper classes move back into urban neighborhoods, they are moving into areas that are likely to have large houses and modest studio apartments on the same block. Sure, there are many neighborhoods in which both the fancy house and the studio apartment are too expensive for many people, but that is simply an issue of supply and demand. There are simply not enough modest apartments in charming urban neighborhoods, and so the price on this kind of housing option becomes temporarily inflated. If this is how we understand the problem, then the solution is to encourage more neighborhoods to gentrify so that the cost of living in this kind of neighborhood goes down.

Justice in the Built Environment

Gleanings

If zoning has had the overall effect of making neighborhoods less just by restricting access to certain areas to a particular class of people, the question is, how to we rectify this situation? Justice concerns with respect to our living arrangements often focus on the level of the private residence—or housing. We need to eradicate homelessness, some will maintain. Others will ask about the fairness of a wealthy person having a large home, while a poor person has a small home. These questions quickly tap into our basic political convictions about the private ownership of land.

However, when we think in terms of the neighborhood instead of just the home, this question becomes more nuanced. One of the ways that the Bible maintains justice is to require that landholders leave gleanings behind so that the poor can share to some extent in the bounty of their land: "You shall not strip your vineyard bare, or gather the fallen grapes of your vineyard; you shall leave them for the poor and the alien: I am the LORD your God."[21]

It is not being suggested in this passage that the owner of the vineyard should sell his property and distribute it to the poor, but rather that he should leave the boundaries and liminal spaces of his vineyard alone, so that the poor can derive some spillover benefit from his wealth.

What I am suggesting here is that we consider the notion of some acceptable level of diversity with regard to different people's private domiciles. But at the same time, we can think of the neighborhood or the spaces in between the houses as the gleanings from which those with fewer financial resources could benefit. The question of justice for the poor with regard to land use so often is expressed simply as a demand for more and better affordable housing. What I am suggesting is that we widen our scope just a bit and think about access to a good neighborhood for everyone as a requirement of justice. In countries where the public realm is more vibrant, there is much less concern with having a large and well-equipped private home; people enjoy the amenities of the public realm.

When development strategies exclude all poor people from a particular neighborhood, they are being denied access to the "gleanings" of a dignified experience of neighborhood life. It may be that we should be less concerned with the size or grandeur of individual houses, and more concerned with how accessible neighborhoods are to a broad representation of social classes.

So, if I had to stick my neck out and suggest a justice imperative with regard to neighborhoods, what I would suggest is an end to "housing-type" exclusive zones where we have one zone for big houses and another zone for condos and apartments; rather, we would have a mix of them on the same block. I would also question the justice of gated neighborhoods. And I would question homes on five-acre lots unless people are growing crops on them, because they fail to leave any kind of common space for those who can't afford to live in a large house.

Public Transit

Another area in which an understanding of the dynamics of the built environment could lead to justice for the poor has to do with investment in public transit. As has been noted, one of the primary ways that injustice has increased in the built environment over the past fifty years is directly related to automobile-dependent development. People who are too poor, too old, too young, or too infirm to own and operate a car are excluded from full participation in society.

In addition to being unjust to these population groups, automobile-oriented development is very wasteful from an environmental standpoint. So far, ideas and innovations having to do with technologies that make automobiles more efficient seem to generate the most excitement. However, things like hybrid cars and electric vehicles, even when they work, tend to be far out of the price range for most of the population. Having a minority of the population driving highly fuel-efficient cars will most likely not have a significant impact on our overall energy use or considerably reduce emissions.

By far the best investment we could make of public funds and private initiative would be to vastly improve our public transit system. A good public transit system serves a much wider range of the population than does automobile-oriented development, and it can bring real environmental benefit as well. A good public transit system also helps support other urban amenities. Major public transit hubs tend to attract higher-density development. And walkable neighborhoods become more viable when public transit increases the pedestrian population in an area. Public transit also has been demonstrated to correlate with better health, as people tend to walk a bit farther during the day as they go from home to bus stop to home again.

Urban Bill of Rights

As we conclude this section on justice, it may be interesting to examine one attempt to articulate what advocacy for justice in the built environment might look like. An online discussion among the New Urbanist community has made the following recommendation.[22]

URBAN BILL OF RIGHTS IN A DEMOCRACY

NEIGHBORHOOD:

1. The right to neighborhoods that are safe, functional and desirable, including:
2. The right to the fulfillment of ordinary needs within a 15-minute walk. These needs include access to fresh food, childcare, primary school and green public space.
3. The right to sidewalks shaded by trees.
4. The right to streets illuminated at night.
5. The right to healthy and comfortable buildings.
6. The right to nightlife in the urban cores.
7. The right to streets that are safe, pleasant, habitable public spaces, day and night.
8. The right to buildings that enfront the streets contributing to the quality of the public space of the neighborhood.

Engagement

HOUSING:

1. The right to socially and economically integrated housing, including:
2. The right to neighborhoods that contain a mix of housing types designed for households of various sizes, types and income levels.

TRANSPORTATION:

1. The right to convenient and dignified public transportation, including:
2. The right to convenient access to buses, rail and bike paths.
3. The right to walk or to take public transportation to work.

CULTURAL ASSETS:

1. The right to the preservation of and access to cultural assets.

OPEN SPACE:

1. The right of access to large natural spaces, including:
2. The right of access to the shoreline.
3. The right of access to all natural bodies of water including creeks, streams, rivers, lakes and oceans.

SOLITUDE:

1. The right to solitude and privacy, including:
2. The right to a greenbelt in close proximity to living areas.
3. The right to get out of the city into the country.

CLEANLINESS:

1. The right to a clean city, including:
2. The right to adequate means for disposing of items in an environmentally responsible way.
3. The right to clean air.

PREDICTABILITY:

1. The right to predictability in the evolution of the city.

PUBLIC PROCESS:

1. The right to a comprehensible and accessible public process for decisions regarding the public realm, including:
2. The right to regulations that are intelligible and the right to having them explained.
3. The right to fully participate in the municipal decision-making process at the neighborhood, city and metropolitan levels.

A Balanced Solution

Classic Conflicts in Development

In this chapter, we have looked at thriving, environmental stewardship, and justice in the context of the city. These three issues are of concern not only to Christians, but in fact each one of these goals represents classic kinds of issues around which the concerns of professional planners tend to cluster. Scott Campbell has devised a schematic that shows not only how these three areas represent three differing views of the city among planners but also where conflicts among these three points of view are likely to emerge.[23]

The first point on his schematic is economic development. Those who prioritize this goal understand the city as a "location where production, consumption, distribution, and innovation take place." A second point is environmental protection. Those who prioritize this goal see the "city as a consumer of resources and a producer of wastes." A third point is social justice. Those who prioritize this goal see "the city as a location of conflict over the distribution of resources, of services, and of opportunities."[24]

If we place these distinct points of emphasis on the three points of a triangle, we can then locate all three of the classic conflicts that tend to arise when planners and various stakeholders attempt to enact their visions for the city. The *property conflict* is the classic conflict (we have already seen it in the problem of gentrification) that tends to erupt between those advocating economic development and those advocating social justice. On the one hand, we see those who want the right to maximize return on their privately owned property, and on the other we see those who want to protect the housing rights of people who have lived for a long time in a particular neighborhood.

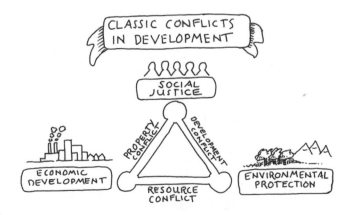

The *resource conflict* is a classic conflict between those in favor of economic development and those advocating environmental protection. Some people see natural resources as productive inputs that need to be developed for consumption and profit, and some people are concerned about the renewability of those resources and want their use to be limited.

The *development conflict* is perhaps the thorniest of all three of these classic conflicts. This conflict exists between those seeking social justice and those protecting the environment. In this conflict we see those wanting to protect the environment running up against those who see their jobs being threatened by people whom they perceive to be environmental elitists.

The point in recognizing these classic conflicts is not to become cynical or to adopt a fatalistic point of view, but rather to reduce our surprise when these kinds of issues come up and to help us better prepare for the public process. Campbell further makes the claim that true sustainability in the city can come about only when a balance is reached in making progress on these three goals. Even if a planner is not particularly interested in justice or the environment, he or she would be well advised to understand the perspective of those who are, and to make concessions for these concerns in whatever proposal he or she brings to the table. This gets us back to where we began this section. True sustainability is not a simple issue of minimizing resource use, but rather involves navigating a delicate balance among human needs, fears, and aspirations.

Faithfulness in the Space Between

I think that Campbell's schematic is of particular interest to Christians, because the God we worship cares about human thriving, environmental stewardship, and justice. We are called to work for all three of these goals, but we do so recognizing that we should expect to encounter frustration and conflict along the way, both from those who oppose the goals of God's kingdom and from those who happen to be working on a different side of the triangle than we are.

The good news for Christians is the confidence we have in knowing that when Christ returns, he can and will bring all three of these goals to fulfillment when he takes his rightful place as judge of the universe. In the meantime, we don't just sit around and wait for his return, we take up his cause and work for these goals as we look for foretastes of his return.

This is the kind of strategy that we must adopt in this "space between" the incarnation and the eschaton. John Stott articulates this attitude:

So then, although it is right to campaign for social justice and to expect to improve society further, in order to make it more pleasing to God, we know that we should never perfect it. Christians are not utopians. Although we know the transforming power of the gospel and the wholesome effects of Christian salt and light, we also know that evil is ingrained in human nature and human society. We harbor no illusions. Only Christ at his second coming will eradicate evil and enthrone righteousness forever. For that day we wait with eagerness.[25]

For Further Reading

Borgmann, Albert. *Crossing the Postmodern Divide*. Chicago: University of Chicago Press, 1992.

Campbell, Scott. "Green Cities, Growing Cities, Just Cities? Urban Planning and the Contradictions of Sustainable Development" in Scott Campbell and Susan S. Fainstein, *Readings in Planning Theory*. Oxford: Blackwell Publishers, 2003.

Florida, Richard L. *The Rise of the Creative Class: And How It's Transforming Work, Leisure, Community and Everyday Life*. New York: Basic Books, 2004.

Frumkin, Howard, Lawrence D. Frank, and Richard Jackson. *Urban Sprawl and Public Health: Designing, Planning, and Building for Healthy Communities*. Washington, DC: Island Press, 2004.

Glaeser, Edward L. *Triumph of the City: How Our Greatest Invention Makes Us Richer, Smarter, Greener, Healthier, and Happier*. New York: Penguin Press, 2011.

MacIntyre, Alasdair C. *Dependent Rational Animals: Why Human Beings Need the Virtues*. Chicago: Open Court, 1999.

Owen, David. *Green Metropolis: Why Living Smaller, Living Closer, and Driving Less Are Keys to Sustainability*. New York: Riverhead Books, 2009.

Steiner, Christopher. *$20 Per Gallon: How the Inevitable Rise in the Price of Gasoline Will Change Our Lives for the Better*. New York: Grand Central, 2009.

Wolterstorff, Nicholas. *Until Justice and Peace Embrace: The Kuyper Lectures for 1981 Delivered at the Free University of Amsterdam*. Grand Rapids: Eerdmans, 1983.

9

Loving Place

In the musical *Fiddler on the Roof,* there is a touching scene involving the lead character, Tevye, and his wife, Golde. Tevye has just informed Golde that he has given consent for their daughter Hodel to marry a young man named Perchik. This is concerning to Golde, because Perchik is poor and doesn't have good prospects. But Tevye informs his wife that this is a new world, and now love, not just prospects, has become an important consideration in marriage. And Hodel loves Perchik.

This conversation leads Tevye to ask Golde, "Do you love me?" Golde and Tevye grew up in a different world, where love was not a very important part of a marriage. Their parents arranged the marriage, and they first met on their wedding day. Golde, apparently, has not given much thought to whether or not she loves Tevye, and so her first impulse is to evade the question.

When Tevye persists, Golde begins to consider the question but can do so only in terms of the things she has done for Tevye and the family. She doesn't answer his question directly, but rather provides a litany of tasks she has performed for him including the washing of clothes, cleaning the house, providing children, and milking the cow.

Her second attempt at framing the question involves claiming her formal role: "I'm your wife." But this is not enough for Tevye, and he asks the question one more time. This time, Golde finally comes to an answer in her own mind: "For twenty-five years I've lived with him / fought with him, starved with him / Twenty-five years my bed is his / If that's not love, what is?"[1]

Having concluded that somehow even though these things listed are not among the most notable accomplishments a family might achieve in a lifetime, somehow they do add up to something that we can call love, she informs Tevye, "I suppose I do." Tevye, pleased with this response, tells Golde, "I suppose I love you, too."

This conversation between Tevye and Golde reveals a tension inherent in the institution of marriage. As we noted in chapter 5, a marriage can be seen in vocational terms. Marriage is a task that we willingly take on. It is a covenantal partnership between two people who have agreed to work together to strengthen societal bonds by raising responsible children to adulthood. Marriage is ultimately based on this covenant and isn't necessarily validated only by this thing known as love.

And yet most of us do want our marriages at some level to be characterized by love. It is a bit of a mystery, however, how to account for this love. Where does it come from? How does it grow? Our love does grow over time as we set about the major tasks of life. But love also grows out of those less noteworthy aspects of our life together—fighting and enduring hardship, living in close proximity, and sharing a bed.

The question of love is expected in considerations of marriage, but our experience of the built environment can also involve love. When we travel to a faraway place, we often feel homesick for the *place* we have come to love. Love bonds us to the place we live. But our love also can shape the place we live. G. K. Chesterton claims that love is a key element to a city becoming great: "Men did not love Rome because she was great. She was great because they had loved her."[2]

In the previous chapter, we looked at the important work that we take on when we seek to engage the built environment as disciples of Jesus Christ. We considered the question of thriving and the question of environmental stewardship, and we looked at justice. In this chapter, we look at some of the less tangible aspects of our experience in the built environment.

The foci of this chapter—specifically, belonging and beauty—would not be considered things that we *accomplish* in the built environment. Rather, these are often the things that take place while we are thinking about other more pressing issues. But these aspects are very important; in many cases these are the things that engender our love for the places we live. And, conversely, when something just doesn't seem right in the built environment, often we can diagnose the problem in one of these two areas. We begin with the question of belonging.

Engagement

Belonging

What does it mean to belong somewhere? If we take a clue from the *Cheers* theme song, belonging has to do with having a place "where everybody knows your name." This insight can be broken down into two components. There is a relationship aspect; being surrounded by people who know us well enough to call us by name is important. But there is also a locational aspect to consider. The eponymous bar in *Cheers* is a specific place. When we go to that place on a particular day, we don't know who will be there, but we can be reasonably sure that many of the people who are there will know us by name. The first section of this chapter explores the idea of this sense of belonging someplace in the built environment.

Strangers

Over the past couple of years, Brad Keighley has noticed an increasing feeling of dread when he opens up the morning paper. He's been reading more and more stories of crime in his neighborhood. Cars and houses are getting broken into on a fairly regular basis. And he sees undecipherable graffiti cropping up here and there as he drives to work. He used to enjoy walking in the neighborhood, and now he finds himself being much more fearful when he is even a block away from his house.

When his children were younger, it seemed as if he knew most of the families in the neighborhood. But families have moved over the years, and now he knows just a few of his neighbors. And he doesn't seem to see even the neighbors he knows very often, probably because they are also fearful of venturing too far from their homes.

Not only are the people in his neighborhood unfamiliar to him, they also look different from the people he used to know. Brad has never considered himself to be racist, but deep in his innermost thoughts, he has to admit that he was more comfortable when most of his neighbors were white.

Recently, he put a lock on his garage and upgraded the alarm system in his house. He'd even thought about purchasing a handgun to keep in his bedroom, but he thinks that might push his wife right over the edge. This used to be such a nice neighborhood. What can be done about all of these strangers living here now? Bradley doesn't feel like he belongs here any longer.

Euclid *on Strangers*

Bradley doesn't feel that he belongs in his own neighborhood because it has become overrun with strangers. This way of framing the problem is not the only way of understanding what is going on. But it is a fairly common perspective. And we can trace it at least as far back as the *Euclid v. Ambler* case.

One of the implicit values embedded in functional zoning as a planning tool has to do with the place of strangers in society. I have already suggested why a slaughterhouse or a foundry might not be a good fit in a mostly residential neighborhood, but the zoning code of the town of Euclid excluded all commercial activity—including the coffee shop and corner grocery.

Why would anyone want to intentionally bar a coffee shop from one's neighborhood? We already noted that part of the rationale for such exclusion had to do with protecting our children from the potential threat of society. However, another aspect of the exclusion has to do with protecting our neighborhoods from a particular undesirable element known as "the stranger." According to the majority opinion of *Euclid*, "A place of business in a residence neighborhood furnishes an excuse for any criminal to go into the neighborhood, where, otherwise, a stranger would be under the ban of suspicion."[3]

The logic here is that a coffee shop is a dangerous place in your neighborhood because it provides a safe place for a stranger to hang out. A neighborhood is safer when strangers don't have a place to go, and therefore feel ostracized. Note also how the language also implies that a stranger is likely to be a criminal.

This implicit suspicion of strangers is expressed not only in the lack of commercial establishments in exurban subdivisions but also in the design of such neighborhoods. The curvilinear streets without a clear network of blocks make it very difficult to navigate the streets unless you live there or know someone who does. And, as we have noted, the cul-de-sac limits our exposure to strangers because they prevent our streets from being pathways that lead to other places. The connectionalism of the grid layout may make walking more interesting, but it also makes it more likely for you to encounter a stranger near your home.

A concern about strangers also explains why homes are oriented socially toward the backyards. The front yard is for display, but the backyard is where people hang out and socialize. If one does become lost in a exurban subdivision, it can be very hard to find another person in order to ask directions. There are few people on their front lawns; there are no people on front porches. And there are not shopkeepers who can help us find our way.

The Fluidity of Strangers

At one level, the logic behind discouraging strangers from visiting our neighborhoods makes sense. Some strangers are dangerous. The presence of strangers can make us feel uncomfortable because we don't know anything about them. Where the logic of *Euclid* begins to break down is that, in most cases, the label of *stranger* is not as fixed as we might assume. With few exceptions, no one is a stranger everywhere. In general, people are known in some contexts and in other contexts they become strangers. We are strangers in more places than we are not. Strangers are not even fixed in a particular location. A person who is a stranger today may be an acquaintance tomorrow and a friend in the matter of a few months. And people that we once knew fairly well may become strangers to us if we do not interact with them over an extended period of time.

The problem with the legacy of *Euclid* is that in allowing our fear of strangers to shape policy decisions, we have created a situation in which people who live close to one another tend to become more estranged over time, and there are very few opportunities for strangers to become known in an unfamiliar community. Such a policy is not only unwise but, more important, unbiblical.

A Theology of Strangers

The Bible has quite a bit to say about strangers and estrangement, one of the clearest being that we are to be kind to them. The primary reason for us to adopt this attitude toward the stranger is that this is how God also acts.

> The LORD watches over the strangers;
> he upholds the orphan and the widow,
> but the way of the wicked he brings to ruin.[4]

For the LORD your God is God of gods and Lord of lords, the great God, mighty and awesome, who is not partial and takes no bribe, who executes justice for the orphan and the widow, and who loves the strangers, providing them food and clothing.[5]

As chapter 10 from Deuteronomy continues, a second related reason for showing kindness to strangers comes to light. The Israelites had been strangers once themselves and can empathize with the plight of the stranger.

You shall also love the stranger, for you were strangers in the land of Egypt.[6]

You shall not oppress a resident alien; you know the heart of an alien, for you were aliens in the land of Egypt.[7]

Part of what it means to love the stranger is for him or her to receive the benefits of being a part of God's covenant community:

Six days you shall do your work, but on the seventh day you shall rest, so that your ox and your donkey may have relief, and your homeborn slave and the resident alien may be refreshed.[8]

In fact, God has made provision for the outsider to become an insider.

If an alien who resides with you wants to celebrate the Passover to the LORD, all his males shall be circumcised; then he may draw near to celebrate it; he shall be regarded as a native of the land. But no uncircumcised person shall eat of it; there shall be one law for the native and for the alien who resides among you.[9]

A track record of caring for the stranger was one of the ways for a person to establish his righteousness. When Job makes his defense against his accusers, two times he mentions his kindness to strangers.

> I was a father to the needy,
>   and I championed the cause of the stranger.[10]

> the stranger has not lodged in the street;
>   I have opened my doors to the traveler.[11]

In the New Testament, the gentiles are identified as aliens and strangers to the covenant. And through Christ they are reconciled and become members of the community, as in this passage from Ephesians:

Remember that you were at that time without Christ, being aliens from the commonwealth of Israel, and strangers to the covenants of promise, having no hope and without God in the world. But now in Christ Jesus you who once were far off have been brought near by the blood of Christ. For he is our peace; in his flesh he has made both groups into one and has broken down the dividing wall, that is, the hostility between us.[12]

This helps to explain why followers of Christ are also told to show kindness to strangers:

for I was hungry and you gave me food, I was thirsty and you gave me something to drink, I was a stranger and you welcomed me.[13]

Contribute to the needs of the saints; extend hospitality to strangers.[14]

Do not neglect to show hospitality to strangers, for by doing that some have entertained angels without knowing it.[15]

Engagement

As we saw in the Ephesians quotation above, it is our sin that estranges us from God and from one another. Outside of Christ, our status is that of strangers and aliens. Christ's death on the cross, then, defeats the power of sin and reconciles us to God. We are to help spread this ministry of reconciliation by letting others know that they too can be reconciled:

> All this is from God, who reconciled us to himself through Christ, and has given us the ministry of reconciliation; that is, in Christ God was reconciling the world to himself, not counting their trespasses against them, and entrusting the message of reconciliation to us.[16]

Reconciliation in the New Testament is primarily about our relationship with God. But it is clear that one of the benefits of our being reconciled to God is that we can also be reconciled to one another. In fact, it is an indication of a problem if we continue to be estranged from someone else in our community.

> So when you are offering your gift at the altar, if you remember that your brother or sister has something against you, leave your gift there before the altar and go; first be reconciled to your brother or sister, and then come and offer your gift.[17]

In summary, then, Scripture instructs us to empathize with the stranger, because we were once estranged ourselves, to show kindness to strangers, to create opportunities for strangers to become members of the community, and to work to redeem the estrangement between humans and God and between individual humans. Each one of these directives has implications for the built environment.

Reducing Estrangement via Third Places

We can begin a reconsideration of how strangers are treated in the built environment by returning to *Euclid*. Whereas *Euclid* allowed communities to banish commercial establishments in residential neighborhoods so that strangers would not feel welcome, we can advocate for certain kinds of commercial establishments that help to build relationships. The clearest articulation of this kind of establishment comes from Ray Oldenburg, who coined the term "third place."

According to Oldenburg, a third place is a place that is not home and is not the place of work. The third place is where people can gather informally and be themselves. These places, like coffee shops and pubs, allow people who live or work in the same neighborhood to get to know one another in a nonthreatening way. Third places help create connections among residents in an area, they create places where strangers can feel welcome, and they help to socialize us to the rules of our communities.

Almost any place can function as a third place, but some kinds of places function better than others for this purpose. Oldenburg therefore articulates eight characteristics of third places. I paraphrase these characteristics here:[18]

- *On neutral ground.* Everyone must feel welcome at a third place. No one is the host and no one is the guest. People can come and go as they please.
- *The third place as leveler.* Social distinctions that exist outside of the third place should have no place within. There should be no distinction between management and workers, upper class and lower in a third place.
- *Conversation is the main activity.* An ongoing and lively conversation is the focus of a third place. Therefore, no one voice should dominate; the art of spirited conversation should be paramount.
- *Accessibility and accommodation.* A third place should have relatively long hours and a steady stream of patrons, so that one can go alone at any time and be reasonably sure of finding others there.
- *The regulars.* A group of regular patrons gives each third place its distinctive character. But there should be enough openness that a newcomer can become a regular over time.
- *A low profile.* Good third places are often plain and do not generally impress the newcomer. They are the opposite of slick.
- *The mood is playful.* Humor, joy, and winsomeness are paramount. People who tend to take themselves too seriously learn to adapt or they won't feel comfortable in a third place.
- *A home away from home.* A third place is very different from a home, but it is similar in the sense of comfort and support one feels in a third place.

One of the easiest ways we can reduce estrangement and encourage the development of relationships is to seek to support third place establishments throughout our communities.

Hospitable Homes

As we observed in chapter 4, the housing type that developed for exurban subdivisions was designed not to encourage interaction with the public. The

Engagement

cul-de-sac/arterial-street model minimizes the possibility of a stranger walking in front of one's house on the way to somewhere else. And the houses reinforce this by having thresholds that are intimidating or impossible for strangers to cross (front doors protected by sweeping lawns and garage doors). The houses in the exurbs turn their backs on the public realm in front and are oriented toward the backyard.

The exurban neighborhood and home tend to shun the stranger rather than welcome her. This setup makes it very uncomfortable for a stranger who happens to find herself in a particular subdivision. Generally, this is not noticed by the residents of such subdivisions, because they feel at home in their area, but one becomes confronted by this lack of hospitality in design when one becomes lost in another subdivision. Not only do those who begin as strangers not feel welcome in certain communities, some of these design features can increase the estrangement of those who live in relative proximity to one another. When everyone enters their homes through the garage door and spends time indoors or in the backyard, it can lead to a situation where neighbors lose contact with one another. Of course, families with young kids can mitigate this kind of dynamic, but those who don't have kids, or whose kids have left the home, can feel isolated.

Obviously, one solution to this problem is for families to choose to live in neighborhoods and homes that are built in the more traditional style. There remains a great deal of housing stock in these kinds of pre-WWII neighborhoods. And it is becoming increasingly common for new neighborhoods and houses to be developed with a greater sensitivity to sociability and connection.

Adaptations can be made to increase the hospitality of home and neighborhood. We noted the adaptations that Mexican Americans in East Los Angeles made to their typical middle-class homes by adding a fence and front gate to create defensible space that turned out to be sociable space. There may be other kinds of adaptations that can be made in this direction. Randy Frazee suggests the simple step of bringing the family swing set from the backyard to the front yard as a way to connect with the neighborhood.[19]

Adaptations can even be made at the neighborhood and regional levels. One of the more interesting examples of this is the BeltLine project in Atlanta. For years Atlanta developed on a cul-de-sac arterial plan that left neighborhoods disconnected from one another and from the public spaces of the city. The BeltLine project is an attempt to undo that strategy by superimposing a traditional street grid over the existing cul-de-sac network, thus reconnecting neighborhoods to each other and to public spaces. In this way, Atlanta has made an explicit effort to build up the connectionalism of their city. This project has been very successful and may serve as an important model for other communities.

City Gates

While hospitality to the stranger is a clear biblical mandate, it can be a bit complicated in a contemporary setting. Christine Pohl makes the point that in premodern cultures, a family's act of hospitality was couched within the protective bounds of a more tightly knit community than we experience today. A true stranger would typically be met by elders at the gate on his or her way into town. The stranger thus would be subject to an initial screening by the community before anyone would even be in a position of offering hospitality.

And if someone were to offer hospitality to this stranger, others in the community would be aware of the situation and able to help if things became difficult. Since our society is much less cohesive now, opening our homes to true strangers can be a much more risky proposition. We can speak of gates and gatekeeping today in a more abstract sense as a community-protecting activity. Pohl's study on hospitality helps demonstrate how the community as a whole has traditionally played a role in helping people take responsibility for one another.[20]

Several Old Testament accounts show hospitality beginning in a public place where the community gathered regularly. The stranger was first encountered there and then invited into an individual household. Drawing from the practices surrounding the city gate in premodern cultures, Pohl asserts that the larger community today might help to break down some of the strangeness of those that we encounter in public as a way of lessening the vulnerability that people experience in new encounters.

> Without intentionally building some minimal connections, it is unlikely that we will welcome the most vulnerable people into our homes or churches, even if we accept responsibility to offer hospitality to strangers and recognize its significance for them. We need to find or create contemporary equivalents of the city gate, community rituals, and small group meetings in which we can build preliminary relations with strangers.[21]

A food bank or a ministry of meals can provide a safe place for people to get to know some of the more vulnerable members of our community without putting themselves or their families at risk. One can express hospitality within the context of an emergency shelter or a food bank. And in some cases, such settings allow for the hospitality to comfortably extend to a more personable setting, such as a walk around the block or a shared meal in one's home.

Hospitable Practices

As we think about ways neighborhoods and homes can be more or less hospitable to strangers, it is important that we remember the issue of physical determinism that was raised in the introduction to part 2. Having a neighborhood with a good grid network of streets and homes that are oriented outward toward the public will not necessarily lead to residents acting more hospitably to strangers or more neighborly to one another. At some level people still need to be motivated to make these kinds of connections if they are going to take place. On the other hand, a person or family who is highly motivated toward hospitality and neighborliness can be extremely welcoming and help create deep and lasting connections in even the most insular kind of community. I have heard numerous inspiring stories of residents of exurban communities that watch out for one another and bring baked goods to welcome newcomers to the neighborhood.

We saw at the beginning of this chapter that God calls us to be welcoming to the stranger and to pursue the ministry of reconciliation. Therefore, Christians who live in hospitable homes and neighborhoods and those who live in insular homes and neighborhoods must seek to develop and sustain hospitable and neighborly practices regardless of what kind of physical setting they happen to find themselves in.

Space for Relationships

Most of what we have been talking about with regard to the built environment has been the importance of place to human thriving and to Christian discipleship. However, as mentioned in chapter 4, space is not altogether bad. We all need space when our lives feel too crowded with people, things, and responsibilities. And space is important for the forming of relationships. As we make the transition from thinking about hospitable places to hospitable practices, it will be helpful if we spend some time thinking about the role space plays in forming relationships.

One of the positive trends within the church over the past few decades has been the small-group movement, which has been an attempt to counteract the sometimes formal and impersonal setting of gathered worship by providing more intimate settings for people to develop stronger relationships with one another and with God. While this has been a good development, there is some concern that the development of small groups is only the first step toward providing the kinds of spaces we need in order to develop a full range of relationships.

Joseph Myers has been one of the more compelling voices to point out some of the limitations of the small-group movement.[22] Myers is not opposed to small groups but recognizes that they don't present a kind of "magic bullet" solution to every problem faced by the church. Myers's argument is worth reading in its entirety, but I address just one part of it here.

Small groups do not accomplish the promise of fulfilling all facets of a person's search for community. Small groups deliver on only one or two specific kinds of connection. A person's search for community is more complex than this. The truth is that people can experience belonging in groups ranging in size from two to two thousand or more.

Myers identifies the lack of a sense of belonging to be the core issue that is behind the impetus of the small-group movement. What is missing is the notion that our need to belong actually is experienced at a number of different levels. Small groups address only one level of our need to belong, and we need to account for all of our levels of belonging.

The levels of belonging that Myers identifies are public, social, personal, and intimate. For each kind of belonging, Myers describes a different kind of space that facilitates this level of relationships.

Public belonging refers to the kinds of relationships we share with those whom we may not know personally, but with whom we share some common interest or identification. People who experience a sense of public belonging with one another are not strangers, exactly, because what it means to be a stranger is to not experience any connection.

Fans rooting for the same team experience a sense of public belonging. Owners of the '65 Mustang identify with one another in a public way. And people worshiping together in a very large church experience this as well.

A sense of *social* belonging is the setting for small talk. Myers calls this kind of relating "neighborly." This is the level of relationships at which we will offer small snapshots of our lives and perhaps ask for small favors. The settings at which social belonging is cultivated are often dismissed as trivial, but they are more important than many people understand. We crave this kind of relating, and we miss it when it is not there.

Social space is significant. Connecting with people at a social level is part of how we decide whether we want to grow deeper with them. And social space is important for our own identity formation. As we "explain" who we are in these kinds of settings, we practice shaping the identity by which we are known to others.

Personal belonging is the level of relationship at which we share private information about ourselves. Those with whom we experience a personal sense of belonging we call close friends. When we hear the word *community*, we think of our experience of personal belonging. It is important to note, however, that personal space is not the same as intimate space.

We may feel very close to our best friend, but we need to maintain a level of relationship that is even closer to account for our relationship with our spouses. *Intimate* belonging involves those relationships "in which another person knows the naked truth about us and yet the two of us are 'not ashamed.'"[23] We tend to overuse the term *intimate* to describe everything that is closer than public belonging. To experience the fullness of human community, we need to feel that we belong to others in the public, social, personal, and, possibly, the intimate realms. And many of our specific relationships need to work at two or more levels in order to be successful.

Providing Space

Myers's observations about these different levels of relationship and belonging yield a number of useful insights. The first is that people have distinct needs that are met at each one of these levels. The problem that can occur in a church that has an amazing worship service and a healthy small-group program is that little attention may be paid to people's needs for social space.

Another insight is that there are different rules for relating to one another that are keyed to the different levels of relationship implied by a particular space. Some of the more common social errors that are committed have to do with people's misunderstanding of the kind of space that they are in.

Myers tells the experience he had while shopping at a vitamin store. He was feeling uncomfortable with a salesperson who was invading his space and using too loud of a voice for the setting. Myers came to the realization that the salesperson was completely misreading the kind of relational space they were in. People shopping for vitamins are often looking for items that may be related to their personal or even intimate lives and this salesman's strategy was appropriate for social or even public spaces.

And last, Myers notes that each of our individual relationships may be expressed on more than one level. We relate to our spouses at an intimate level, but we relate to them at the personal, social, and even public levels as well. We might compliment our spouse for the great job she is doing at her job, but doing so publicly in front of a large group of people has an entirely different effect.

Myers's insights are pertinent to the built environment insofar as we can think of the region between the buildings not only as places in which we inscribe the meaning of our lives, but also as spaces that can help meet our needs for public, social, and even personal belonging.

Beauty

Advocating Beauty

Angela Harper has had an eye for beauty for as long as she can remember. As a child she loved to paint and draw and found herself frequently getting lost in her parents' dusty old *History of Art* textbook that was kept under the coffee table in the living room. She thinks that she might have become a great artist herself, or perhaps even an art teacher, but somewhere along the way, life took her in a different direction, and she spent her most active years keeping up a home and raising children.

Now that the children are out of the house and are largely financially independent, Angela is making up for lost time. She is on the board of directors for the local art museum, and she has been the primary impetus for an endowed series that sponsors well-known artists for public lectures. She sees herself as an advocate for beauty in her town.

This year, however, she is experiencing a minor identity crisis. Her good friend from church had asked if she would be willing to help organize and finance a medical team that would travel to Haiti to help children orphaned by the earthquake of 2010. She said that she would love to but couldn't because all of her time and money are tied up with the museum and especially with the lecture series.

Her friend had read a bit about this year's sponsored artist, whose work was admittedly challenging and very controversial. And she wondered how an artist who produces "art" that isn't even beautiful could possibly be more important than giving Haitian children much-needed medical attention.

Angela didn't want to admit this, but her friend's argument was getting through to her. Angela also didn't really like the work of this year's artist. But she knew that wasn't supposed to matter, since good art doesn't have to be beautiful, and besides, beauty is in the eye of the beholder. Also, she felt that if no one supports professional artists, the arts die, and then where would we be as a society? She managed to brush off her friend's response, but she felt a little less sure of her role as an advocate for beauty in her city.

Angela's story reveals a few cultural assumptions that are typically made with regard to beauty. We can summarize them with the following statements. Beauty is:

- in the eye of the beholder,
- completely independent of moral considerations,
- something created only by a professional class known as artists,

- a specialized pursuit, displayed in special places, for the enjoyment of a specially cultivated elite.

In the following two sections, we examine each of these assumptions.

A Theology of Beauty

Historically, it has been common for both secular and Christian philosophers to recognize truth, goodness, and beauty as transcendentals that are neither arbitrary nor accidental.[24] That is to say, these thinkers believe that aspects of these three areas of consideration are not subject to individual taste or the spirit of the age. There are differing reasons behind assigning these three transcendental status, but for Christian theologians, at least, the transcendentals tend to be grounded in God's character or God's revelation.

For the most part, one would still expect to find strong support for the transcendental status of truth and goodness among conservative Christians who hold a high view of the authority of Scripture. But this is not necessarily true of beauty. Robert P. Mills, who teaches humanities at a conservative Christian college, claims that the overwhelming majority of his students believe that beauty is in the eye of the beholder. That is to say, they believe that beauty is simply a matter of taste and is not subject to any authority, God or otherwise. Mills believes that this is because the idea that beauty is in the eye of the beholder has become so pervasive in our culture that it simply goes unchallenged among secular and Christian students.[25]

So it may require some justification on my part to even have a section entitled "a theology of beauty." If beauty is simply "in the eye of the beholder," what would be the point of dragging God into this conversation? Let me ask, therefore, that we at least recognize that the idea that beauty is only in the eye of the beholder is one of those cultural truisms, so commonly accepted that rarely does anyone feel the need to defend it. I am asking that, for the purpose of this next section, we forget for a moment that we already know the answer to this question, and consider the possibility that there are at least some aspects of beauty that may be subject to God's authority.

As justification for this experiment, let me simply mention that the Bible does talk about beauty. In the NRSV, the English word *beauty* is mentioned 32 times, and *beautiful* 58 times. This is not nearly as common as *love* (586 times) or *faith* (275 times). But it is at least as common as *repentance* (31 times) and *repent* (45 times). And few Christians would suggest that God doesn't care about repentance. Since the Bible talks about beauty, it may be helpful to our discussion to find out what it has to say.

God Is Beautiful

As we search the Scriptures for references to beauty, one of the most significant things we discover is that beauty is a characteristic of God.

> In that day the Lord of hosts will be a garland of glory,
> and a diadem of beauty, to the remnant of his people.[26]

> One thing I asked of the LORD,
> that will I seek after:
> to live in the house of the LORD
> all the days of my life,
> to behold the beauty of the LORD,
> and to inquire in his temple.[27]

God is beautiful, and therefore our worship of God should be characterized by beauty, "Honor and majesty are before him; strength and beauty are in his sanctuary."[28] This is true with regard to the ideal setting for the worship of God, and it has a bearing on how God instructed the Israelites to construct even their temporary setting for the worship of God:

> You shall make a curtain of blue, purple, and crimson yarns, and of fine twisted linen; it shall be made with cherubim skillfully worked into it. You shall hang it on four pillars of acacia overlaid with gold, which have hooks of gold and rest on four bases of silver.[29]

Proximate Beauty

One notable thing about these references (as well as the other references to beauty in the Scriptures) is that beauty is nowhere described as being in the eye of the beholder. Psalm 27 makes reference to "the beauty" of the Lord. It does not say that a specific group of people happened to see God as beautiful. To affirm that God simply *is* beautiful regardless of whether God is seen to be beautiful by a certain group of people is a radically countercultural statement.

The way this issue can be framed philosophically is to ask whether beauty is objective or subjective. To say that beauty is objective is to affirm that there is something about the thing itself that is inherently beautiful. That is to say, the thing conforms to some timeless standard known as beauty. To say that beauty is subjective is to say that something is beautiful when it is seen to be beautiful by a particular viewer.

According to Robert P. Mills, it was assumed that beauty was objective from at least the time of Plato until the Enlightenment. People held to the objective view for different reasons, but that was the reigning assumption about beauty for a few thousand years of human history. Although a few thinkers began to challenge beauty as objective, the death blow to this perspective was delivered by Kant, who saw beauty as entirely subjective as well as detached from truth and goodness. Mills quotes a telling passage from Kant.

> If someone reads me his poem or takes me to a play that in the end fails to please my taste, then he can adduce Batteux or Lessing, or even older and more famous critics of taste, and adduce all the rules they established as proofs that his poem is beautiful. . . . I will stop my ears, listen to no reasons and arguments, and would rather believe that those rules of the critics are false . . . than allow that my judgment should be determined by means of a priori grounds of proof, since it is supposed to be a judgment of taste and not of the understanding of reason.[30]

Apart from Kant's references to Batteux and Lessing, I suspect that his argument would be received well by students (Christian or non-Christian) in a college classroom today.

The problem with the subjective view of beauty is not only that it seems contrary to the biblical witness; in many cases it simply doesn't hold up to experience. This is especially true with regard to the built environment. As Witold Rybczynski points out, when people are asked to identify their favorite buildings, there is more than a 50 percent chance that they will name one built during the relatively brief period of history in which the City Beautiful approach was predominant.

> In a 2007 national poll that asked people to name their favorite buildings in the United States, the leading choices include the Jefferson Memorial, the Lincoln Memorial, the Supreme Court of the United States, the National Gallery of Art in Washington D.C., the Philadelphia Museum of Art and the Chicago Tribune Tower—all built between 1925 and 1943.[31]

Part of what got this debate off in the wrong direction is another Enlightenment thinker, Descartes, who insisted that all knowledge be verified by the criterion of absolute certainty. That is to say, if one has any doubts about something, then one doesn't really know it to be true. And since it can be difficult to define with absolute certainty the criteria for defining absolute beauty, the tendency has been to retreat entirely to the realm of the subjective, that is, to claim that beauty is entirely in the eye of the beholder.

There are a couple of ways to reframe this debate that can help us to avoid such an either-or approach to such an important question. In the first place, we can make a distinction between epistemology and ontology. Ontology has to do with what *is*, and epistemology has to do with how we *know* what is.

This distinction allows us to suggest that there may be some kind of absolute standard for beauty, but to also acknowledge that it can be known with certainty only by God. We have difficulty knowing and articulating with any certainty what this standard is, but this is because of our limitations as humans, not because there is any problem with the concept of beauty. Since we are creatures made in God's image, it shouldn't surprise us that we may respond positively to that which is objectively beautiful even when we can't quite articulate or pin down what makes it so.

Another thing that we can suggest to refine this debate a bit more is that there may be both objective and subjective aspects to beauty with regard to different kinds of objects and situations. There may be some objective features that make one object more beautiful than another. However, this could be augmented by personal taste or one's history with a place. If one of the buildings happened to be the setting of one's happy childhood, one could come to the point of declaring that building more beautiful than another even though that other building is more objectively beautiful.

These kinds of moves are not unique to questions of beauty and the built environment; in many fields there are attempts to get away from allowing the impossible criteria of absolute certainty to impede practical action. The term *proximate* is often used to signal that this kind of move is being made. One hears discussion of proximate truth or proximate justice, meaning we know enough to take responsible action but don't know with absolute certainty. In the same way, it can be helpful for discussions of the built environment to talk about proximate beauty.

God Wants Us to Experience Beauty

Another thing that we discover when we explore the concept of beauty in Scripture is that beauty in the world is not accidental; God makes things beautiful on purpose. "Out of the ground the LORD God made to grow every tree that is pleasant to the sight and good for food."[32] John Calvin, who has a reputation for being aesthetically dismissive, expounds on the significance of this passage.

> Now if we ponder to what end God created food, we shall find that he meant not only to provide for necessity but also for delight and good cheer. Thus the purpose of clothing, apart from necessity, was comeliness and decency. In grasses, trees, and fruits, apart from their various uses, there is beauty of appearance and pleasantness of odor [cf. Gen. 2:9]. . . . And the natural qualities themselves of things demonstrate sufficiently to what end and extent we may enjoy them. Has the Lord clothed the flowers with the great beauty that greets our eyes, the sweetness of smell that is wafted upon our nostrils, and yet will it be unlawful for

our eyes to be affected by that beauty, or our sense of smell by the sweetness of that odor? What? Did he not so distinguish colors as to make some more lovely than others? Did he not endow gold and silver, ivory and marble, with a loveliness that renders them more precious than other metals or stones? Did he not, in short, render many things attractive to us, apart from their necessary use?[33]

From this we can make two assertions about the built environment. The first is that beauty is perhaps as important as food and shelter to people. Virginia Postrel helpfully challenges the "hierarchy of needs" approach that makes beauty a lesser need than food and shelter:

> Human beings do not wait for aesthetics until they have full stomachs and a roof that doesn't leak. They do not pursue aesthetic needs "only when basic needs have been satisfied." Given a modicum of stability and sustenance, people enrich the look and feel of their lives through ritual, personal adornment, and decorated objects.[34]

This is an important thing to keep in mind when we consider the justice implications of resource allocation. Much of the extremely ugly and dehumanizing public housing that has been built in this country has been justified on the basis of a reductionist logic that sees the provision of shelter as more important than beauty. This can be in part attributed to Kant, who not only made aesthetics entirely subjective but also prioritized ethics over aesthetics. Also, the increasing ugliness of the public realm has had a disproportionate impact on the poor because many poor people are deprived of beautiful private places to live and cannot afford to escape into the realm of natural beauty.

To extrapolate a bit from the basic point that God designed trees to be pleasing to the sight, we can more cautiously assert that God may have also provided things within creation that are pleasing to our other four senses as well. The Bible celebrates the fragrance of a field,[35] a husband's enjoyment of his young wife's breasts,[36] and the importance of good wine at a celebration.[37] As we think about providing beautiful things within the built environment, we then might add that, if possible, things should be beautiful to many of our senses. With regard to the built environment, this can have an impact on the kinds of materials with which we build. Wood paneling smells more pleasing than wallboard, and natural stone feels better than concrete.

Beauty's Effect

Another thing we discover about beauty in the Bible is that our desire for beauty can draw us out of isolation toward intimate relationship with others and with God:

O taste and see that the LORD is good;
    happy are those who take refuge in him.[38]

Until the day breathes and the shadows flee,
    I will hasten to the mountain of myrrh and the hill of frankincense.
    You are altogether beautiful, my love;
    there is no flaw in you.[39]

Certainly, our sexual desire seems to work that way. In cultures where traditional attitudes toward marriage are strong, young people often overcome their fear of commitment to marriage at least partially because of their strong desire for sexual intimacy with the beloved. This sexual desire also leads naturally to procreation and childbirth, thus nudging two potentially isolated individuals to widen their circle further by the inclusion of children.

It's a bit difficult to see how this very private use of beauty can relate to the built environment (especially in its public manifestations), except in a negative way. Advertisers have for years understood the power of erotic attraction to sell us consumer products. Graham Ward suggests that as we have moved beyond the modern rationalist city, we have now begun to construct postmodern cities of desire that are enlivened by this erotic desire.[40] It's important when critiquing such commercial uses of sexual desire to keep in mind the basic goodness of our sexual appetites and to make our critique from the standpoint of the relational and covenantal purchase (or lack thereof) afforded by such awakening of desire.

Our desires can also lead us to desire a relationship with God. St. Augustine made much of this connection— "Thou awakest to delight in Thy praise; for Thou madest for Thyself, and our heart is restless until it repose in Thee"[41]—as did C. S. Lewis. Lewis found his experience of earthly desire to be an important element in his conversion: "It is difficult to find words strong enough for the sensation which came over me . . . [an] "enormous bliss" of Eden . . . of desire; but desire for what?"[42]

Here we find more possibilities within the built environment than with erotic desire, because the object that elicits the desire for God can be different from the actual God for whom one's desire is awakened.[43] Lewis's experience of desire involved a strictly natural object, but one can imagine someone having a similar experience while watching the pattern of shadows on a beautiful old building or morning sunlight streaming into a plaza.

It is important to acknowledge that not all of the references to beauty in the Bible are positive. The desire for beauty can lead us into life-giving and covenantal relationship with another and with God, but it can draw us away from relationship with others and away from God as well.

So when the woman saw that the tree was good for food, and that it was a delight to the eyes, and that the tree was to be desired to make one wise, she took of its fruit and ate; and she also gave some to her husband, who was with her, and he ate.[44]

When Shechem son of Hamor the Hivite, prince of the region, saw her, he seized her and lay with her by force.[45]

It was not the beauty of the tree or the physical allure of Dinah that caused the disobedient actions described above. However, in both cases sin warped the actors so that their responses to beauty were tragically twisted and set off chains of events with profoundly catastrophic consequences. There are examples of such sad perversity throughout Scripture.

Does the fact that beauty can lead us into covenantal relationship as well as away from covenantal relationship make it a morally neutral value? I do not think that this is a necessary conclusion. One of the elements that distinguishes Christianity from some of the major Eastern religions (Buddhism, for instance) is its basic affirmation of sensuous desire. Whereas Buddhism sees desire as leading to suffering and encourages its adherents to renounce desire, Christianity leads its adherents to redirect misplaced desire to a more appropriate object. We see this impulse in Paul's advice to unmarried widows: "But if they are not practicing self-control, they should marry. For it is better to marry than to be aflame with passion."[46]

John Navone develops this line of thinking in his distinction between true beauty and seduction: "Seductive beauty, as opposed to true beauty, is the attractiveness or allure of the apparent good that would undermine human excellence and its concomitant joy and gladness."[47]

The misdirection of desire is not always the case of a passive object of desire and a sinful subject aroused in lust. The Bible also warns against putting too much effort into self-adornment for the purpose of impressing or attracting others.

Charm is deceitful, and beauty is vain, but a woman who fears the LORD is to be praised.[48]

As mentioned above, it is a bit difficult to apply the notion of misdirected desire to the built environment, but the distracting role of beauty has a more direct application. A beautiful image, even if it doesn't lead to an impure desire, can also be a distraction from obedience to God. "The Israelites said to them, 'If only we had died by the hand of the LORD in the land of Egypt, when we sat by the fleshpots and ate our fill of bread; for you have brought us out into this wilderness to kill this whole assembly with hunger.'"[49] The distinction between manna in the desert and fleshpots in Egypt is aesthetic, not just caloric. The Israelites were using the aesthetic attractions of Egyptian food as a rationale for disobedience to God.

Beauty, Truth, and Goodness

To bring this discussion back to where we began, we can recall that beauty historically was considered in conjunction with the other transcendentals of truth and goodness. There are a number of problems that ensue when beauty is removed from its place in this list. As Hans Urs von Balthasar asserts, "Our situation today shows that beauty demands for itself at least as much courage and decision as do truth and goodness, and she will not allow herself to be separated and banned from her two sisters without taking them along with herself in an act of mysterious vengeance."[50]

In the first place, truth, goodness, and beauty depend on one another for their vitality. Without goodness, we forget why seeking truth is important. And without beauty, we can find it hard to be motivated toward the good. In the second place, beauty without reference to truth and goodness can be corrupted to seduction and deception. Things that are "merely beautiful" can lead us away from truth and goodness, and over time such things will lose even their beauty.

Beauty in Everyday Life

The Grand Narrative of the Arts

To address the final two questions raised by the case study at the beginning of the chapter, it will be helpful to introduce Nicolas Wolterstorff's concept of "the grand narrative of the arts." Wolterstorff contends that the way we understand art in the modern West is different from how most cultures currently and throughout history have understood the role of art in everyday life.

He describes the set of almost universal and implicitly accepted truisms about art that shape our modern Western understanding, "the grand narrative of the arts." The driving force behind this narrative is the notion that the sole purpose for art is for the sake of disinterested contemplation. This leads to a whole set of other understandings and practices.

Since art is for disinterested contemplation, we tend to draw sharp distinctions between that which is art and that which is useful, which we call craft.

And since our art does not have any utility, we must cultivate a special class of professionals known as artists, and we must find ways to support them in their work.

Because we need to contemplate art without distraction, we must also create special settings where art is contemplated. These places, known as museums, galleries, and concert halls, are the appropriate settings in which to contemplate art.

These aspects of "the grand narrative of the arts" are so common within our culture that they are almost universally accepted as normal and unremarkable. But Wolterstorff notes that this situation has not pertained in most contexts throughout the world and throughout history. In most contexts, there is no clear line between what is art and what is a useful thing. Art is included in everyday life, and there is no professional class of artists and no special place for the contemplation of art.

Useful Beauty

This has two important implications for our focus on the built environment. The first is that the built environment is one of the exceptions to the rule. We accept architecture as an area of art even though we recognize the usefulness of buildings. Wolterstorff contends (and I agree) that this understanding should be extended to include urbanism as well as architecture. "I am profoundly convinced that if we are concerned that our fellow human beings should find some sensory refreshment in their lives, then it is the city that we must first of all pay attention to, and not those isolated objects that we call works of art."[51]

The other area where we have allowed art to be somewhat is liturgical art. We recognize the artistic merit of a piece of music even if it has been composed primarily to be performed in a setting of worship.

Another way that Wolterstorff's insight can be useful to our purposes is with regard to the way art functions in a society. In our culture, which unquestioningly accepts "the grand narrative of the arts," we feel that the artist must be allowed complete freedom from societal pressure or constraint when pursuing her or his artistic vision. But where art is not the exclusive purview of a particular class, and where art is a more normal part of everyday life, there is a greater connection between the artist and community. Instead of art as a one-way communication from artist to society, in other cultures art is more of a dialogue between them.

In the following section, we explore some of the ways that the built environment can be a setting for a kind of beauty that is not just for the purpose of contemplation, but is the context of everyday life for most people.

Beauty in the Built Environment

The Aesthetics of the City

After making the case that the grand narrative of the arts tends to ignore the aesthetic quality of the urban space of our cities, Wolterstorff makes an attempt to account for the kinds of things that make for an aesthetically pleasing city. He cites three factors. The first is the *unity and variety* of the urban space itself.

> The characteristics that make for aesthetic excellence in urban space are no different from those that make for aesthetic excellence generally. Other things being equal, the more strongly unified the space, the better. When space is allowed to leak out all over, so that the degree of unity is very low, we can scarcely even experience it as shaped space. And other things being equal, the more rich, complex, varied, contrasting the spaces, the better. When some spaces are distinctly bay-like and others distinctly channel-like; when some of the channels are narrow and others broad, ceremonial, and processional in character; when some of the channels are straight as an arrow and others are curved; when some are absolutely horizontal and others sway up and down; when the bays come in different shapes and when some are given a centralizing directionality toward dead center and others off-center; when some of the channels are given closure at the ends (the Mall in Washington) and others are allowed to stretch to the vanishing point—that's when the space of the city becomes rich, and so far good. And thirdly, a good space, other things being equal, has a certain intensity of character—whether agitated or serene, whether billowing (like the Spanish Steps in Rome) or rigidly stately, whether fast or slow.[52]

Because the bulk of writing on aesthetics on the built environment has to do with the buildings themselves, which Wolterstorff dismissively refers to as facade, he notes formal architecture as significant to the aesthetic quality of the city, but focuses his attention on other aspects of *the spaces between the buildings*.

> Since none of us has to be reminded that the quality of the facades contributes to the aesthetic quality of the city, let me move on to a third contributing factor—the way light pervades the spaces. A space may be dimly lit or brightly lit, uniformly lit or varying in its lighting, varying in the lacy fashion of the light under a locust tree in strong sunlight or varying in the stark fashion of the light and shadow on the Acropolis, lit from above or lit from the level of street lamps. From the lighting within our own homes we are all aware of the way in which the character of a room changes drastically depending on how it is lit. When dealing with light in urban spaces, we are of course dealing with something

in constant change. The shape of the space and the character of the facades is fixed; variations in light introduce slow but ceaseless movement.[53]

And last, Wolterstorff considers the *dramatic quality* of the spaces between the buildings.

> The city itself tends also to give to the very sequence of our movement through it a certain kinetic, dramatic quality, a building up and relaxing of tension. It is true of course that we all have our own personal paths and goals as we traverse the city, quite independent of the structure of the city. But in addition, the channels of a city build up a tension within us—the more so, the more constricted they are—and the bays of a city relax that tension. We move through the narrow, clotted street of Bruges jostled by the crowds and then suddenly are sprung loose into that wonderful open plaza. That sequence, no matter what one's personal mission on a certain day, inescapably introduces a dramatic quality into the sequence of one's movements. When a city fails to impart dramatic sequence to one's movements through it, when it fails to build up and then relax tension and thus introduce variety and unity right into the sequence of one's movements, then it is, other things being equal, aesthetically poor.[54]

While there may be many different ways to develop a set of evaluative criteria to determine proximate beauty, Wolterstorff's notion of unity, variety, and drama in the space between the buildings provides a helpful example of the kind of work that needs to be done.

Harmonious Architecture

Wolterstorff passes over the aesthetic quality of the buildings themselves as having been too much the focus of attention when writing about the aesthetic quality of cities. However, when we read more carefully, we discover that much of the writing about architecture actually avoids making objective value judgments about the buildings themselves. There is plenty of commentary about whether a particular building is a good or poor example of the Romanesque style. And much is written about how certain buildings help mark the transition from one style to another. But there is mostly silence on the question of whether one style is aesthetically to be preferred over another or to justify why the high-style buildings are more aesthetically valuable than vernacular or even mass-produced buildings.

Into this silence, Jonathan Hale brings a helpful contribution. Hale believes that there are fundamental aspects of putting buildings together that make them more or less aesthetically pleasing that transcend questions of style. He doesn't think of style as unimportant; he just believes that there are fundamental issues that must be understood before thinking about style. To support this point, he makes an analogy between architecture and music.

Proportion is to architecture as the scale is to music. Ratios are the strings of the harp on which you play the music. If you don't have a harp, or if you don't tune it, you are not going to get much music. You may get some interesting strange plunks and clanks—and some music, and some architecture, does that. But in our modern age we still love to hear or see the old systems of harmonious proportions. We prefer music based on the diatonic or other harmonious scales because those scales come from harmonic laws that are inherent in living nature. What I call magic in architecture is not prestidigitation, not supernatural emanations, but music. But the kind of power you can get in music is lost to architecture if you leave out the harmonic relationships only proportioning systems can provide. Proportion is the nature of architecture. There is an innately understood grammar of shape. And that grammar, unlike speech, is expressed in all living things. Euclidian shapes—cones, cubes, spheres—are often used to make architecture, but the deep patterns come from life forms. Most of all, they come from the human body and face.[55]

With this analogy in mind, Hale points to a few basic elements of beauty in buildings. The first is *regulating lines*. Regulating lines are what tie the various elements of a building (and even its setting) into a coherent whole.

Regulating Lines

The most common type of regulating line is a diagonal connecting key points on a rectangle. The eye relates any element placed along that line to the whole even if the line is invisible. The regulating line might become the diagonal of a window; it might continue up beyond the wall to determine the shape and location of the chimney. Lines parallel to it might become the roof slope. The roofline, carried through space to the ground beyond the building, might determine the location of a gate or an outbuilding, or it might point to a natural object such as a boulder.[56]

Hale observes that organizing a building according to regulating lines is imperative to the beauty of a building, but there is something intuitive to how this is accomplished. Even good architects who organize building in this way often are unaware that they are doing so during the design phase. Bad architects, on the other hand, often fail to respect regulating lines in their efforts to force a particular style on a building or meet a client's demands for certain features, or they may simply be working in the wrong scale.

In addition to providing an objective metric for harmonious beauty, regulating lines also reveal something more fundamental about the role of individual buildings in the built environment. Part of the reason that regulating lines were a consideration in the placement of windows was that the architect was thinking about the building from an exterior perspective. That is to say he or she was thinking about how the details of the building contributed to the public realm outside of the building. In our current cultural context, an architect will typically place windows from an inside out perspective; windows are placed in order to frame a pleasing view for the resident within. How the window adds to or detracts from the experience of harmonious beauty for the people on the outside looking in is no longer an important consideration.

The second aspect of beauty in buildings is the use of the *golden section*. The golden section is the ratio between the length and width of a rectangle that is pleasing to the eye. The golden section is 1 to 1.618 or it can be expressed in whole numbers as 3 to 5. Not only do we naturally prefer rectangles that correspond to this particular ratio, examples of this ratio can be found throughout nature.

The golden section also can be used to expand patterns in pleasing ways. One can use a golden section to expand a rectangle in such a way that a perfect nautilus curve is created when a line is drawn through the corners of the rectangle. The golden section can be used to create a perfect five-pointed star, and it can be used to create a pentagram. The rose window on Chartres cathedral is made up of golden section lines.

These patterns work, not for mystical reasons, but rather because these patterns correspond with the patterns that we perceive in nature and the patterns that are inherent in our own createdness.

One purpose of pattern is to ground the building in nature and connect it to our bodies by imitating the ordering discipline of life forms, especially our own. I believe that to be recognized as a place, a building must embody the harmonic patterns of life forms. Talk of "harmony" and "embodying life forms" rubs some people the wrong way. The word "harmony" has been sentimentalized, but no other term is so apt. I mean it in the musical sense, not in the sense of "have-a-nice-day."[57]

Chaotic Beauty and Planned Ugliness

As we begin to think about the objective features that make an urban environment beautiful, we need to be careful about the dangers of overconfidence in this area. Getting back to an earlier observation, we can explore the possibility of confidence in the ontological reality of beauty but still have the humility to recognize the gaps we have in our epistemology. We do not, in every case, understand how to make the built environment more beautiful. And sometimes our sin and human frailty can cause our aesthetic judgment to be faulty. For these reasons, I will conclude this chapter on aesthetics with a few cautionary words.

The first caution to be aware of is the way that questions of "aesthetic judgment" can function as a mask for more sinister motives. In chapter 4, I spoke favorably of the City Beautiful movement, which was an attempt to bring some of the formal aspects of civic art into American cities. But not everyone who cares about the built environment shares my convictions.

One of the primary examples of the beaux arts school of civic art is the reconstruction of Paris under Napoleon IV and his city engineer, Van Hausmann. This application of beaux arts principles is one reason that we find Paris such a beautiful city today. However, we need to also recognize that Van Hausmann was ruthless in displacing hordes of Parisians in order to create his wide boulevards. Also, Napoleon's primary goal in creating such wide boulevards was more pragmatic than aesthetic. He knew that wide boulevards would make it very difficult for the disgruntled citizenry of Paris to express their frustration by erecting blockades in the streets. Some have therefore suggested that the beaux arts style is more suitable for autocratic regimes than for an open democracy.

For these and other reasons, not everyone who is attuned to urban beauty likes the City Beautiful movement. One notable example is Jane Jacobs, who called this movement "an aesthetic cult." Jacobs greatly prefers the messy beauty that emerges when neighborhoods grow organically through the individual initiative of its citizens.

The question of organic beauty versus formal beauty is beyond the scope of this study, but it provides interesting fodder for discussion. Also, it is probably important when entering into such discussion to not automatically assume

Engagement

that God is on the side of formal beauty. Certainly, God is a God of discipline and order, but salvation history has revealed to us a God whose creativity can also be expressed in the wildness of the flower in the field, and who sometimes breaks down things that express the hubris of humanity.

Another kind of caution is to recognize the hidden role that aesthetics can play when it is not explicitly on the table. John Calvin in Switzerland and the Puritans in America are commonly understood to have been anti-aesthetic in their sensibilities. But more recent scholarship has challenged that judgment. The Calvinist/Puritan impulse is now understood not to be anti-aesthetic, but expressing a particular kind of aesthetic:

> A Calvinist aesthetic exists. . . . From the architecture, from church furnishings, from the congregational music, from the Geneva gown of the pastor himself, everything breathes *simplicity, sobriety,* and *measure*—which are precisely the qualities that Calvinist aesthetics demand of the art-object.[58]

This case helps us to realize that even those who are reticent or dismissive of the significance of beauty may have a strong aesthetic sensibility that governs their actions and decisions. In the case of Calvinism/Puritanism, this aesthetic sense has had a good outcome. There is a kind of severe beauty that we can appreciate in something like the Puritan meetinghouse, for instance.

Where this becomes a cautionary example is when we think back to the way that functional zoning was universally adopted and had been the default tool among planners for much of the twentieth century, despite the fact that it is one of the least efficient and most unsatisfying ways to organize human communities. We've already attributed the popularity of this practice to some unique material factors in this country during the twentieth century, to the influence of expert culture, and to the philosophical ideals of the *CIAM*. But aesthetics may have also been a factor in the strong hold that zoning held among the planning community.

Even though, on the ground, a perfectly zoned community can be wasteful and banal, a kind of aesthetic can be seen on the surface of the planners' map. Instead of portraying the city as a incoherent jumble of streets and buildings, a zoning map makes the city look clean and organized. Everything is color-coded and expressed in geometric shapes. Of course, most planners would be appalled at the suggestion that their attachment to zoning as a planning tool can be attributed to an unexpressed aesthetic judgment—albeit a highly abstracted rationalistic aesthetic. But I think that we need to be open to the various ways that aesthetic concerns can shape even the most "rational" judgments.

Friendship, Beauty, and Attachment to Place

Historically, people have put up with the inconvenience of living in proximity to one another because of the advantages these kinds of settings offer to their individual plans and goals. They have sought the safety of numbers. They have desired economic opportunities and the availability of goods and services. Others, especially those who have been guided by Scripture, have been motivated to temper these individual goals with communal values such as justice and environmental responsibility. All of these things are important and are part of the "purposes" of the city.

But they don't fully explain how we come to feel that we belong in the places we live, how we become attached to specific locations, and how we come to even love them. While we are working on these other plans and goals, other things are happening, often outside the scope of our attention. We are becoming familiar to our neighbors, and they to us. We are, hopefully, making friends. And we are finding beauty, not just in specialized settings, but in our everyday life. And if our cities and neighborhoods, like Tevye, were to press the question of whether we love them, hopefully our answer will be, "I suppose I do."

For Further Reading

Alexander, Christopher, Sara Ishikawa, and Murray Silverstein. *A Pattern Language: Towns, Buildings, Construction*. Center for Environmental Structure series. New York: Oxford University Press, 1977.

De Gruchy, John W. *Christianity, Art, and Transformation: Theological Aesthetics in the Struggle for Justice*. Cambridge: Cambridge University Press, 2001.

Dyrness, William A. *Reformed Theology and Visual Culture: The Protestant Imagination from Calvin to Edwards*. Cambridge: Cambridge University Press, 2004.

Finney, Paul Corby, ed. *Seeing beyond the Word: Visual Arts and the Calvinist Tradition*. Grand Rapids: Eerdmans, 1999.

Frazee, Randy. *The Connecting Church: Beyond Small Groups to Authentic Community*. Grand Rapids: Zondervan, 2001.

Hale, Jonathan. *The Old Way of Seeing*. Boston: Houghton Mifflin, 1994.

Kunstler, James Howard. *Home from Nowhere: Remaking Our Everyday World for the Twenty-First Century*. New York: Simon and Schuster, 1996.

Kwartler, Michael. "Legislating Aesthetics: The Role of Zoning in Designing Cities." In *Zoning and the American Dream: Promises Still to Keep*, edited by Charles M. Haar and Jerold S. Kayden. Chicago: Planners Press, American Planning Association in association with the Lincoln Institute of Land Policy, 1989.

Mills, Robert P. "Beauty, the Beholder, and the Believer." *Theology Matters* 15, no. 5, 2009, 1–16.

Myers, Joe. *The Search to Belong*. Grand Rapids: Zondervan, 2003.

Oldenburg, Ray. *The Great Good Place: Cafés, Coffee Shops, Community Centers, Beauty Parlors, General Stores, Bars, Hangouts, and How They Get You through the Day*. New York: Paragon House, 1989.

Engagement

Pohl, Christine D. *Making Room: Recovering Hospitality as a Christian Tradition*. Grand Rapids: Eerdmans, 1999.

Pollan, Michael. *A Place of My Own: The Education of an Amateur Builder*. New York: Random House, 1997.

Postrel, Virginia I. *The Substance of Style: How the Rise of Aesthetic Value Is Remaking Commerce, Culture, and Consciousness*. New York: HarperCollins, 2003.

Wolterstorff, Nicholas. *Art in Action*. Grand Rapids: Eerdmans, 1980.

Conclusion

A Geography of Rest

So then, a Sabbath rest still remains for the people of God; for those who enter God's rest also cease from their labors as God did from his. Let us therefore make every effort to enter that rest, so that no one may fall through such disobedience as theirs. (Hebrews 4:9–11)

Begin Here (Again)

Let's return to the question asked at the very beginning of this book: Where are you? If you are in your (or somebody else's) home or in a car, you will have to use a bit of imagination here, because I want you to consider your role once you leave your private domain. If you are (or if you are imagining you are) outside of the realm over which you have exclusive control (say, a coffee shop), what legitimates your presence where you are? The place where you are sits on land that belongs to somebody. How is it that they have come to give you permission to be here? Let us consider a couple of possibilities.

You may be where you are in the capacity of a consumer. You may be in a coffee shop or a bookstore, and the owner allows you to be here because you have purchased or are likely to purchase what they are selling. This is also true if you are a student in an academic setting. If you are on the campus, in a classroom, or in the college library, you are allowed to be where you are because you pay for that right when you pay your tuition.

Perhaps you are allowed to be where you are in the capacity of a producer. Maybe you are a teacher and are reading this on campus or at your office. Maybe you are a journalist, an architect, or a city planner and are reading this at your place of work.

These kinds of settings are the most likely places for you to be as you sit and read a book. This is because the economy provides the primary lens for viewing reality. It is the economy that informs us as to how we are doing as a country. Is the economy growing or stagnant? Is the market up or down? Important decisions about production and resource distribution are relegated to the free market.

Because of this, we tend to be seen as significant in our society insofar as we are making a contribution to the economy as a producer or a consumer. There are good reasons for this arrangement, and, given the alternatives, it may be that this is the best way to organize our lives together. The downside of this is that it creates a situation where we feel significant only when we are doing something useful for the economy.

Theologically, this is somewhat problematic, because God created us as creatures with inherent worth. We are "very good" because we are in the image of God. Our value and significance come first and foremost from who we are, rather than from what we do. The question that concerns us in this conclusion has to do with how the built environment functions as a place to *be* rather than to *do*.

The answer to "Where are you?" just may be that you are in a public place right now. It may be that you are in a public library or sitting in a public space of the city, such as a park, a plaza, or a bench near the street. And it may even be that it is a gracious public space. That is to say, you feel comfortable where you are, and your dignity as a human creature is being affirmed by the beauty of the setting even if you aren't contributing a whit to the economy at the present time.

If this is the case, you are in the minority and you are in a somewhat unusual place. Most of us don't stumble across these kinds of settings very often. The physical setting of the public realm has been given scant attention over the past half-century. We explored some of the reasons for this neglect in chapter 6, but now consider what this means theologically.

The Sabbath

In chapter 4, we discovered that one of the foundational rhythms through which our lives find their proper cadence is the Sabbath. Our lives are supposed to be shaped by a rhythm consisting in six days of work and one day of rest. This rhythm coordinates our communal life as we gather for worship week in and week out. But, as we saw in chapter 7, there is more to the Sabbath than just gathering for worship. The Sabbath helps us to nurture our intimate relationships, and it provides respite from the hectic pace of the week.

The Sabbath pattern governing our labor and rest is different than the daily rhythm of work and sleep, in that it is more voluntary. That is to say we can choose to ignore it. A person who ignores his or her need for sleep will eventually fall asleep involuntarily. But people may choose to ignore the mandate for weekly rest and restoration their entire lives.

The Sabbath command therefore can be seen as an invitation to a deliberate practice. And it is through such practices that we truly learn some of the most fundamental truths from Scripture. It is easy to understand our Christian commitments in exclusively cognitive terms, but we need to include our minds and our bodies to get a complete picture of the life of faith. Part of what we know of God's faithfulness, we come to know tacitly. The practice of keeping the Sabbath provides a regular way to train our bodies to tacitly know something important that God wants us to know. The next question we need to explore is what it is specifically that we learn by practicing the Sabbath.

Sabbath Lessons

To answer the question about what we learn when we practice the Sabbath, we can first go back to the Sabbath command as we find it in Scripture. The command is part of the Ten Commandments, which are given in two slightly different forms in the Old Testament. These two versions of the command convey slightly different reasons for the giving of it. In Exodus, the Sabbath command is linked to God's activity in creation.

> Six days you shall labor and do all your work. But the seventh day is a sabbath to the LORD your God; you shall not do any work—you, your son or your daughter, your male or female slave, your livestock, or the alien resident in your towns. For in six days the LORD made heaven and earth, the sea, and all that is in them, but rested the seventh day; therefore the LORD blessed the sabbath day and consecrated it.[1]

One way of understanding this reason for the command is that the Sabbath is a day for remembering that our goodness is rooted, not in the productive work we can accomplish, but rather in the fact that we have been created by a good and loving God. The Sabbath is a day to enjoy being part of a good creation.

In Deuteronomy, the Sabbath command is linked to God liberating God's people from their captivity in Egypt.

> Six days you shall labor and do all your work. But the seventh day is a sabbath to the LORD your God; you shall not do any work—you, or your son or your

daughter, or your male or female slave, or your ox or your donkey, or any of your livestock, or the resident alien in your towns, so that your male and female slave may rest as well as you. Remember that you were a slave in the land of Egypt, and the LORD your God brought you out from there with a mighty hand and an outstretched arm; therefore the LORD your God commanded you to keep the sabbath day.[2]

This reason for the command can be understood as the Sabbath being a day to remember that our well-being is ultimately in God's hands. The Israelites were not strong enough to deliver themselves from captivity to the Egyptians, so they had to depend on God to accomplish this for them.

In the same way, our tendency is to try to solve all of our problems by just working a bit harder. This is how we naturally deal with any shortages we may encounter, and this is even how we are tempted to deal with our sin. We are tempted to believe that the stress of our lives stems from the fact that there is not enough time in each day and week to solve all of the problems we face. To not work on the Sabbath, therefore, is a bold assertion in the midst of a frenetic culture that we don't have to "do" everything, because we are trusting God, who is capable and willing to deal with all of the problems we face.

Living the Sabbath

Practicing the Sabbath teaches us tacitly two important truths. We have inherent value because God made us and declared us good. Second, our confidence comes, not from our own capabilities, but from God's faithfulness. We learn these things anew as we practice the Sabbath, but of course we recognize that these things are not only true on the Sabbath. They are true seven days a week, and the Sabbath provides a regular place to be reminded of these truths.

When the Sabbath is functioning as it should, then, it spills out into the rest of our lives. When we do our work on the other six days, we do so differently because of the Sabbath. We work hard, but we remember that our work isn't what makes us valuable. We do our very best at what we have been called to do, but we realize that our ultimate trust is always in God's competence, not in our own.

The Sabbath helps us to work in a less stressful way, since it lowers the stakes of the work that we do. But the Sabbath can also help us learn to rest in the midst of the working week. Even on the six days in which we work, there are times when it is possible to rest. We can rest while we sleep. We can

Conclusion

rest at mealtimes. And we may find that we can enjoy some time alone or with those we love.

When we don't know that our value and our confidence are grounded in a faithful God, our temptation is to raid those natural times of rest and make them more productive. We can get by on less sleep, and we can get work done during mealtimes. We can fill our lives and the lives of our children with such frenetic activity that we almost never find time just to enjoy being alone or spending time together. But the lessons that we learn on the Sabbath can help us fight such temptations.

A Place for Rest

We can learn how to rest from Sabbath practices, but these lessons can be either supported or contradicted by the built environment that surrounds us. Places that invite us to rest and to engage with one other and with the world that surrounds us without demanding that we give something productive in return can be described as places of shalom. We are more likely to find places of shalom in environments built before the proliferation of automobile culture. But in recent years we have begun to see new places being built with a greater sense of shalom. Below is a sketch of plans for a new development in Chico, California, involving a church, a ball park, and a mix of uses all held together with places of shalom in the spaces in between.

Image by Seth Harry

The availability of places where we are invited to stop and enjoy our rest provides a tacit reminder of what is important. If these places invite us to stay because we are consumers or producers, we will learn to see ourselves as valuable only insofar as we contribute to the economy. If our public spaces are ugly or inconvenient, we learn tacitly that our value as human beings is minimal.

The kinds of environments that have been built by functional zoning also tend to contradict the lessons we learn on the Sabbath. By encouraging us to put great distance between where we work and where we live, and by spreading out the places we shop, play, and worship, our built environment encourages us to spend inordinate amounts of time in our cars.

This time spent in our cars cuts into the time that we could spend enjoying ourselves alone or with those that we love. This layout also tends to scatter the people in our lives, as well as reduce them to their functional roles. The young man that serves our coffee is unlikely to also be our neighbor when we live in different subdivisions. Likewise, our coworkers are unlikely to have kids who go to the same school as ours.

It is interesting, therefore, to evaluate our built environment from the perspective of how well it helps us to practice our Sabbath rest throughout the week. From this perspective, then, ask yourself again, "Where are you?" Where is the closest place that you are invited to rest, regardless of your status as a producer or a consumer? How much time would you need to spend in your car to enjoy face-to-face time with some of the people who are most important to you right now?

These questions are important, not only because they reveal how much of our everyday life supports or contradicts the lessons that we are supposed to learn on the Sabbath. But also because they reveal how well the built environment in which we live and move helps to orient us toward our ultimate destination. This line of inquiry brings to mind once again the glimpse of shalom provided by the prophet Zechariah:

> Thus says the Lord of hosts: Old men and old women shall again sit in the streets of Jerusalem, each with staff in hand because of their great age. And the streets of the city shall be full of boys and girls playing in its streets.[3]

The Sabbath is not just a respite from the "real life" that we encounter the other six days of the week. The Sabbath is in many ways more characteristic of our "real life" than are the days in which we work. The work that we are called to now is connected to the particular time in which we live. We live now in the space between the cross and the Parousia, and we are invited to partner with God in the plan to redeem all of creation. This work is uneven, it can involve drudgery, and it can be beautiful and fulfilling. But this kind of work will come to an end when Christ returns. There may be work for us under the reign of Christ, but it will be devoid of drudgery. And there will most certainly be rest—a Sabbath's rest for all eternity.

The question that we need to be asking of our built environment—that is to say, of the space between the buildings—is, how well does this environment point to and remind us of the Sabbath rest that is to come? How does this place measure up to the standard of shalom?

At the beginning of this journey, I confessed that my goal was to change the way you look at everything. My hope is that by now you have learned to attend to the spaces between the buildings. And in these important spaces you are beginning to see new possibilities for the redemption of all of creation as you wait expectantly for Christ to reign over all in the space between.

For Further Reading

Dawn, Marva J. *Keeping the Sabbath Wholly: Ceasing, Resting, Embracing, Feasting.* Grand Rapids: Eerdmans, 1989.

Wirzba, Norman. *Living the Sabbath: Discovering the Rhythms of Rest and Delight.* The Christian Practice of Everyday Life. Grand Rapids: Brazos, 2006.

Notes

Introducing the Built Environment

1. Philip Bess, *Till We Have Built Jerusalem: Architecture, Urbanism, and the Sacred* (Wilmington, DE: ISI Books, 2006); Timothy Gorringe, *A Theology of the Built Environment: Justice, Empowerment, Redemption* (Cambridge: Cambridge University Press, 2002); Nicholas Wolterstorff, *Art in Action* (Grand Rapids: Eerdmans, 1980); Nicholas Wolterstorff, *Until Justice and Peace Embrace: The Kuyper Lectures for 1981 Delivered at the Free University of Amsterdam* (Grand Rapids: Eerdmans, 1983).

2. James Rojas, "The Enacted Environment: The Creation Of 'Place' By Mexicans and Mexican Americans in East Los Angeles" (Massachusetts Institute of Technology, 1991).

3. Spiro Kostof and Greg Castillo, *A History of Architecture: Settings and Rituals*, 2nd ed. (New York: Oxford University Press, 1995).

4. Richard J. Mouw, *When the Kings Come Marching In: Isaiah and the New Jerusalem*, Rev. ed. (Grand Rapids: Eerdmans, 2002).

5. Albert M. Wolters, *Creation Regained: Biblical Basics for a Reformational Worldview*, 2nd ed. (Grand Rapids: Eerdmans, 2005).

6. Genesis 1:28.

7. Mark Henrie, "From Green Fields to the Grey Town," *The University Bookman*, no. 1, 42: 6–12.

8. Ibid.

9. Andrés Duany, "New Urbanism: The Case for Looking Beyond Style," *Metropolis* (April 2011): 74–79.

Part I: Orientation

1. I first heard this question and answer sequence from David Gruesel on September 11, 2008 at a discussion in Kentlands, MD, sponsored by the Washington Institute.

2. See Cornelius Plantinga, *Engaging God's World: A Christian Vision of Faith, Learning, and Living* (Grand Rapids: Eerdmans, 2002).

Chapter 1: Who Are You?

1. Pedestrian and Bicycle Information Center, www.walkinginfo.org/facts/facts.cfm.

2. Center for Disease Control and Prevention, "Fire Deaths and Injury Fact Sheet," http://www.cdc.gov/HomeandRecreationalSafety/Fire-Prevention/fires-factsheet.html.

3. Philip Bess, *Till We Have Built Jerusalem: Architecture, Urbanism, and the Sacred* (Wilmington, DE: ISI Books, 2006), 116.

4. Genesis 2:7–9.

5. Deuteronomy 6:5.

6. Ephesians 5:15.

7. Philippians 3:17.

8. Colossians 2:6.

9. 1 Thessalonians 4:1.

10. Exodus 13:3.

11. Deuteronomy 8:2.

12. Michael Polanyi and Amartya Sen, *The Tacit Dimension* (Chicago: University of Chicago Press, 2009).

13. Robert Venturi, Denise Scott Brown, and Steven Izenour, *Learning from Las Vegas* (Cambridge: MIT Press, 1977).

14. Jan Gehl, *Cities for People* (Washington, DC: Island Press, 2010), 33.

15. Ibid., 34–35.

16. Ibid.

17. Ibid., 41.

18. Ibid., 236.

19. Ibid.

20. The Charter of the New Urbanism, http://www.cnu.org/charter.

21. Andres Duany, Elizabeth Plater-Zyberk, and Jeff Speck, *Suburban Nation: The Rise of Sprawl and the Decline of the American Dream* (New York: North Point Press, 2000).

22. Exodus 32:4.

23. Isaiah 46:1–2.

Chapter 2: Where Are You?

1. Some material from this section first appeared in Eric O. Jacobsen, "Place" in *The Global Dictionary of Theology*, eds. William A. Dyrness, Veli-Matti Kärkkäinen, Juan F. Martinez, and Simon Chan (Downers Grove, IL: IVP Academic, 2008).

2. Walter Brueggemann, *The Land* (Philadelphia: Fortress Press, 1977).

3. John Inge, *A Christian Theology of Place: Explorations in Practical, Pastoral, and Empirical Theology* (Aldershot, Hampshire, England: Ashgate, 2003), 6.

4. George Ritzer, *The Globalization of Nothing* (Thousand Oaks, CA: Pine Forge Press, 2004).

5. Gaston Bachelard and M. Jolas, *The Poetics of Space* (Boston: Beacon Press, 1994).

6. Martin Heidegger, *Poetry, Language, Thought*, trans. Albert Hofstadter (New York: Perennial Classics, 2001), 163.

7. John 4:9.

8. Craig Bartholomew, *Where Mortals Dwell: A Christian View of Place for Today* (Grand Rapids: Baker Academic, 2011).

9. Genesis 12:1.

10. Numbers 35:34.

11. Brueggemann, *The Land*, 175.

12. John 14:21.

13. Matthew 18:20.

14. John 14:2.

15. Daniel Solomon, *Global City Blues* (Washington, DC: Island Press, 2002), 71.

16. Nicholas Wolterstorff, *Art in Action* (Grand Rapids: Eerdmans, 1980).

17. Philip Bess, *Till We Have Built Jerusalem: Architecture, Urbanism, and the Sacred* (Wilmington, DE: ISI Books, 2006), 116.

18. Richard Sennett, *The Fall of Public Man* (New York: W. W. Norton, 1996), 13.

19. Nicholas Lash, *Theology on the Way to Emmaus* (London: SCM Press, 1986), 42.

20. Material for this section first appeared in Eric O. Jacobsen, "Building for Memory: How Church Buildings Can Express God's Faithfulness," *Reformed Worship*, March 2008. Reprinted from *Reformed Worship* © 2008 Faith Alive Christian Resources.

21. John 4:21b.

22. Matthew 18:20.

23. Exodus 13:3.

24. Exodus 3:6.

25. Hebrews 12:1.

Chapter 3: What Are You?

Much of this chapter first appeared as an article in the *Journal of Markets and Morality* 6, no. 1 (Spring 2003).

1. I was introduced to the term by Howard Ahmansen at a conference on Christianity and New Urbanism in Seaside, Florida.

2. Genesis 2:18.

3. Colin E. Gunton, *The One, the Three, and the Many: God, Creation and the Culture of Modernity* (Cambridge: Cambridge University Press, 1993), 163.

4. Ibid., 164.

5. Ibid., 168.

6. James Howard Kunstler, *The Geography of Nowhere: The Rise and Decline of America's Man-Made Landscape* (New York: Touchstone, 1994), 185–86.

7. Dietrich Bonhoeffer, *Life Together* (New York: Harper & Row, 1954).

8. Ibid.

9. Ibid., 28.

10. Eugene H. Peterson, *Under the Unpredictable Plant: An Exploration in Vocational Holiness* (Grand Rapids: Eerdmans, 1992).

11. Ibid., 89.

12. John Updike, "Slum Lords," in *Americana: And Other Poems* (New York: Knopf, 2001), 84.

13. I will marry couples who are members of another church on behalf of their pastor or congregation.

14. H. Richard Niebuhr, *The Kingdom of God in America* (New York: Harper & Row, 1959), 193.

Chapter 4: When Are You?

Some material in this chapter first appeared in "An Over-Ruralized Eschatology" in *Comment*, December 2010.

1. Romans 5:8.

2. Alasdair MacIntyre, *After Virtue: A Study in Moral Theory*, 2nd ed. (Notre Dame, IN: University of Notre Dame Press, 1984), 206–7.

3. Ibid.

4. Isaiah 28:23–29, cited in Albert M. Wolters, *Creation Regained: Biblical Basics for a Reformational Worldview*, 2nd ed. (Grand Rapids: Eerdmans, 2005).

5. Proverbs 8:1–11.

6. Christopher Alexander, Sara Ishikawa, and Murray Silverstein, *A Pattern Language: Towns Buildings, Construction*, Center for Environmental Structure (New York: Oxford University Press, 1977).

7. Daniel Solomon, *Global City Blues* (Washington, DC: Island Press, 2003), 72.

8. Le Corbusier Charter of Athens 194 (New York: HarperCollins, 1971), para 74.

9. Ibid., para 77.

10. Ibid., para. 80.

11. Proverbs 15:14.

12. We will explore this movement more fully in chapter 6.

13. Some material from this section first appeared in Eric O. Jacobsen, "An Over-ruralized Eschatology" in *Cardus* online (Dec. 24, 2010).

14. For "laid bare," see NIV; for "disclosed," see NRSV. Also see Malachi 3:2–3 for refiner's fire.

15. Wolters, *Creation Regained*, 45–46.

16. Eugene Peterson, unpublished sermon Dec. 1, 2002, First Presbyterian Church, Missoula, MT.

17. Colin E. Gunton, *The One, the Three, and the Many: God, Creation and the Culture of Modernity* (Cambridge: Cambridge University Press, 1993).

18. James Rojas, "The Enacted Environment: The Creation Of 'Place' By Mexicans and Mexican Americans in East Los Angeles" (Massachusetts Institute of Technology, 1991).

19. John 1:12–13.

20. Eugene H. Peterson, *Working the Angles: The Shape of Pastoral Integrity* (Grand Rapids: Eerdmans, 1987), 67–68.

21. Psalm 121:3–4.

22. Hebrews 10:24–25.

23. Nicholas Wolterstorff, "The Theological Significance of Going to Church and Leaving and the Architectural Expression of That Significance," Theology and the Built Environment, Second Colloquium, Calvin College, 2004, 1.

Part II: Participation

1. Jeremiah 29:4–7.

Chapter 5: Family

1. Robert Goizueta, *Caminemos Con Jesus* (Maryknoll, NY: Orbis Books, 2003), 50–51.

2. *Village of Euclid, Ohio, et al. v. Ambler Realty Co. No. 31* (1926).

3. Dolores Hayden, *Redesigning the American Dream: Gender, Housing, and Family Life* (New York: W. W. Norton, 2002), 87.

4. Lawrence J. Stone, *The Family, Sex, and Marriage in England, 1500–1800* (New York: Harper & Row, 1977), 7. Cited in Robert Fishman, *Bourgeois Utopias: The Rise and Fall of Suburbia* (New York: Basic Books, 1987), 33.

5. Ibid.

6. Fishman, *Bourgeois Utopias*, 29.

7. Ibid., 35.

8. William Cowper, *The Task*, Book 3, "The Garden" (London: Kessinger Publishing, LLC, 2004), 49.

9. Ibid., Book 1, "The Sofa," 23.

10. Fishman, *Bourgeois Utopias*, 56.

11. Ibid., 64.

12. Ibid., 45.

13. Ibid., 66.

14. Ibid., 66–67.

15. Ibid., 70.

16. Witold Rybczynski, *Makeshift Metropolis: Ideas about Cities* (New York: Scribner, 2010), 74–75.

17. Richard Sennett, *The Uses of Disorder: Personal Identity & City Life* (New York: W. W. Norton, 1992), 169–70.

18. Christine D. Pohl, *Making Room: Recovering Hospitality as a Christian Tradition* (Grand Rapids: Eerdmans, 1999).

19. Hebrews 13:2.

20. James Rojas, "The Enacted Environment: The Creation of 'Place' by Mexicans and Mexican Americans in East Los Angeles" (Massachusetts Institute of Technology, 1991).

21. Zechariah 8:4–5.

22. Christopher Alexander, Sara Ishikawa, and Murray Silverstein, *A Pattern Language: Towns, Buildings, Construction*, Center for Environmental Structure (New York: Oxford University Press, 1977), 216.

23. Richard J. Mouw, *Uncommon Decency: Christian Civility in an Uncivil World* (Downers Grove, IL: InterVarsity Press, 1992).

24. Lenore Skenazy, *Free Range Kids: Giving Our Children the Freedom We Had without Going Nuts with Worry* (San Francisco: Jossey-Bass, 2009), 6.

25. Ibid.

Chapter 6: Politics

1. Anthony Flint, *Wrestling with Moses: How Jane Jacobs Took on New York's Master Builder and Transformed the American City* (New York: Random House, 2009), xiii.

2. Richard Sennett, *The Uses of Disorder: Personal Identity & City Life* (New York: W. W. Norton, 1992), 130.

3. Ibid., 142.

4. Robert Neelly Bellah, *Habits of the Heart: Individualism and Commitment in American Life* (New York: Harper & Row, 1986).

5. Matthew 5:45.

6. Andy Crouch, *Culture Making: Recovering Our Creative Calling* (Downers Grove, IL: InterVarsity Press, 2008).

7. I don't actually know whether or not Jacobs considered herself to be a Christian. She did work alongside the local Catholic parish on some of her projects, however.

8. Robert Fishman, *Bourgeois Utopias: The Rise and Fall of Suburbia* (New York: Basic Books, 1987), 11.

9. *Village of Euclid, Ohio, et al. v. Ambler Realty Co. No. 31* (1926).

10. Le Corbusier, *The City of Tomorrow and Its Planning* (Mineola, NY: Dover, 1987), 5.

11. Ibid., 179.

12. Charles Jencks, *The Language of Post-Modern Architecture* (New York: Rizzoli, 1984), 9.

13. Jane Jacobs, *Death and Life of Great American Cities* (New York: Vintage, 1961).

14. Ibid., 17.

15. Ibid., 15.

16. Ibid., 432.

17. Ibid., 447.

18. George Lakoff and Mark Johnson, *Metaphors We Live By* (Chicago: University of Chicago Press, 2003).

19. Jacobs, *Death and Life of Great American Cities*, 13.

20. Rem Koolhaas, "Whatever Happened to Urbanism," *Design Quarterly*, no. 164 (1995): 28–31.

21. Jacobs, *Death and Life of Great American Cities*, 32.

22. Ibid., 56.

23. Ibid., 82.

24. Ibid., 52.

25. Ellen Dunham-Jones, "The Generation of '68 Today: Bernard Tschumi, Rem Koolhaas and the Institutionalization of Critique," paper presented at Constructing Identity: "Souped-Up and Unplugged," Association of Collegiate Schools of Architecture, 1998.

26. Sarah Williams Goldhagen, "Extra-Large," *The New Republic*, July 2006.

27. Daniel Zalewski, "Intelligent Design: Can Rem Koolhaas Kill the Skyscraper?" *The New Yorker*, March 2005, 9.

28. Goldhagen, "Extra-Large."

29. Zalewski, "Intelligent Design," 2.

30. Ibid., 9.

31. Goldhagen, "Extra-Large."

Chapter 7: Church

1. It should be noted that this is the official position of the Orthodox Rabbis, but not all Orthodox Jews abide by this regulation.

2. Avram Hein et al., "Reflections on the Driving Teshuvah," *Conservative Judaism* 56, no. 3 (2004).

3. Ben Zion Bokser, "The Halachah on Travel on the Sabbath," in *Tradition and Change,* ed. Mordecai Waxman (New York: Burning Bush Press, 1958), 393.

4. David Novak, *Law and Theology in Judaism* (New York: Krav, 1974). Reprinted in Elliot Dorff, *Conservative Judaism: Our Ancestors to Our Descendants* (New York: Youth Commission, United Synagogue of America, 1977), 180.

5. Bokser, "Halachah on Travel on the Sabbath," 397.

6. David Golinkin, "Riding to the Synagogue on Shabbat," http://www.responsesfortoday.com.

7. Bokser, "Halachah on Travel on the Sabbath," 397.

8. Robert L. Smith cited in Hein et al., "Reflections on the Driving Teshuvah," 42.

9. Ibid.

10. Ibid.

11. Ibid.

12. Anne C. Loveland and Otis B. Wheeler, *From Meetinghouse to Megachurch: A Material and Cultural History* (Columbia: University of Missouri Press, 2004).

13. Darrell L. Guder and Lois Barrett, *Missional Church: A Vision for the Sending of the Church in North America*, The Gospel and Our Culture series (Grand Rapids: Eerdmans, 1998).

14. John 20:21b.

15. Alan J. Roxburgh, *Missional: Joining God in the Neighborhood* (Grand Rapids: Baker Books, 2011).

16. Ronald F. Thiemann, *Constructing a Public Theology: The Church in a Pluralistic Culture* (Louisville: Westminster John Knox, 1991), 43. My thanks to Richard Mouw for bringing this concept to my attention.

17. James K. A. Smith, *Desiring the Kingdom: Worship, Worldview, and Cultural Formation* (Grand Rapids: Baker Academic, 2009).

18. Nicholas Wolterstorff, "The Theological Significance of Going to Church and Leaving and the Architectural Expression of That Significance," unpublished paper presented at Theology and the Built Environment, Second Colloquium, Calvin College, 2004, 15.

19. 1 Corinthians 11:21.

20. M. Francis Mannion, "The Church and the City," *First Things* 100 (2000): 35.

21. Ibid., 32.

Part III: Engagement

1. Gordon Lynch, *Understanding Theology and Popular Culture* (Malden, MA: Blackwell, 2005).

2. Paul Tillich, *Systematic Theology*, vol. 1 (Chicago: University of Chicago Press, 1973), 64.

3. Don S. Browning, *A Fundamental Practical Theology: Descriptive and Strategic Proposals* (Minneapolis: Fortress, 1991).

Chapter 8: The Sustainable Environment

1. Edward L. Glaeser, *Triumph of the City: How Our Greatest Invention Makes Us Richer, Smarter, Greener, Healthier, and Happier* (New York: Penguin Press, 2011), 1–2.

2. Richard L. Florida, *The Rise of the Creative Class: And How It's Transforming Work, Leisure, Community and Everyday Life* (New York: Basic Books, 2004).

3. Ibid., 6.

4. "More Bicycling Means Safer Streets," *New Urban News* (Jan./Feb. 2011), 7.

5. David Owen, *Green Metropolis: Why Living Smaller, Living Closer, and Driving Less Are Keys to Sustainability* (New York: Riverhead Books, 2009), 1–3.

6. Psalm 104:10–13.

7. Colossians 1:15–20.

8. Romans 8:19–22.

9. Revelation 21:1.

10. Revelation 22:2.

11. Cited in Morton White and Lucia White, *The Intellectual versus the City* (New York: Mentor, 1962), 28.

12. Lazare, "America's Undeclared War," cited in Owen, *Green Metropolis*, 19–20.

13. Ibid., 47.

14. Ibid., 46.

15. Psalm 97:1–2.

16. Isaiah 1:17.

17. Isaiah 5:8.

18. *Village of Euclid, Ohio, et al. v. Ambler Realty Co. No. 31* (1926).

19. Michael Kwartler, "Legislating Aesthetics," in *Zoning and the American Dream: Promises Still to Keep*, eds. Charles M. Haar and Jerold S. Kayden (Chicago: Planners Press, American Planning Association in association with the Lincoln Institute of Land Policy, 1989), 205.

20. Lance Freeman, *There Goes the 'Hood: Views of Gentrification from the Ground Up* (Philadelphia: Temple University Press, 2006).

21. Leviticus 19:10.

22. "Urban Bill of Rights" February 2005 DRAFT Message posted to– PRO-URB@LISTSERV .UGA.EDU The Practice of New Urbanism.

23. Scott Campbell, "Green Cities, Growing Cities, Just Cities? Urban Planning and the Contradictions of Sustainable Development," in Scott Cambell and Susan S. Fainstein, *Readings in Planning Theory* (Oxford: Blackwell Publishers, 2003), 435–58.

24. Ibid.

25. John R. W. Stott, *The Contemporary Christian: Applying God's Word to Today's World* (Downers Grove, IL: InterVarsity Press, 1992), 390.

Chapter 9: Loving Place

1. Sheldon Harnick and Jerry Bock, *Fiddler on the Roof*, 1964 by Alley Music Corporation and Trio Music Company, Inc.

2. G. K. Chesterton, *Orthodoxy*, rev. ed. (Fairfield, IA: 1stworld Pub., 2009), 63.

3. *Village of Euclid, Ohio, et al. v. Ambler Realty Co. No. 31* (1926).

4. Psalm 146:9.

5. Deuteronomy 10:17–18.

6. Deuteronomy 10:19.

7. Exodus 23:9.

8. Exodus 23:12.

9. Exodus 12:48–49.

10. Job 29:16.

11. Job 31:32.

12. Ephesians 2:12–14.

13. Matthew 25:35.

14. Romans 12:13.

15. Hebrews 13:2.

16. 2 Corinthians 5:18–19.

17. Matthew 5:23–24.

18. Ray Oldenburg, *The Great Good Place: Cafes, Coffee Shops, Community Centers, Beauty Parlors, General Stores, Bars, Hangouts, and How They Get You through the Day* (New York: Paragon House, 1989), 20–42.

19. Randy Frazee, *The Connecting Church: Beyond Small Groups to Authentic Community* (Grand Rapids: Zondervan, 2001).

20. Christine D. Pohl, *Making Room: Recovering Hospitality as a Christian Tradition* (Grand Rapids: Eerdmans, 1999), 95.

21. Ibid., 96–97.

22. Joseph R. Myers, *The Search to Belong: Rethinking Intimacy, Community, and Small Groups* (Grand Rapids: Zondervan, 2003).

23. Myers, *The Search to Belong*, 50.

24. Robert P. Mills, "Beauty, the Beholder, and the Believer," *Theology Matters* 15, no. 5 (2009).

25. Ibid.

26. Isaiah 28:5.

27. Psalm 27:4.

28. Psalm 96:6.

29. Exodus 26:31–32.

30. Cited in Mills, "Beauty, the Beholder, and the Believer," 7.

31. Witold Rybczynski, *Makeshift Metropolis: Ideas about Cities* (New York: Scribner, 2010), 84–85.

32. Genesis 2:9a.

33. John Calvin, *Institutes of the Christian Religion*, 3.10.2.

34. Virginia I. Postrel, *The Substance of Style: How the Rise of Aesthetic Value Is Remaking Commerce, Culture, and Consciousness* (New York: HarperCollins, 2003), 44.

35. Hosea 14:7.

36. Proverbs 5:19.

37. John 2:10.

38. Psalm 34:8.

39. Song of Songs 4:6–7.

40. Graham Ward, *Cities of God* (New York: Routledge, 2000).

41. Augustine, *The Confessions of St. Augustine* (New York: Book League of America, 1936), I i.

42. C. S. Lewis, *Surprised by Joy* (New York: Harcourt, Brace, Jovanovich, 1955), 16.

43. Some might argue that this works with erotic desire as well—that pornography or voyeurism can increase desire for one's beloved—but I am unconvinced.

44. Genesis 3:6.

45. Genesis 34:2.

46. 1 Corinthians 7:9.

47. John J. Navone, *Toward a Theology of Beauty* (Collegeville, MN: Liturgical Press, 1996), 30.

48. Proverbs 31:30.

49. Exodus 16:3.

50. Hans Urs von Balthasar, Joseph Fessio, and John Kenneth Riches, *The Glory of the Lord: A Theological Aesthetics*, 7 vols. (San Francisco: Ignatius Press, 1983), 18.

51. Nicholas Wolterstorff, *Until Justice and Peace Embrace: The Kuyper Lectures for 1981 Delivered at the Free University of Amsterdam* (Grand Rapids: Eerdmans, 1983).

52. Nicholas Wolterstorff, *Art in Action* (Grand Rapids: Eerdmans, 1980), 180.

53. Ibid., 181.

54. Ibid.

55. Jonathan Hale, *The Old Way of Seeing* (Boston: Houghton Mifflin, 1994), 58.

56. Ibid., 47–48.

57. Ibid., 67.

58. Donald Davies, *A Gathered Church: The Literature of the English Dissenting Interest, 1700–1930* (Oxford: Oxford University Press, 1978). Cited in Wolterstorff, *Until Justice and Peace Embrace*, 134.

Conclusion

1. Exodus 20:9–11.

2. Deuteronomy 5:13–15.

3. Zechariah 8:4–5.

Index

aesthetics 15–17, 46, 111, 171, 178, 256, 257, 260, 262–63, 266–68. *See also* beauty; visual
affordable housing 24, 150, 233
agency 105, 121, 131–32, 134, 147, 150, 155, 179, 189, 193, 204
agrarian. *See* rural
air-conditioning 71, 113, 141, 199
Alexander, Christopher 110, 153
"already and not yet" 122, 132, 212
apartment buildings 47, 52, 79, 140, 142, 167, 177, 192, 225, 229–30, 232–33
applicationist method 208–10
appreciative inquiry 115
architects 15–16, 18, 63, 84, 97, 111, 113, 150, 153, 167, 171, 177, 179, 265
artifact 16, 73, 210, 215, 225
arts, grand narrative of 260–62. *See also* civic art
askesis 89–92, 97, 138, 185
aspect ratio 62, 67
Athens Charter 112, 164. See also *CIAM*; modern architecture
Augustine, Saint 258
automobile 25, 33–39, 42–43, 46, 48–50, 52, 54, 64, 80, 82, 113–14, 117, 125, 131, 140, 142–43, 157, 166, 184–88, 191, 199, 203–4, 207–8, 220, 226, 233–34, 275
autonomous individualism. *See* individuality
axial lines 67–68, 96, 192

Babylon 132–34
beauty 32, 90, 96, 110, 129, 201, 240, 252–68, 272. *See also* aesthetics
Beaux Arts 16, 67, 266
Bellah, Robert 160
belonging 241, 250–51, 268
bike lanes 215–20, 235
blessing 109, 161
Bonhoeffer, Dietrich 88–89
boulevard 14, 66, 96, 98, 266
Brueggemann, Walter 56, 59

cadence 127, 183, 198, 272

call of God 30–32, 37, 54, 59, 72, 101, 119, 151, 193, 195–96, 207, 227–28, 237, 249, 274, 276. *See also* vocation

call to worship 198–203

Calvin, John 256, 276

Campbell, Scott 236–37

car. *See* automobile

celebration 51, 94, 96, 128, 201, 244, 257

childhood 57, 120, 178, 183, 256

children 20, 22, 82, 120, 133, 135–36, 137–39, 142–46, 151, 154–55, 174, 210, 227, 229, 239–42, 252, 258, 275

church
  adapted 191
  embedded 189–92, 195, 199
  insular 189–92, 195, 203
  missional 193–94, 196

CIAM 112–13, 125, 162, 164, 267. *See also* modern architecture

City Beautiful 67, 225, 266

city planning. *See* planning, city

civic art 16–17, 67, 266

civic righteousness 161

civic virtue 158–62, 180, 196

civility 154

Clapham Community 145–49

cognitive knowledge 38–39, 273

coherence 68–69, 85–87, 126, 183

commitment 85, 89, 94–95, 139, 258

commodity 32, 76, 87, 89, 123

common grace 109, 160–62. *See also* grace

connectivity 43–49, 140

consumer 11, 47, 83–84, 95, 202, 207–9, 226, 236, 258, 271, 272, 276

consumption 176, 197, 208, 229, 236–37

convenience 43, 48, 210, 226

conversation 136, 153, 246

correlationist method 208–11

covenant 38, 59, 94, 128–29, 174, 203, 208, 240, 243, 244, 258–59

creation mandate 20, 119, 122, 223

creative class 218–19

critical correlational model 211

critical mass 84–85

cross 75, 96, 122, 245

cul-de-sac 43, 52, 136, 140, 220, 242, 247

cultivation 120, 214–15, 223

cultural mandate 20, 127, 139, 211

curb radii 33–35

delight 32, 36, 43, 119, 256, 258–59

density 90, 166, 218, 225–26, 230–32, 234

Descartes, René 255

design 5, 18, 51, 88, 91, 95, 111, 147–50, 153, 177, 192, 242, 247, 265
determinism, physical 82–83, 131, 249
dignity 45, 227–28, 272
dismissal (liturgical) 202–4
displacement 226, 231
distraction 259, 261
domestic 133–34, 145–46, 204
dominion 20, 223, 225
driving teshuvah 184–88
Duany, Andrés 23–24, 51
durability 73, 110, 116, 138
dwelling 143, 207, 217–18, 222, 229–30

Eden 37, 59, 118, 258. *See also* garden
elitism 22, 111, 148, 179, 218, 237, 253
enacted space 17–18, 124, 174, 200
enactment 72, 105, 131, 173, 174–75, 178, 183, 199
enclosure 61–65, 67, 141, 192
engagement 25, 40, 43, 55, 72, 103, 145, 151, 153, 159, 173–74, 177–78, 189, 194, 195, 197, 199, 207–12, 240, 275
environment 14, 71, 207–9, 215, 218–19, 221–26, 234–37, 268. *See also* stewardship
epistemology 255–56. *See also* knowledge
eruv line 184
eschatology 104–5, 118, 119, 122–23, 126, 132, 153, 179–80, 212, 237
estrangement 203, 243, 245–47
ethics 188–89, 209, 257
Eucharist. *See* Lord's Supper
Euclid v. Ambler Realty 47–48, 113, 143–44, 163, 229–30, 241–43, 245
evangelicals 118–19, 144–47, 161, 189, 197, 207–8
everyday life 29–30, 38, 76–77, 104, 118, 120, 122, 130, 144, 150, 170, 180, 197, 207, 260–61, 268, 276
evil 120, 161, 225, 238
expert 112–16, 162, 164, 168, 267
extended families 137–38, 150, 153, 155
exurb 24, 34, 43, 48–52, 113–14, 120, 140, 143, 147, 184, 186, 189, 207, 220, 230, 232, 242, 246–47, 249. *See also* suburb

fabric buildings 15, 68, 192
fall, the 90, 104, 146
Federal Highway Act (1956) 48, 164
fence 49, 81, 136, 141, 149, 152–53, 201, 247
Fishman, Robert 145, 148, 156, 163
Florida, Richard 218–19
folly 113, 114, 129
food bank 248
footprint 25, 195–96, 201, 225
forgiveness 100, 128
fortress mentality 195

fossil fuels 207–9, 222
frailty 266
freedom 26, 32, 55, 88, 97–98, 107, 113, 149, 153, 186, 224, 226, 261
Freeman, Lance 231
friendship 13, 71–73, 108, 133, 136, 143, 152, 174, 199, 203, 212, 219, 227, 243, 250–51, 252, 268
front door 66, 71, 81, 91, 133, 141, 152, 191, 247
functional zoning 36, 47, 143, 163, 166, 168, 242, 267, 276
fundamental ethical decisions 188–89. *See also* ethics
funeral 129

garage door 141, 247
garden 18–20, 30–31, 37, 59, 82, 99, 118–22, 133, 147–48, 214–15, 224
Garden City 168–69
gate 108–9, 152–53, 201, 247, 248, 265
gathering 16, 18, 22, 60, 72–73, 81, 88, 93, 97, 124, 127–28, 134, 154, 187, 191, 198–99, 201–2, 245, 248, 249, 272
Gehl, Jan 40–42, 45
gentrification 227, 229–32, 236
geography 12–13, 31, 95, 219, 271
Glaeser, Edward 217–18
gleanings 232–33
glory 19, 60, 118, 123, 128, 224, 254
Goizueta, Roberto 137–38
golden section 265
goodness 106, 119, 122, 253, 255, 258, 260, 273
grace 88–89, 96, 100, 109, 132, 160–62
gratitude 101, 123, 132
grid, street 43, 49, 52, 79, 140–41, 218, 220, 242, 247, 249
growth 44, 56, 121, 163, 217–19
Gunton, Colin 86–87, 121, 123

Hale, Jonathan 263–65
harmony 19, 30, 150, 179, 180, 215, 266
Hayden, Dolores 144, 210
health 35, 98, 121–22, 143, 220, 224, 234
high style 111, 113, 263
history 16–17, 19, 20, 32, 35, 51, 54, 60, 72, 73–77, 85, 92, 97, 99, 100, 105, 111–12, 119, 124, 127, 128, 149, 164, 179, 180, 223, 255–56, 260
Holy Spirit 32, 37, 83, 86, 200
home
  as haven 144, 151, 154–55, 210
  single-family 49, 52, 140, 148, 154, 229–30
homelessness 232
hospitality 91, 133, 151–52, 244, 246–49
Housing Act (1954) 164
Howard, Ebenezer 168–69
human scale 50, 80
hypostases 86

identity 52, 56–59, 82, 87, 89, 127, 132–33, 137–38, 174, 197, 201, 250
idolatry 53–54, 93–95, 96, 99
image of God 20, 30, 87, 179, 212, 214, 223, 256, 272
individuality 75, 82–84, 86–87, 89–90, 92–93, 95, 97, 101, 105, 113, 123, 128–29, 132, 138, 150, 169, 184, 188, 193, 201, 203, 207, 209, 222, 225, 258, 268
infrastructure 46–48, 202, 217
Inge, John 56
inherent worth 272
institutional power 158–59
intergenerational 82, 153

Jacobs, Jane 45, 157–60, 162, 168–79, 183, 266
justice 30, 72, 75, 215, 226–29, 232–34, 236–38, 243, 256–57, 268

Kant, Immanuel 255, 257
kehillot 187
kindness 133, 243–45
kingdom of God 20–22, 73, 96, 98, 119, 122–23, 237
knowledge 38–39, 107–8, 110, 112, 114, 119, 159, 195, 211, 255. *See also* epistomology
Koolhaas, Rem 171–72, 175–79
Kunstler, James Howard 23, 87, 100

Lash, Nicholas 72, 198
lawn 152, 227, 242, 247
la yarda 153
Le Corbusier 166, 170, 175, 179
LEED 221. *See also* environment
Lewis, C. S. 258
light 32, 59, 124, 125, 155, 258, 262–63
liturgy 72, 128, 183, 196–97, 199, 203–4
locomotion 200, 202
Lord's Supper 31, 128, 200–202
love 35, 37, 59, 89, 93, 94, 103, 116, 127, 128, 139, 154, 239–40, 243, 258, 268, 275, 276
Lynch, Gordon 130, 208

MacIntyre, Alasdair 105
mall. *See* shopping mall
market forces 53, 69, 79–81, 83–85, 92, 95, 124, 165, 272
marriage 87, 89, 93–94, 129, 133, 138–39, 208, 239–40, 258
memory 57, 72–76, 82, 120
middle class 137, 140, 142, 150, 152–53, 230, 247
Mills, Robert P. 253–55
modern architecture 80, 91, 97, 100, 114, 116, 166
money 92, 94, 99, 212, 216, 219–20, 252
monument 15–16, 60, 66–69, 71, 140–41, 190, 192
Moses, Robert 157–59, 162
Mouw, Richard 154

museum 15, 88, 118, 178, 252, 261
Myers, Joseph 250–52

Nash, John 148
natural environment 14–20, 32, 35, 106–7, 113–14, 125, 149, 150, 199, 223, 225
neighborly behavior 83, 131, 249
New Jerusalem 118, 204, 275
New Urbanism 23–24, 50–51, 79–100, 109, 131, 232, 234. *See also* urbanism
New York City 47, 157–58, 163, 166, 177, 221–22, 224–26
nostalgia 120–21, 147, 178
novelty 75

obedience 20, 30, 37–39, 118, 119, 121, 122, 193, 259
objectivity 98, 254–56, 263, 265–66
Oldenburg, Ray 245–46
ontology 255, 266
outdoor hallway 64–66, 141
outdoor room 64–65, 191
Owen, David 221–22, 225

paleo-urbanism 80, 84, 86, 95. *See also* urbanism
parish 193–96
parking 13, 42, 63–64, 66, 67, 114, 116–17, 190–91, 203, 226
parousia 276
particularity 86–87
patina 74–75, 76
pedestrian 34, 42, 45, 50, 51–52, 54, 80–81, 140, 142, 155, 190, 220, 234. *See also* walking
pedestrian shed 51–52, 140
performance 71–72, 128, 133, 139, 176, 183, 197–98, 218, 261
perichoresis 86–87, 89, 94, 132, 138, 193
personhood 132, 137
Peterson, Eugene 90, 122, 126
placelessness 57, 60, 69–70
placemaking 60, 79
planners, city 17, 44–45, 50, 63, 114, 168–70, 172, 175, 216, 236, 267
planning, city 16–17, 23, 45, 47, 51, 64, 84, 92, 112–15, 159, 162, 164, 166–68, 170–72, 179–80
plaza 15, 16, 18, 30, 64, 66, 67, 108, 176, 258, 263, 272
Pohl, Christine 151, 248
polis 23, 134, 158–63, 180
politics 98, 107, 109, 126, 134, 139, 145, 146–47, 157–80, 229, 232
poor, the 166, 168, 218, 228–30, 232–33, 257
porch 70, 80–81, 141, 160, 201, 242
Postrel, Virginia 257
practices 69, 71, 72, 74, 90, 107, 109, 111, 113–14, 121, 123, 127–28, 131, 149, 184–187, 194, 197–98, 199, 202–4, 248, 249, 273–76
preservation 16, 91, 116–18, 120, 232, 235
private realm 70, 133–34, 143, 146, 147, 152
proclamation 103, 119, 199

production 83, 215, 236, 272
prosperity 217–18, 219
proximity 12, 14, 49, 57, 91, 100, 134, 174, 179–80, 187, 225–26, 235, 240, 247, 268
Pruitt-Igoe project 167
public life 69, 72, 109, 113, 144, 146, 176, 191–92, 196
public place 18, 125, 176, 194, 248, 272
public realm 29–31, 45, 49, 51, 70–72, 75, 98, 108–9, 133–34, 141, 147, 159, 176, 183, 203–4,
    233, 235, 247, 257, 265, 272
public transit 45, 50, 136, 209, 222, 225, 226, 233–34
Puritan 267

reconciliation 26, 201, 223–24, 244–45, 249
redemption 20, 26, 30, 59, 60, 87–88, 95, 104–6, 118–19, 121–22, 123, 126, 129, 132, 138, 147,
    150, 151, 155, 180, 189, 193, 204, 224, 245, 277
reductionism 169, 257
regulating lines 264–65
repentance 103, 253
respite 272, 276
rest 127, 244, 271–77. *See also* Sabbath
retail 36, 57, 80, 191
retirement 135, 137, 142, 217
revolution 121, 176
rhythm 32, 123–28, 175, 178, 183, 191, 198–99, 272–73
righteousness 88, 108, 161, 228, 238, 244
Rojas, James 124–25, 152–53
root metaphor 172, 175
rural 51, 63, 120, 189, 215, 222, 225

Sabbath 127, 184–88, 271–77. *See also* rest
sacrament 200, 203
salvation 26, 54, 59, 60, 74–75, 96, 104–6, 109, 124, 126, 128–29, 200, 267
sculpture, buildings as 15
seduction 99, 259–60
segregation, income 52, 230, 232
self-repair 173, 175–76, 178
semiotic memory 74, 82
Sennett, Richard 151, 159
setback of building from street, 49, 67, 96
shalom 26, 30–31, 32, 72, 118, 120–21, 133–34, 147, 179, 214–15, 275–77
shevut 186
shopping mall 136, 143, 191, 192, 197, 207
sidewalks 12, 33–34, 42–43, 49, 52, 66, 71, 90–91, 117, 153, 173, 174–75, 183, 190, 199, 203,
    216, 218, 234
simulacra 76
sin 18, 32, 59, 76, 83, 87–89, 92, 96, 99, 103–7, 119–23, 129, 147, 161, 200, 245, 266, 274
siting of buildings 31, 149, 189, 195
small group 136, 227, 248–51
Smith, James K. A. 197

social capital 160–62, 174–75, 180, 201–2, 211
socioeconomic class 52, 166, 201, 214, 228–29. *See also* poor, the
Solomon, Daniel 60, 66, 68, 112, 160, 190
sovereignty 122, 126–27, 179–80, 188
space
  carved 61–62
  leaking 63–64
spatial tropes 64–65
spirituality 96, 98–99, 119, 146–47, 194, 204, 225
stakeholders 116, 164, 236
stewardship 20, 207–8, 215, 221, 223–26, 236–37, 240. *See also* environment
stranger 56, 141, 152–53, 155, 163, 227, 241–50
streetwall 65, 68, 70–71, 141, 147, 191–92
subdivision 23, 43, 80, 131, 136, 140, 207, 209, 242, 246, 247, 276
suburb 22–23, 47–51, 147–50, 185. *See also* exurb
sustainability 213–15, 226, 237
SUV 207–9
synagogue 184–89, 196

tacit knowledge 38–39, 211, 273–76. *See also* knowledge
taste, aesthetic 46, 110, 149, 171, 178–80, 253, 255–56. *See also* aesthetics
taxes 216–20, 227
technology 13, 57, 113, 123, 125, 150, 161–62, 165, 170, 190, 219
tehumin 185
television 141
Thiemann, Ronald 196
third place 245–46
threshold 70–71, 133, 141, 152–53, 190–91, 199, 201, 247
thriving, human 14, 26, 32, 37, 77, 82, 100, 107, 118, 215–20, 224, 229, 236–37, 240, 249
time 17, 32, 56–57, 92–93, 100, 104–5, 113, 122–24, 125–29, 132–33, 186, 198, 200
town fabric 60–72, 83, 117, 140, 142, 147, 190–92, 211
tradition 87, 93, 97, 107, 109–12, 114, 121, 149, 183, 194, 198, 200–201
transcendentals 253, 260
transformation 14, 56, 172–73, 175–76, 178, 238
transgressive 175–78
trees 199, 216, 224, 225, 234, 256–57, 262
Trinity 86. See also *perichoresis*
two kingdoms 20–21, 98

unified kingdom 21
urbanism 15, 51, 80, 92, 95, 112, 149, 226, 261. *See also* New Urbanism; paleo-urbanism
urban planning 16–17, 112, 115, 162–63, 179
urban renewal 116, 158, 163–64, 166–68, 230–32
utilitarian 110–11, 190–91, 203

vernacular 110–11, 113, 149, 263
visual 42, 70, 74, 80, 90. *See also* aesthetics
vitality 160, 260

vocation 22, 119, 132–33, 165, 224, 240. *See also* call of God
voyeurism 176–78

walkable communities 23, 46–47, 49, 131, 209, 234
walking 35, 37, 40, 42–43, 51, 70, 81, 84, 87, 91, 144, 154–55, 184–85, 187–88, 195, 199, 203,
    225, 227, 241–42, 247. *See also* pedestrian
welcoming 81, 151–52, 249. *See also* hospitality
"What Would Jesus Drive?" 207–8
Wilberforce, William 145
wilderness 19, 38, 215, 219, 221, 225, 260
windows 40, 70–71, 264–65
wisdom 36, 46, 50, 84–85, 90, 92, 97, 100, 105–18, 121, 149, 153, 166, 168, 217, 225
Wolters, Albert 106, 121
Wolterstorff, Nicholas 127–28, 199, 260–63

zoning 35–36, 46–48, 50–52, 63, 101, 113, 143–44, 160, 162–64, 166, 168, 229–30, 232, 242,
    267